THE
COUNTRY LOVER'S
COMPANION

First published by Odhams Press Ltd.

This edition published 2006 by Bounty Books, a division of Octopus
Publishing Group Ltd 2–4 Heron Quays, London E14 4JP.

ISBN-13: 978-0-753713-58-7
ISBN-10: 0-753713-58-6

A CIP catalogue record for this book is available from the British Library.

Printed and bound in Dubai.

All efforts have been made to trace the copyright holders prior to publication, but this has not always
been possible. If notified, the publisher would be pleased to rectify any errors or omissions at the
earliest opportunity.

THE
COUNTRY LOVER'S
COMPANION

*The wayfarer's guide
to the varied scenery of Britain and
the people who live and work
in the countryside*

Bounty Books

Colour Plates

Contents

VILLAGE OF THE ISLE OF WIGHT

The Isle of Wight is twenty-four miles long and thirteen miles broad and lies off the coast of Hampshire, from which it is divided by Spithead and the Solent. It contains countryside of great variety, ranging from chalk downlands to level land rich in soil and varied in agricultural products. Above all the Isle of Wight contains within its small compass a number of charmingly situated villages. This aerial view shows Godshill.

6

Introduction

WE LIVE on one of the most beautiful islands in the world. It is a fact that we are always forgetting. But there is another fact, even more important, which we are also always forgetting (which, perhaps, many people never realize), and that is that man made this island of ours one of the most beautiful places in the world.

It is not, I think, very difficult to appreciate scenery. It is easy enough to write a descriptive and topographical account of certain features of the British countryside. You need only the detached view of the connoisseur. But that is less than half the picture. The British rural scene was made with hands and, therefore, if the canvas is to be complete, the painter must be included in the picture.

The British countryman is the greatest landscape artist in the history of art. He it was who made our island, and it has taken him rather more than four thousand years to do it. Or rather, he has remade our island, since Nature presented him with two superlative tools for the job—geology and climate. It is the changeability of the weather within the bounds of our climate and the diversity of the rock-formations within the boundaries of our seas that give to the British landscape its unique quality—extreme variety within a very small compass. There is a continent of varieties within the narrow limits of this little island. It is the supreme achievement of the British countryman that, in remoulding Britain, he remained conscious always of that variety, faithful always to the medium in which he worked. The result is a whole so complete that it is now difficult to decide whether he made the country or the country made him.

Yet, when we speak of the British countryman, we must remember that many races have contributed to his making. If there is a continent of varieties in our landscape, there is no less a continent of varieties in our people. The diversity of race has been just as important in the moulding of the British rural scene as the diversity of soil or the caprice of the weather.

It is true that much of this diversity of race has disappeared with the development of modern communications, with the spread of the towns, with universal education. Urbanization has inevitably a levelling tendency. But it would be quite wrong to think that all diversity has disappeared. Many different races, speaking many different languages and having many different customs, contributed to the making of Britain. Traces of them are still to be found all over the place.

The most obvious difference, of course, is in colouring—the fair hair and blue eyes of the Nordic races, the dark eyes and swarthy complexions of the Mediterranean races. Everyone is aware of that broad distinction. The knowledgeable man will relate the distinction to history; will know that the broad-shouldered, flaxen-haired, blue-eyed people so characteristic of the East Riding of Yorkshire are a legacy of the Norsemen who settled in this part of Britain; will know that the thick-set, fair-haired, blue-eyed people of middle height so characteristic of eastern Hampshire are a legacy of the Jutes who conquered this region more than a thousand years ago; will know that the small dark people of Wales are descendants of the Iberians, who were in these islands even before the Celts came. But the observant man will relate this distinction not only to history but to soil. The Celts were a people who mistrusted valleys and lived on the open tops of the chalk hills; you may still find typical Celts on the Downs and the Chilterns. The fair-haired Saxon preferred the valleys; you will still find a preponderance of fair-haired people in the valleys of the south.

FROM THE CHALK-LANDS TO THE HEATHS

Indeed, the change as you come off the chalk of Hampshire and Wiltshire down to the acid heathlands of the New Forest, Cranborne Chase, and the Dorset heaths is quite remarkable—a change not only in the type of man, but also in the breeds of domestic animals, in architecture, in custom, in folk-lore, in speech. There is as big a change between Salisbury and the Solent as there is between the East Riding of Yorkshire and the mountains of Cardiganshire. Myself, I think that you can carry the distinction still further, for you can often relate it to occupation. The Iberians (the Ancient Britons) were a small dark people with long faces and hooked noses, and they were a pastoral people. The type has persisted in many places outside Wales, especially in some of the villages of Hampshire, Dorset, and Somerset. And today in these villages you will find that among those men who handle sheep and cattle and horses, the majority are small and dark.

In just the same way, diversity of language has persisted in the face of universal education and ease of communication. As you travel Britain it is easy to pick out the speech of the different invaders—the clipped "u" of the Saxon and the long "u" of the Anglian—and to distinguish them from the quick lilting speech of the Celt. But it is when the countryman talks of his country crafts that these regional differences in speech become most marked. We may now all speak the same language when it comes to politics or football "pools," but when we talk "shop" there are times when we can scarcely understand each other. Consider sheep: the Cumberland man will call them gimmers, the Leicestershire man threaves, the Sussex man ewes. Or consider the different names for so common a thing as grass in a hayfield—fog, eddish, aftercut, aftermath.

In just the same way different customs have survived in different areas of Britain. Morris dancing, mumming, mothering, the May-day pole—these still linger on, though they are becoming less common year by year. But the traditional customs connected with land, and the Church festivals, and the

BASTION OF ENGLAND

Through every civilization that has infused fresh blood into the racial strain of the British people, Dover has been an important link with the Continent and a vital bastion in the defence of the island kingdom. Dover Hill was fortified in Roman days and the remains of a Roman lighthouse tower can be seen on the right beside the Saxon church of St. Mary in Castro.

SCOTLAND'S TRADITIONAL DRESS

The kilt is the traditional national costume of Scotland, but is now the dress of everyday life only in remote parts of the countryside. On ceremonial occasions, however, every Scotsman is proud to don his traditional dress. Every clan has its own tartan, every regiment its own special insignia. These three photographs show three characteristic uniforms—on the left is a bowman of the Royal Company of Archers, which is the King's Bodyguard for Scotland; in the centre is a competitor in the Highland Dancing competition at the Highland Games, Cowal, Argyllshire; and on the right a Scottish piper of the Glasgow Police Pipe Band in full array.

seasons of the year, though not always observed nowadays with full ceremony, are most certainly not forgotten. Sometimes they survive only as children's games—Nuts-in-May, Peg-top, and Ring-a-Ring-o'-Roses are good examples —sometimes only as stories, but they survive.

In the same way folk-lore survives, too. Undoubtedly ancient lore is strongest in Wales and the Highlands of Scotland, for in both there is an unbroken tradition dating back to very early times and preserved in the original language of the people. Similarly you will find that ancient customs and ideas persist more strongly in Wales and the Highlands than in England. This is due to the many invasions that England has experienced and the consequent mixing of races. But for this very reason the folk-lore that has survived is the more interesting. The superstitions which we, rather shamefacedly, acknowledge today are but the mutilated relics of ancient religious beliefs that may have their origin in Scandinavia or Frisia or in some Pictish camp of the far north. All over this country, differing a little from region to region with the people that settled there, are to be found beliefs and superstitions about birth and childhood, courtship and marriage, death and burial; about the sun and the moon and the stars, about birds and beasts, trees and plants, water and stones; about witches and witchcraft, about luck. And, if you can find them, there are the most magnificent stories about all these things, still to be told in villages of a night in prose or song.

All these things should, I believe, be looked for as one goes about the country, for they add so enormously to the interest of the actual countryside.

The history of Britain's landscape can be summed up in six words—axe, crook, scythe, chisel, plough, and billhook. In other words, what made the countryside was a multitude of crafts contained within one major craft, agriculture. Each craft has its own language and its own customs, yet each differing a little with the people and the region, and all are there for the seeker with an inquiring mind.

Geology and climate have done more for Britain than merely aid man to make it a beautiful place. Together they have given us flora and fauna that are unsurpassed in Europe. There is no need to go to the ends of the earth to taste the full joys of exploration. There is a vast field of interest at our very doors in our wild life, which to be understood must be discovered anew by each one of us individually, a field in which there is plenty of scope for original observa-

DANCING ROUND THE MAYPOLE

May Day ceremonies are among the traditions of old England that have survived with the greatest vigour. The Maypole ceremony is very ancient in origin; it was once the custom for the men of one village to try to seize the maypole of a neighbouring village even at the cost of bloodshed. Today all that survive of ceremonies which started as celebrations of the coming of the summer and the growth of the crops are dances round the maypole, the choosing of a May Queen, and other picturesque but harmless pageants. This charming scene is at Kingsteignton, South Devon.

tions. Fields, woods, streams, and rivers, and lakes and ponds, moors and hills, sea-shore and marsh, each have their own particular wild life which changes with the seasons. Thus it does not matter what the season or what the weather, there is always something of interest to observe in the British countryside—if you know where to look and how to look.

There are not, it is true, many different sorts of mammals living wild in Britain today, and most of those that there are are very shy and difficult to observe. But there are more, and they are more widespread than casual observation would lead one to think. For example, it is commonly thought that the deer are confined to the wilder regions of the West of England and the Highlands of Scotland, whereas, in fact, there is scarcely a county without its population of wild deer. However, mammals do require a good deal of experience and a good deal of skill for their observation, and for the man who is not a fairly accomplished naturalist, it is better to concentrate on the birds and insects.

British bird life is prodigal in its wealth. Nowhere else in Europe will you hear so much song, nowhere else in Europe will you find birds so tame, so easy of approach, nowhere else in Europe within so small an area will you see so many different sorts of birds. Nor does the season make any difference. So far as actual numbers go, we certainly have more birds to watch in the winter than in the spring. Nobody need ever be dull or bored in the British country-side, for a lifetime can be spent in learning the different calls and songs of the birds and fitting them to their owners. It is an exciting and rewarding pursuit.

For that matter, examination of any piece of waste ground is exciting enough to thrill the heart of any explorer. You have but to bend down to become aware of a vast bustling life amid the grass roots and the flowers. The recognition of the insects and the identification of the flowers is in itself an absorbing occupation.

All these things are necessary for a proper appreciation of the wonderful country that is Britain. For all these things—the soil and the climate, the flowers and the grasses and the trees, the birds and the beasts, the humble beetle no less than the noble red deer—affect in no small measure the lives of the people who live in the countryside their forefathers made. They are at the very least the backcloth of the stage on which we live and play our parts.

No man can ever hope to know it all. But it is within everyone's power to learn some of it, and thereby to increase enjoyment of a priceless heritage. In this book various authors, each an authority on his particular subject, write of different regions and different aspects of the British countryside. The book is more than a guide: it is in truth a companion, helpful, friendly. But to become a country lover, as opposed to a country visitor, depends in the final assessment on oneself. All this interest is there for you to seek out if only you know what you are looking for and where to find it. This book will tell you that. But this book cannot give you eyes that see. The final key to great treasure is in each individual's own keeping.

BRIAN VESEY-FITZGERALD

YORK MINSTER

The city of York is to the north of England what Canterbury is to the south.
The minster is one of the most magnificent of Britain's medieval churches and
is the largest of the English cathedrals. It is on the site of a church built in
the seventh century. Since the year 627 it has been the see of an archbishop.
Apart from its importance as a religious centre, York has a long history as
a garrison town. It was first fortified in Roman times; many parts of its
medieval walls are still standing, as well as four of the gates or bars, of which
this photograph shows Bootham Bar.

THE VIEW FROM GREEN CRAG

The Lake District of Cumberland and Westmorland contains in miniature all the majesty of the Scottish Highlands and a quality of its own that is like nothing else in Britain. This view from Green Crag shows Buttermere and Crummock Water, with the mountain rising cliff-like from the water's edge.

The Landscape and the People

THERE is unending interest in the British countryside. The country lover, although he spends the leisure of a whole lifetime in exploring it, can never come to the end of its hidden places or feel that his interest is diminishing. To get out and about in the highways and byways, along the lanes and across the footpaths, to drowse in sequestered village streets and explore the historic places of old towns—those are the constant ambitions of every true country lover.

In order to appreciate fully the infinite variation of country types we must know something of the races which have contributed to the making of the rural people. In broadest outline it may be said that the people of the extreme west are Celtic, those of the central districts Saxon, and those of the extreme east Northmen or Norse. The great element of truth which lies in this generalization is that the older races, that is to say, the races which came to Britain earliest, survive among the mountain valleys of the west and in the south-western peninsula. That is because, with constant migrations from the Continent, earlier inhabitants of Britain have generally retreated before the invaders and taken refuge in a country in which they were impregnable.

The earliest people who lived in Britain comprised a race whose weapons and implements were made of stone and who lived perhaps fifty thousand years ago. It is often said that these earliest people of Britain have died out completely. That may be so, but they at least started a tradition which may have been absorbed by later races.

When we come to the New Stone Age, which was drawing to its close about four thousand years ago, we are by then at least talking of people whose descendants have made some contribution, however small, to the racial stock of the British people. The evidence of archaeology is that this late Stone Age people was driven into the far west and north-west by a bronze-using race who migrated from Europe in search of fresh pastures. In fact the story of early civilizations is a story of the successful discovery of new metals, first bronze, then iron, and with recent times steel, each producing an "industrial revolution" which brought into use weapons for which those of earlier times were no match.

Thus armed warriors of each new civilization were able to carry all

15

before them. In some cases this meant absorbing the previous culture so that by the fusion of the new and the old a new régime was created which combined some of the best qualities of both. But it also meant the retreat of the more primitive people to the mountain country, with their consequent survival for hundreds and even thousands of years as a distinct race with their own customs and way of life.

This is well illustrated by the story of the Stone Age people, who, driven into what is now Scotland, Wales, and Cornwall about 2000 B.C., were still fighting on against the Romans in the first century A.D. The natural inference is that in parts of Highland Scotland, and perhaps in Wales, too, there are living now some who are descended from these Stone Age people through their successors, the Pictish and Scottish tribes.

After the primitive civilization founded on the discovery of bronze had lasted nearly fifteen hundred years in Britain, there came tribes from Europe who had mastered the use of iron. These established firmly the strains in the population which are called Celtic. With iron weapons they brought a civilization more developed than any which had preceded. They were in occupation in Britain when the Romans came to conquer a new province across the Strait of Dover. To the Romans, with their advanced culture, they appeared as woad-painted savages. All the evidence suggests, however, that they were far from this, but rather a people still mainly concerned with raising

PERTHSHIRE VALLEY

Some of the loveliest and most lonely country in the Scottish Highlands falls within the boundaries of Perthshire. This is the winding road to Glen Artney that follows the valley of the Keltie Water in south-west Perthshire. The valley is a fertile cleft in the heather-covered moors near Callander, the opening scene of Sir Walter Scott's *The Lady of the Lake*. The surrounding hills form one of the most extensive deer forests in Scotland.

I. AUTUMN IN A BEECH WOOD OF THE WYE VALLEY

II. ULLSWATER, SECOND LARGEST OF THE ENGLISH

LAKES, DIVIDING CUMBERLAND FROM WESTMORLAND

III. DAHLIAS ON A FLOWER FARM NEAR BOSTON, LINCOLNSHIRE

a meagre living from the land, yet with that leavening of culture and religion, custom and observance which denotes a civilized people.

Not only were these Iron Age Britons in occupation when the Romans came in the first century A.D. but they remained substantially in occupation throughout the four centuries of Roman rule. There were never enough Romans in Britain to affect substantially the racial characteristics of the people. Rather the British people were Romanized and absorbed the culture and institutions of the Romans. They reached a new peak of prosperity and their numbers increased, they had scope for leisure as well as work. Britain for the first time was a country civilized in the modern sense of the term.

Such is the background of the British people, a background all the more important in view of the misleading impression that the British people are exclusively Anglo-Saxon. What happened was that when the Roman defenders finally left Britain open to the attacks of savage tribes who dwelt in Western Europe, these earlier inhabitants of Britain retreated gradually, as Stone Age man had over two thousand years before, in face of the unceasing attacks of the invaders. These in turn absorbed the culture of the previous inhabitants of Wales, west Scotland and south-west England, and these areas became and remain the Celtic Britain of tradition.

FROM A SCOTTISH MOUNTAIN TOP

This remarkable panorama is the view from the summit of Ben Lawers, the highest of the Perthshire mountains, which commands one of the finest views in Scotland. The peak nearest the camera is Ben Ghlas (the green mountain) and behind, to its left, can be seen the western end of Loch Tay. In the distance, from left to right, are the peaks known as Ben Lomond, Stobinian, and Ben More, Ben Lui, and Ben Cruachan.

Here the people were undisturbed alike by the Saxon invaders, by the Viking marauders, and even by the Norman invasion. It was not until far into the Middle Ages that they began to have intercourse with the people of the lowlands. To this very day there is race consciousness and national pride among the peoples of Cornwall, Wales, and Scotland which derives surely from this early background, enhanced and hardened in the case of Wales and Scotland by a long series of bloody wars which were waged between them and the English before the three countries were united under a single crown. An Englishman must prove himself in a Welsh home before he is accepted. Nor is this attitude confined within the erstwhile national boundaries. Monmouthshire is perhaps more Welsh than Wales.

From the time of the Anglo-Saxon invasions the story of the lowlands is entirely different from that of the west and north and the legacy of tradition is correspondingly different, too. What we call the Anglo-Saxons consisted of three distinct peoples, the Angles, the Saxons, and the Jutes, to mention only

DEESIDE

All the magnificence of the eastern Highlands of Scotland is epitomized in this view from the slopes above Deeside looking into the Pass of Lochnagar. The serried ridges of the Grampian mountains, their bare slopes snow-covered for much of the winter, make an effective background to the rolling densely wooded country that falls away to the River Dee. Most of the trees in this part of Scotland are conifers, which have a vigorous growth in the rather bleak climate at an altitude between 1,000 and 2,000 ft. In the left centre among the trees is the house called Birkhall on the Royal Deeside estate. The house was used regularly as a holiday retreat by the present King and Queen when Duke and Duchess of York, and it was here that Princess Elizabeth and the Duke of Edinburgh spent part of their honeymoon.

IN THE SCOTTISH HIGHLANDS

Almost the whole of west Scotland is covered by the Grampian mountains, which rise abruptly from the west coast and extend eastward as far as the fringe of the coastal plain and southward as far as the valleys of Clyde and Forth, in which lie Glasgow and Edinburgh. Some of the wildest country is in Ross and Cromarty, where this scene occurs on the road to Skye as it passes Loch Duich and the Five Sisters of Kintail. The countryside is almost entirely barren in the uplands and has always been thinly populated.

the principal parts of what was a diffuse invasion by numerous tribes from the Continent.

At first these warrior peoples harried the east coast, sailed up the eastern estuaries and sacked the Romano-British towns which they found, plundered what they could find, and then returned across the North Sea. Later they began to settle in Britain and, though the settlements at first were scattered and intermingled, a pattern soon began to appear.

The Angles settled principally in East Anglia. The names Norfolk and Suffolk, incidentally, mean the country of the north folk and south folk, respectively. Within the kingdom of East Anglia the Angles were more or less protected by the sea on two sides and by the undrained fens on a third side. So for several hundreds of years the Angles held sway in this countryside without interruption and peopled their kingdom more thickly than most other parts of Britain.

The Jutes never penetrated far inland and settled principally in the Isle of Wight and along a strip of the Hampshire coast. Their influence on the racial strain of modern Britain must be correspondingly meagre.

THE NEEDLES, ISLE OF WIGHT

The most spectacular coastal scenery of southern and south-eastern England is where the white chalk cliffs are broken off abruptly at the sea. It is the white chalk cliffs of Dover that are traditionally known as the White Cliffs of Albion. Beachy Head (see page 327) is another famous point where chalk cliffs rise abruptly from the sea. Hardly less magnificent are those at the western extremity of the Isle of Wight, as this aerial photograph shows. The line of the cliff is continued in a series of stacks known as the Needles, ending at the lighthouse. They are a phenomenon caused by uneven erosion of the sea, which is constantly cutting back the cliffs and undermining them.

The Saxons were the most widespread settlers and very many Saxon tribes were responsible for the founding and development of English villages. The Saxons dwelt mainly by river or seashore and the vast majority of villages in central and southern England were founded by them, sometimes on the site of a previous Romano-British settlement but more often on virgin soil. Much later, petty kingdoms arose within the Anglo-Saxon domain and several of the counties derive their names from these principalities. Sussex is the land of the South Saxons, Essex that of the East Saxons, Northumberland is the kingdom of Northumbria, and so on. The largest of all the Saxon kingdoms, those of Wessex and Mercia, occupied most of the south Midlands and the southern counties. Wessex is a name which has disappeared from the map of England but its memory has been perpetuated in the novels of Thomas Hardy.

Meanwhile from the seventh century onwards there was a new wave of invasion, this time from the Scandinavian countries by the Norsemen or Northmen, or, as they are sometimes called, the Vikings. This was a race of skilled mariners to whom in no small measure is due Britain's medieval prowess in the ways of the sea. Just as the Saxons had been too strong for the earlier British people, so the Saxons in turn were no match for the Norse warriors who, as they had done before them, sailed up the eastern estuaries in their longboats and laid waste their villages and towns. Overrunning the eastern half of England and Scotland, they founded a large number of new villages and towns, including almost all whose names end in "thorpe" or

TREACHERY OF ENGLISH COASTAL WATERS

There are treacherous shallows and shifting sands off the east and south-east coast of England—sandbanks that are covered at high tide but exposed at low. The most infamous of these shifting banks of sand are the Goodwins, on which hundreds of ships have been trapped by running aground to become firmly embedded and so left to be broken up by the first storm that raises a rough sea. This aerial photograph gives a fine impression of the swirling waters and deep-cut channels in the sand.

A WOODLAND CRAFT OF KENT

It is often said that the traditional woodland crafts of Britain are dying out. This is true in the sense that many rural industries have become centralized in the factories of the big industrial towns. Yet side by side with modern industrial development, rural crafts continue to thrive, especially in the wood crafts associated with the Forest of Dean and the beech woods of southern England. This woodland workshop, a primitive lean-to with a roof of corrugated iron and a windbreak of sacking, is in a clearing of the Kentish woods at Hardres near Canterbury, in the centre of the country of the *Ingoldsby Legends*. The craftsman is trimming stakes, which are then arranged in neat stacks outside the workshop ready to be carted away.

"by." Finally after a long war with the Saxons they won nearly half of England, which took the name of the Danelaw and was ruled over by Scandinavian kings as a kingdom separate from the Saxon one.

Yet another strain was introduced into the people when the Norman king, William, claimed the throne of England in 1066 and brought with him numbers of his army and followers. The Normans were a branch of the Norse race (as their name suggests), who had migrated southward to what we call Normandy at the same time as their fellow countrymen were invading the coast of Britain.

These are the foundation on which the British race has been built up.

22

It is, as we have seen, by no means an entirely Anglo-Saxon one. In fact the Anglo-Saxon was only one of many influences which determined it.

Since the eleventh century there has been no major invasion, no great drift of population from the Continent to Britain. Immigration has played its part, especially migration by Flemings, Huguenots, Jews, and others, but the numbers, except perhaps in the case of the Jewish race, are comparatively insignificant. Largely the British race has evolved from the peoples to whom we have referred.

When speaking of the fact that intermingling between the various parts of Britain was on a small scale for several centuries after the Norman "conquest" it must be remembered that reference is made to the mass of the people, not to the few privileged landowners or lords of the manor. From comparatively early times there were no limitations on the latter, either in the way of travel or prejudice. But until recent times the wealthy few have been poles apart from the vast majority of the rural people. Above all, their numbers have been by comparison small, as indeed they still are.

FOREST CHARCOAL BURNERS

Charcoal burning is one of the most ancient of the traditional rural industries of Britain, and has been carried on almost continuously since Roman times. The Forest of Dean in Gloucestershire is one of several areas where charcoal burners are still regularly at work. Here, as one man rakes the charcoal dust off the pit with the keeler board, the other uses the drawing rake to collect the precious "coal." The men have to work quickly, for the charcoal is very hot and there is danger of its catching fire if it is uncovered and comes into contact with the open air.

CHESHIRE SMITHY

Of all the rural workshops that have survived from the distant past to the present, the smithy is probably the most important. Smithies date back to the time when the horse succeeded the ox as the draught animal of the farm. This photograph of a smithy at Christleton in Cheshire shows a collection of horseshoes as well as the way shoes are beaten out.

IN A KENT HOPGARDEN

Every year thousands of Londoners invade hopgardens of Kent for the annual
picking. This photograph shows a hopfield almost ready for the pickers
to strip it. The stilts are an essential part of the equipment of the permanent
workers in the hopfields, and enable the hop tenders to train the vines along
the cross poles in order that they may get sunshine to ripen them.

25

STAMFORD BRIDGE, YORKSHIRE

The Vale of York is the most fertile part of the north of England. In its scenery, its people and even in the number and style of its villages, it is more akin to the pastoral countryside of the south than it is to bleak moors of the north. Stamford Bridge, seen here, is like scores of other villages in the heart of the Vale which depend for their prosperity entirely on the wealth of the land. The graceful mill-house is a reminder of the time when almost every village had its mill, at which the raw material was delivered by each individual farmer and the "finished product" sold to the village baker.

So when the country lover travels in search of fresh interests and a new angle of approach to rural life, he must bear in mind that if he is journeying from Land's End to John o' Groats, or from Flamborough Head to the Pembrokeshire coast, he is passing through a countryside which bears all the outward signs of unity, but which within itself is not so far removed from the time when it was the home of British peoples who not only felt themselves to be different from each other but actually were so. He will notice not only the characteristic signs of racial differences, but an entirely different outlook on life and an entirely different manner of living.

It is not without significance that the Sabbath is observed in completely different ways in different parts of Britain. From one point of view this represents a difference in the attitude of the established Church. From another point of view it reflects a much deeper difference of tradition.

There is another factor. The work and life of the people, whatever their traditions, are inevitably modified by the nature of the countryside in which they live. Just as we have seen that there is a sharp cleavage between the racial characteristics of the people who live in the west and north and those who live in the south and east, so there is an equally sharp cleavage in the kind of life which the nature of the countryside will allow.

The north and west of Britain are the highlands of the country, the south and east the lowlands. In every way, from the farmer's point of view, the one is different from the other; the wealth of the valleys of southern England is a dream never to be fulfilled for the hardy husbandmen of the narrow mountain valleys of Scotland and Wales.

The climate of the mountainous country determines to some extent the productive wealth of the land, and this to a lesser degree is true of different parts of England and eastern Scotland. In East Anglia and south-east England generally the growing season is comparatively hot and sunny and the rainfall comparatively low. These are conditions which make possible the growing of corn crops on a large scale. As a direct result East Anglia comprises most arable farms, including nearly half of the total acreage of wheat grown in the whole country. In the south and east, too, there are many specialized crops like the hopgardens of the Weald of Kent and the orchard-lands which stretch from the North Downs towards the Thames Estuary, representing much invested capital but at the same time assuring a regular interest on the capital and a good standard of living for the farmers, with corresponding benefits for the men who work under them.

VILLAGE OF THE YORKSHIRE DALES

Wharfedale, seen here, is one of the longest and most romantic of the York-shire dales, and Kettlewell, the village in the foreground, one of the largest and most important of the string of ancient settlements that lie in the trough of the valley. In addition to Kettlewell, famous places in Wharfedale include Ilkley—celebrated in the traditional Yorkshire song, "On Ilkley Moor baht 'at"—and Bolton Abbey. At this point the moors of Penyghent slope up on the left, and the Great Whernside forms the sharp skyline in the background. The latter is one of the highest points in the Pennine Chain (2,419 ft.) and marks the watershed between the rivers that flow into the Lancashire plain on the west and into the Vale of York on the east.

LAKELAND SCENES

This view is from Brathay Park near Ambleside, looking across Lake Windermere to Waterhead in Westmorland. Boats ply across the lake from the landing
stage on the farther bank. Behind Waterhead the Lakeland mountains rise
steeply, their lower slopes beautifully wooded and half concealing within
the woodlands a number of large mansions. Higher up the slopes the woods
merge into the expanse of moorland that covers the summit.

If we travel across England from east to west we shall notice the arable
land gradually giving place to pasture. This is because the climate of the West
of England, even the lowlands, is less suitable for corn crops than that of the
east. The rainfall is higher, the summer temperature lower, the sky generally
more cloudy.

By contrast with East Anglia and the south-east, the West Country is
a land of green fields, of thousands of acres under permanent grass, with only
occasional ploughed fields to break the monotony of the scene, just as in East
Anglia an occasional pasture field brings variety to a landscape which in the
main is ploughed land.

In the south, too, are the great tracts of downland, which have their
own traditions of agriculture. The South Downs, the Hampshire Downs, and
the Cotswold Hills are vast sheep-walks, their whale-back ridges covered in
springy turf which is kept for ever short by the sheep who pasture over them.

The picture of farming in east Yorkshire and eastern Scotland is not so
very different from that in southern England, except that wheat is rarely
grown north of the border. Here oats is the staple crop, the basis of porridge,
the "Scottish national food," and barley, some of which goes to the

Scottish whisky distillers. But there is the same mixture of ploughed field and pasture-land and the same intensive cultivation of the soil, the same air of prosperity about the farms and very much the same feeling of security as in the south.

When we come into the highland country it is as though we had come into another world. Here only the narrow valleys are cultivated. The moorlands are totally unproductive by virtue of their poor soil as much as because of their bleak climate and high rainfall.

Though cattle find pasture on parts of the high ground of the south-west, such as Bodmin Moor, there are only mountain sheep on the uplands of Wales and Scotland, and accompanied by their shepherd these must travel far and wide to find enough grass on which to survive. A single unexpected snowstorm may rob at one fell swoop many a farm of its capital resources. The lambing season is always precarious.

There is another factor also. In the lowlands of England and Scotland it is rare for a farm to be more than half a mile from its nearest neighbour. In parts of Wales and Scotland distance means nothing. A farm may be twenty miles from the nearest settlement of any size and twice that distance or more from the nearest town. So hospitality takes on a new meaning, for the rural community, scattered as it is, must depend on its own resources for what

PLOUGHING IN SOMERSET
The fertile earth is turned by the tractor-drawn plough on the hillside near Dundry in Somerset, as another pasture field is reclaimed for root or corn crops. As is so frequently the case when the ground is freshly turned by the plough, seagulls eagerly search for worms and grubs in the soil. These lonely hills are on a spur of the Mendips.

EAST ANGLIAN SCENE

Norfolk and Suffolk together form a natural division of the British scene,
characterized by many little rivers, quiet meadows, and low well-wooded
rolling hills. This view at Earlham near Norwich shows one of the many
streams that flow into the Yare and make the countryside around Norwich
one of the most fertile parts of a very productive land.

communal life it can achieve. Its entertainments are home-made. For weeks
on end the farmer and his family may see no one but themselves. A visit from
a neighbour is an event to be looked forward to and discussed for days afterwards. A visit to the nearest town is something that happens only on very
special occasions. For compensation there is a greater independence of outlook, particularly because a great community of hired agricultural workers is
absent. Most of the farms are managed by the farmer and his sons, not to
mention his wife and daughters, who must play their part to the full in what is
sometimes a really grim struggle for existence.

In the lowlands, however intimate the relations between the farmer and
his men, the fact remains that the farmers, at any rate on the larger farms, are
employers first and foremost. There is a wide gap to be bridged between the
two classes in the rural community, as wide a gap perhaps as exists between
employer and employed in the small business of the towns, even though the
gap is a more intangible one and the relationship between the two more
kindly and tolerant.

There is a strange parallelism between the wealth of the land and the
homes in which the country people live. For reasons which will become

apparent, the village, which is the true unit of the rural population, is comparatively bleak and unbeautiful in most parts of the country where the land is poorest, even though in the midst of the most magnificent scenery. The villages of the Pennine country, of mid-Wales and of the north of Scotland could not be called beautiful by any stretch of the imagination. They are mostly built of local stone or slate, a particularly severe and dull grey in the case of the Pennine country, somehow in keeping with the bleakness and barrenness of the hills which surround the villages.

What a contrast between those remote and desolate places and the calm quiet dignity of a Kentish or Sussex hamlet, with its trim cottages graced by flowering gardens, its thatched roofs and its graceful half-timbered or mellow stone-built cottages.

The husbandman inevitably reflects the nature of his surroundings. The life of dour struggle which faces every farmer of the moorland leaves an impression on his character. The typical moorland farmer is dour, thrifty, inevitably a little morose, kindly because he knows suffering, but somewhat intolerant of strangers and of new-fangled ways. Above all, he must work

WARWICKSHIRE FARMLANDS

Much of the Midlands and West of England is ideal farm country, distinguished by prosperous farmhouses, generous hedgerow timber and a soil that is equally good for growing crops and for pasture. In this aerial view across central Warwickshire the trim hedges mark off the fields into a chessboard pattern, in which the lighter tone of the harvest fields, many of them with their crops already cleared, contrasts with the darker hues of the pasture-lands. In the distance the rich timber gives the impression of forest land and brings back memories of the tree-lined roads that radiate in almost every direction like the spokes of a wheel from Stratford-on-Avon.

MARKET-TOWN OF NORTH WALES

Ruthin is a prosperous town of Denbighshire at the southern end of the fertile
Vale of Clwyd near the beginning of the mountain road that crosses by the
Horseshoe Pass to the Vale of Llangollen. It is the market centre for the
scattered farmhouses and hamlets of the eastern outliers of the Cambrian
mountains. The black-and-white style of the buildings on the left in the picture
is more characteristic of the neighbouring Marcher county of Cheshire than
it is of North Wales. The tapering stone spire of the church, like many large
buildings in this part of the country, is built of local red sandstone.

hard and continuously if he is to derive a living from the unresponsive soil.

The lowland farmer, too, is of necessity hard-working, but his work
is not in the same way the end-all and be-all of life. He is genial, more tolerant,
less unremitting in the pursuit of his goal.

The villages of the lowlands are something more than the homes of the
country people. They are an integral part of the beauty of the landscape.
This is especially true when the villages are built throughout in one style or in one
building material, like the warm grey limestone of Cotswold country. The
church, the manor farm, the rectory, the inn, the two or three larger houses,
and the trim cottages of the rural workers—those are the integral parts of any
and every village in southern and eastern England and Scotland.

There are the black-and-white half-timbered villages of the Welsh Marches of Cheshire, the cobblestone villages of north Norfolk, the flint-built cottages of the downland country, especially the Chiltern Hills, the pargeted and colour-washed homes of Essex villages, and the heavily thatched homesteads of Wiltshire, Somerset, and Devon. Those are only a few of the types of village which will stand out in the memory. Each and every one of them has within itself the possibilities of great beauty, a beauty which is realized in very many.

It is a fact often stated and one which every wayfarer can confirm for himself that the prettiest villages tone in some remarkable way with the colouring and contours of the surrounding countryside. That is easily explained when, as in the Cotswold villages, almost every building is constructed of stone quarried locally. But it is less easy to explain in the case, for instance, of Essex villages, where there was no local building stone and no great store of

WILD WALES

The Conway river rises in the heart of the Cambrian mountains and flows round the slopes of the Snowdon range through Bettws-y-Coed down the broadening valley to the sea near Conway. In its course it comprehends all the typical beauty of the Welsh scene. Near its source it is a mountain torrent, rushing down a rocky bed as far as the falls of Bettws-y-Coed. Thereafter, though it still flows swiftly and after heavy rain on the mountains is a roaring torrent that frequently overflows its banks, it gradually grows more peaceful until below Llanrwst it enters quiet pastoral country and waters a broad fertile valley. This photograph is of that part of the river which lies between Bettws-y-Coed and Llanrwst. On the left are the densely wooded slopes of Cefn Rhydd, rising to a height of 1,453 ft. Dimly seen in the background are the slopes of the Snowdon range, with a sharp skyline against the sky in contrast with the less rugged contours of the foreground. The bed of the stream is covered with stones and fragments of rock carried down by the torrent when the river is in full flood.

timber in the later Middle Ages. Any and every material as it came to hand has been used in the building of the village homes. Yet, in spite of that, villages like Finchingfield and Great Bardfield are absolutely right in their setting of ploughed fields and low rolling countryside.

Many have made the attempt to list the most effective and beautiful villages of Britain. In fact that is a list which every country lover should make for himself, for the perception of beauty is such an individual thing that the choice of one man will never satisfy entirely the tastes of another, and there is no rule of thumb in judging the quality of a village.

Even so, there are a few which must find a place in any such list. Lavenham in Suffolk is outstanding, so are Lower Slaughter and Bibury in the Cotswold country, Castle Combe in Wiltshire, Corfe Castle in Dorset, Newton Blossomville and Turvey in the valley of the Bedfordshire Ouse, and one or more of the fishing villages that lie along the coast of Cornwall and Devonshire, be it Mevagissey or Fowey, Port Isaac or Clovelly.

SOUTHERN PARK-LANDS

A large part of the gracious beauty of southern England is due to the generous park-lands that occur in all the southern counties. There is special grace in the many large parks that have been adapted with only slight modifications from the hills and valleys of the down. This is a typical view of Arundel Park, Sussex, where Nature's landscapes, always park-like in the South Downs, have defied man's efforts to enhance them. The contours of hill and valley, the woods and coppices, combine to form scenery that has well been likened to a landscape garden on a vast scale.

KENT ORCHARD

Many parts of Britain are associated with some particular form of rural
activity, sometimes because of certain qualities of the soil or of the climate,
but sometimes for no other reason than that one locality is the traditional site
of these activities. Since medieval days the county of Kent has been associated
with hopgardens and cherry orchards. Apart from the Vale of Evesham in
Worcestershire and the cider-apple orchards of Somerset, it is the most
important fruit-growing district in the whole of Britain. At this farm near
Singlewell, in the Gravesend district, as on many other fruit farms, a double
use of the land is made by putting sheep to graze beneath the fruit trees.

This is a good beginning to any list of lovely villages, but the northerner
will complain that village beauty is no prerogative of the south. He will call
for the inclusion of fishing villages like Robin Hood's Bay in Yorkshire and
will point out the charms of many a quiet hamlet in the Vale of York and of
the many charming places which lie among the green meadows of the Yorkshire dales, particularly Wharfedale and Wensleydale. To that a southerner
will reply that those, too, have a place, but will ask are these more distinctive
than Devonshire's Buckland-in-the-Moor, or East Dean in Sussex, which
have found no place in this short list. But the only important thing is that
when we set out to explore Britain's countryside we should do so aware of the
people who make it what it is and of the beauty and interest of the places in
which they dwell.

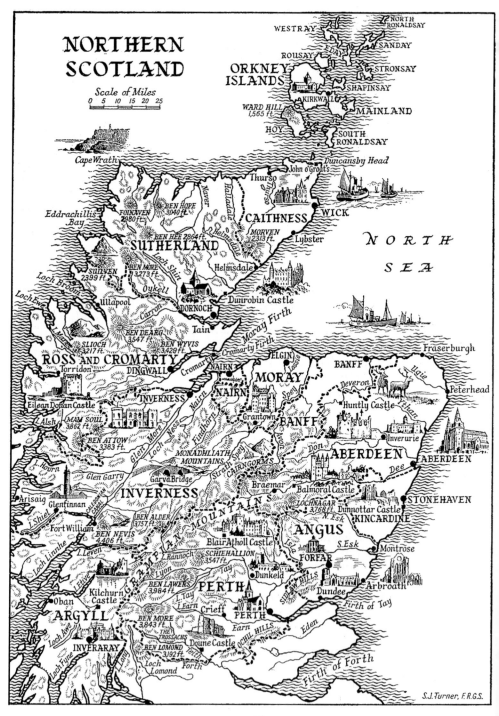

NORTHERN SCOTLAND

Scale of Miles
0 5 10 15 20 25

WESTRAY
NORTH RONALDSAY
EDAY
SANDAY
ROUSAY
ORKNEY ISLANDS
STRONSAY
SHAPINSAY
KIRKWALL
MAINLAND
WARD HILL 1,565 ft.
HOY
SOUTH RONALDSAY

Cape Wrath
Duncansby Head
John o'Groat's
Thurso
River Thurso
Eddrachillis Bay
BEN HOPE 3040 ft.
FOINAVEN 2980 ft.
Halladale
CAITHNESS
WICK
BEN HEE 2864 ft.
SUTHERLAND
MORVEN 2313 ft.
Lybster
Helmsdale
Loch Broom
SUILVEN 2399 ft.
BEN MORE 3273 ft.
Loch Shin
Helmsdale
Loch Ewe
Ullapool
Oykell
Carron
DORNOCH
Dunrobin Castle
Tain
NORTH SEA
SLIOCH 3217 ft.
BEN DEARG 3547 ft.
BEN WYVIS 3429 ft.
Moray Firth
Loch Maree
Torridon
ROSS AND CROMARTY
DINGWALL
Cromarty Firth
Cromarty
ELGIN
Fraserburgh
Eilean Donan Castle
INVERNESS
NAIRN
MORAY
Lossie
BANFF
Peterhead
L. Alsh
MAM SOUL 3862 ft.
NAIRN
Grantown
Spey
Deveron
Ugie
Huntly Castle
BEN ATTOW 3383 ft.
Nairn
Findhorn
BANFF
Ythan
L. Hourn
Glen More
Loch Ness
MONADHLIATH MOUNTAINS
Strath Spey
Don
Inverurie
Arisaig
Glen Garry
Garva Bridge
CAIRNGORMS
ABERDEEN
ABERDEEN
Glenfinnan
CALEDONIAN CANAL
INVERNESS
Braemar
Balmoral Castle
Dee
STONEHAVEN
L. Shiel
Fort William
BEN ALDER 3757 ft.
GRAMPIAN MOUNTAINS
LOCHNAGAR 3768 ft.
Dunnottar Castle
KINCARDINE
BEN NEVIS 4406 ft.
Blair Atholl Castle
N. Esk
ANGUS
L. Linnhe
L. Leven
Rannoch
SCHIEHALLION 3547 ft.
S. Esk
Montrose
L. Etive
Lyon
Tay
Dunkeld
FORFAR
Arbroath
Oban
Kilchurn Castle
BEN LAWERS 3984 ft.
L. Tay
SIDLAW HILLS
Dundee
ARGYLL
L. Awe
BEN MORE 3843 ft.
L. Earn
Crieff
PERTH
PERTH
Earn
Eden
Firth of Tay
L. Fyne
INVERARAY
THE TROSSACHS
BEN LOMOND 3192 ft.
Doune Castle
OCHIL HILLS
L. Long
Loch Lomond
Forth
Firth of Forth

S.J. Turner, F.R.G.S.

The Highlands of Scotland

THERE are countries whose mountains are a direct economic asset, in that they either possess mineral wealth, or are able to support a reasonably prosperous agricultural population. The mountains of the Highlands, however, are singularly uneconomic in these respects—uneconomic, indeed, in almost any respect except in so far as they may be exploited in years to come from the tourist point of view. Their age and geological origin have rendered them more intractable than many hilly parts of the world: from an arable standpoint they are largely useless. As open pasturage for sheep, on the other hand, they have some value, and little isolated communities do contrive to live among them. Where sheep have been driven off to make room for deer, gamekeepers are to be found in place of shepherds.

Where the mountains tend to approach the sea, we find humble hamlets of cottar-fishermen, peasants who derive a modest livelihood from their smallholdings, and from casual and somewhat spasmodic fishing. In recent years, the economic resources of such mountain-dwellers have been appreciably augmented by a revival of spinning and weaving, especially in the production of homespuns, such as tweeds, gloves, scarfs, jumpers, and stockings.

Roughly speaking, the northern mountains of the Highlands are those lying to the north of the Dingwall-Skye railway. The distances to be covered in reaching them are great, which, in territory where population is small and accommodation correspondingly scarce, is a serious drawback to the mountain-lover. However, improvements made during the last few decades in those roads that formerly bore little except slow-moving horse-drawn vehicles now enable one to approach many of the northern mountains by motor-car.

These northern mountains are composed of sandstone. In the Torridon and Assynt districts they are capped with Cambrian quartzite. One instantly feels about the peaks in the far north-west of Sutherland something remarkable and unusual. They seem quite different from those one finds elsewhere in Britain, or even in the Highlands. Take, for example, Foinaven (or Foinne-Bheinn, the White Ben), that mountain-peak situated in the Reay Forest, less than six miles west-south-west of the head of Loch Eriboll, or take Arkle, lying a few miles to the south. In certain lights, the white quartzite, of which these rapidly decaying mountains are composed, gives to them the

37

appearance of something quite fantastic. The hill-climber, especially when approaching their ledges and buttresses, must indeed exercise caution, since their debris is treacherous, and their rocks are brittle and apt to splinter.

If these two peaks do not inspire the beholder with wonder and curiosity, what of Suilven, the Grey Castle, one of the most extraordinary geological formations in all Britain? This mountain lies five miles to the south-east of Lochinver, and is sometimes called the Sugar Loaf. Because of the weirdness of its shape and isolation of its position, it seems to relegate to a place of secondary importance the neighbouring and loftier peaks of Cul More, Cul Beag, and Canisp. Viewed from the east or from the west, Suilven dominates the scene for miles around. From either direction it appears as one massive cone rising steeply from the comparatively flat moorland stretching away on every side of it. Seen from the north or from the south, however, it is, at first sight, less impressive, for then one discovers it to be the western end of a narrow ridge just over a mile and a half in length, and consisting of three main peaks—Castle Liath, in the west; the pointed peak of Meall Mhead-honach, in the centre; and the much smaller mountain of Meall Bheag, in the east. Castle Liath, seen from the ridge, might be the Matterhorn in miniature.

Many other Sutherland peaks are worthy of honourable mention. There come to mind Ben Kilbreck, lying to the south of Loch Naver; Ben Loyal,

SUTHERLAND CROFTERS

The wild barren country of northern Scotland supports only a small number of inhabitants, who by hard work and unremitting energy have won a livelihood from the infertile soil. These crofters at Ledmore are stacking peat to dry. Later the peat will be used for the cottage fire, which is the only means of cooking and heating in most of the crofters' cottages and small farmhouses of northern Scotland. Coal is rarely used in these parts, not only because of its comparatively high price, but because of the difficulty of transporting it from the distant towns along the narrow and difficult roads of the Highlands. The peat "stacks" are designed to allow quick drying.

overshadowing the loch of the same name; and Ben Hope, near the southern end of Loch Hope, that long, narrow, inland loch pouring its excess, by way of a short river, into the northern tides at Loch Eriboll. Ben Hope is the most northerly mountain in Britain exceeding 3,000 ft. The rocky buttresses on its west and north-west faces present some formidable climbs.

Then there are three peaks overlooking Loch Assynt which must not be allowed to pass unnoticed—Quinag, Glasven, and, of course, Ben More Assynt, one of the noblest mountains in the far north. Quinag (the Water Stoup, as the mountain-folk sometimes call it) shares with all the northern

39

Highlands much that is of extreme interest to the geologist in a land remarkable for its isolated masses of very ancient rock.

Four miles south-east of the village of Inchnadamph, which is situated at the head of Loch Assynt, Ben More Assynt rises to a height of well over 3,000 ft. This is one of the most celebrated northern mountains, though, owing to its remoteness, it is much less frequented than most. It lies in the heart of country where roads are scarce, where distances are great.

The name of Assynt is of further significance, since on a spit of land jutting out into Loch Assynt, and at no distance from the modest highway traversing these wild parts, stand the ruins of Ardvreck Castle. Montrose, after his defeat at Carbisdale, fled to Sutherland. He was captured in Assynt and brought to Ardvreck, where lived Neil MacLeod, laird of Assynt. Justifiably or otherwise (and into this highly controversial matter we need not go meanwhile), Neil delivered the fugitive into the hands of his enemies, who, in May, 1650, executed him at Edinburgh.

EXPLORING THE NORTHERN HILLS

Remote as are these northern mountains, it must not be imagined that they are wholly inaccessible. On the contrary, roads permitting of an average speed of 20 miles per hour reach out toward them. But, as accommodation among them is scarce, and population exceedingly scanty, it is as well that one should select some such starting-point as Bonar Bridge or Lairg, both of which are on the main line. From these places, on a long, summer day, one can penetrate far into this region by motor-car, though it is advisable that food should be carried, and also sufficient petrol for the return journey. Lodgings can sometimes be had at little places farther afield, as at Inchnadamph, for instance, on the road to Assynt, or at the fishing village of Lochinver, on the west coast of Sutherland, where the Assynt road ultimately leads. Inchnadamph, however, is the better centre from which to embark on exploration of these northern hills.

When we pass southward into Ross, we are in a region of mountains that would seem to be without end. The centre of the county is one jumbled confusion of them, and of the short, elevated valleys and long, narrow, inland lochs lying between them. The peaks are far too numerous to admit of our naming even a representative number of them.

For our present purpose, therefore, one can do little more than mention some of the groupings, such as the Strathcarron and Achnashellach Hills; the Applecross Hills (which include the famous Bealach nam Bo, or Pass of the Cattle, over which, at an altitude of over 2,000 ft., runs what is probably the highest droving road in Scotland); the Torridon Mountains, with such peaks as Alligin and Liathach, the Grey One; the Maree Hills, between which the loch of that name wedges its way; the groups known as An Teallach, the Fannichs, and the Coigach Hills; and those mountains of Kintail, located in the south-west corner of the county.

Not one of these groups is without peaks that can present hazards to those whose delight it is to spend a holiday arduously, searching out the most

THE MOUNTAINS OF KINTAIL

There is an old drove-road to Skye by way of Glenelg. It winds its way through the mountains of Kintail, and is here seen coming down to the head of Loch Duich, in Ross-shire. The old road has been resurfaced and is now fit for light motor traffic, though in many places the difficult nature of the country prevents the road from being widened.

GLEN COE

Glen Coe links the road that follows the banks of Loch Leven with the central Highlands. This photograph gives an impression of the magnificent but austere scenery that characterizes this high pass and the precipitous slopes of the enclosing hills. Glen Coe is the scene in Scottish history of the massacre of the Macdonalds by the Campbells in 1692. The government issued a proclamation promising pardon to all clans who laid down their arms. The Macdonalds of Glen Coe were late in giving their formal surrender. They were visited by troops of William III led by Captain Campbell, hereditary enemy of their clan, whom they entertained. At a pre-arranged signal the members of the Macdonald clan were put to the sword.

difficult and dangerous routes by which they may be conquered. Take, for instance, An Stac, that mountain in Coigach usually spoken of as Stac Polly. It is only a little over 2,000 ft. high, yet famous mountaineers and cliffsmen are greatly attracted to those sharp and shattered pinnacles which prompted Professor Heddle to describe this peculiar mountain as "a porcupine in a state of extreme irascibility."

Perhaps the loveliest of the mountains of Ross are those of Kintail, clustered round the head of Loch Duich, in Wester Ross. They include that fine range of peaks known as the Five Sisters of Kintail. Scour Ouran (Sgurr Fhuaran) is the loftiest of them, whilst Sgurr na Ciste Duibhe and Sgurr na Carnach, two of the remaining four, are well over 3,000 ft. From a point roughly a mile above Invershiel, a small, rural township situated at the head of Loch Duich, the summit of Scour Ouran may be reached by what is the longest slope of uniform gradient in Scotland—3,500 ft. of grassy buttress.

Kintail and Loch Duich are the epitome of scenic loveliness. Furthermore, they enshrine much highland legendary and tradition, much history and romance. It was gratifying, therefore, when so considerable a proportion of mountainous Kintail—roughly 15,000 acres—was purchased recently by

42

the National Trust for Scotland from donations made by a generous and anonymous supporter, with a view to enabling the Trust to acquire mountainous territory to be held and preserved, henceforth, for the benefit and enjoyment of the nation. The area involved embraces some of the finest mountain scenery in Britain, and is traversed by rights-of-way well known to hillmen and mountaineers. It is inhabited mainly by crofters, and carries, in addition to deer, great numbers of sheep belonging to them. The principle of administration is the same as in the case of the Dalness estate, that beautiful property between Glen Etive and Glen Coe purchased by the Trust.

Deer-stalking, in the accepted sense of the term, has ceased, though it will be necessary to keep down the number of deer by employing, at any rate for a time, the stalkers formerly engaged there. At all times the public will have full right of access to these mountains. No new paths are to be constructed and no directional signs erected. Every effort will be made by the Trust to retain the entire area in its original state, primitive and undeveloped. On the other hand, facilities will be allowed, within reason, for hostels, camping-sites, and such other forms of accommodation as may be thought justifiable. But all such will be confined to the fringes of the shore-road, in order that the wilder, remoter, and more mountainous parts shall continue unspoilt by anything in the form of a human habitation.

In addition to the rights-of-way already alluded to, the whole of Kintail

GLEN ETIVE, ARGYLLSHIRE

From Loch Etive north-east to the mountains of Argyll this road hugs the lowest ground of Glen Etive on the way to Rannoch Moor. In the background are the two peaks known as the Shepherds of Lorne. In the foreground are the pasture-fields of the glen marked out by low stone walls and distinguished by stunted trees and some more extensive plantations of conifers. Rannoch has many literary associations. It figures in Munro's historic novel *John Splendid* and is the scene of many incidents in Robert Louis Stevenson's *Kidnapped*.

WESTERN LEWIS, OUTER HEBRIDES

The Outer Hebrides contain some of the loneliest countryside in Britain. With a small and decreasing population, their only activities are fishing, spinning and weaving, and a meagre agriculture which the poverty of the soil and wetness of the climate constantly threaten. The famous Harris tweed is woven in the small cottages to be found throughout Harris and Lewis. Here at Carnish, in Western Lewis, is a number of two-storeyed crofters' cottages built in recent years to replace older structures.

and of the regions bordering upon it is intersected by a network of mountain-tracks and hill-paths, many of which are known only to the highland shepherds following their solitary calling in this wild countryside, and, perhaps, to the natives who tread them when afoot among the hills and lochs separating them from relatives and friends. These mountain-ways are intricate: they lead in all directions. Many of them are worn hard by the trotters of sheep and the hoofs of deer.

Kintail, the country of the Wild MacRaes, a small clan dependent upon the MacKenzies of Seaforth, is as rich in legendary and history as any part of the Highlands. So, also, is the mountainous country encircling it. The natives will tell you that the great notch in the hills known as the Hunter's Pass was caused by a giant hunter who, when hurrying from Glen Elg to Strathglass, jumped from the Mam Ratagan, hoping to clear Ben Attow, that massive mountain lying immediately to the north of the Five Sisters, and soaring to a height not far short of that of Scour Ouran.

Then, when travelling down Glen Elg toward Kylerhea, the ancient ferrying-place for Skye, you may see, on the skyline on the right-hand side of the glen, a large boulder which looks as though at any moment it might come toppling down. Now it was prophesied by Coinneach Odhar, the Brahan Seer (he who foretold, among other things, the decline of the Sea-forths), that when this boulder does come hurtling down the hillside, a man passing through Glen Elg will be killed by it. According to the natives the

44

victim's name will be John MacRae, and he will be riding a white horse.

High up among the Five Sisters of Kintail is a pass that the highland shepherds call by a Gaelic name denoting Pass of the Spaniards—a curious name to find amidst these great mountains. Yet the reason for it is a historical one. In 1719 there was a Jacobite Rising, of which comparatively few may have heard. To historians it is known as "The Nineteen," having occurred between "The Fifteen" and the final rebellion known as "The Forty-five." In the autumn of 1718, Philip V of Spain, through his minister, Cardinal Alberoni, sent the Jacobites some three hundred Spanish troops, together with much ammunition, money, and stores. At the Battle of Glenshiel, fought near Bridge of Shiel, and at a spot marked on many maps by a pair of crossed swords, the Jacobites and their Spanish allies came to grips with the Hanoverians and were routed. Many of them fled to the mountains around them, the Spaniards for the most part seeking refuge among the Five Sisters, and in the direction of the Pass, the name of which commemorates their abortive efforts to assist the Jacobites in their rebellion.

Of all the wonderful panoramas in the Scottish Highlands, there is one of

IN GLEN BANCHOR

The mountains and rolling foothills of Inverness-shire include some of the most beautiful scenes in Scotland but give only a poor return for the farmer's labour. This photograph of Glen Banchor shows mile after mile of utterly barren countryside, apart from the group of small trees high up the glen and the rough grass which provides a meagre pasturage for sheep. The size of the flock being driven in for the annual dipping by two shepherds and their dogs shows how Scottish farmers make the best possible use of the land available.

surpassing beauty. It is that of the Five Sisters of Kintail as seen from the Mam Ratagan, the summit of the steep mountain-road leading over from Loch Duich to Glen Elg. No mountain-lover should quit this life until he has seen it, and perhaps pictured for himself the journey that confronted the ponderous Dr. Johnson in 1773 when, accompanied by Boswell and the highlanders who led their tired ponies, he travelled astraddle from Glen Shiel to Glen Elg by way of the ancient drove-road linking the Isle of Skye with the Scottish mainland and the Falkirk Trysts.

Another panorama exquisite in its loveliness and situated in the same locality is the meeting-place of Lochs Alsh, Long, and Duich, as seen from the heights behind Ardentoul, on the hill-track between Totaig and Bernera of Glen Elg, with Beinn na Caillich to the left, the hills about Dornie and Kyle of Lochalsh to the right and, afar off, in the centre, the Red Hills of Skye.

WIDELY SCATTERED HAMLETS

The mountains on the east side of Ross are neither so numerous nor yet so prodigious as are those on the west. Nevertheless, we must not forget Ben Wyvis, that lofty tableland, measuring some six miles by three, dominating the scene north of the Beauly Firth, and to the west of the Cromarty Firth. Its highest point is 3,429 ft. above sea-level. To all intents and purposes, it appears a simple and friendly mountain. Yet its corries and caverns, as also some of the glen-routes by which it may be approached, are gruesome.

As in the case of Sutherlandshire, secondary roads enable one to travel awheel through much of mountainous Ross-shire. Ben Wyvis is no great distance from Dingwall, the county town, situated on the main line between Inverness and the far north of Scotland. Westward from Dingwall, with mountains on every side, runs the railway to Kyle of Lochalsh, on the threshold of Skye, sending branches into the remoter and even more mountainous parts, few of which cannot now be reached by the careful motorist. He may find accommodation at such places as Achnasheen and Kinlochewe, Lochcarron and Applecross; but as the country is so thinly peopled, and the distance between hamlets often great, he would be well advised to carry both food and spare petrol, especially if he be a stranger untutored in mountain ways and in the best means of utilizing such information as may be obtained *en route* from cottars or gamekeepers.

If there be any part of the Scottish Highlands with more than its due share of mountains it is Inverness-shire. They continue southward from Ross, right across the entire county, down through Argyll to its south-western extremities, and occupy most of Breadalbane, as much of western Perthshire is called. Indeed, they sweep tumultuously southward right into the Stirlingshire parish of Buchanan. There, at an altitude of over 3,000 ft., they culminate in Ben Lomond, a peak illustrious in the song and story of the Gael.

From the summit of Ben Lomond, to quote from an old gazetteer, the view "in aggregate, diversity, brilliance, and picturesque magnificence is equalled by no view in all the United Kingdom." This view has something suggestive of a holy mountain; and in this context one recalls, from among its

46

THE FALLS OF MORAR

This swift-flowing river is the outlet of Loch Morar, the deepest of the Scottish lochs (more than 1,000 ft. deep in places). It is crossed by the traditional route from Fort William to Mallaig, which carries both road and railway, and is itself part of the most direct route for travellers from central Scotland to the Isle of Skye. This and other well-wooded streams and rivers of western Inverness-shire give some of the finest fishing in Scotland, or even in Britain.

voluminous memories and associations, the ascent made in 1796 by the Rev. Charles Simeon and James Alexander Haldane, who, on the top of it, "impressed by the grandeur of the surrounding scenery, kneeled down and solemnly consecrated their future lives to the service of Almighty God."

The western regions of Inverness-shire—Lochiel and Lochaber, Knoydart and Moidart, Morar and Arisaig—with their lovely sea-lochs penetrating far between the hills, are as mountainous as any part of the Highlands. The same may be said of Sunart and Ardnamurchan, Ardgour and Morven, the impinging districts of Argyll. Indeed, but for the Sound of Mull, the heights of Morven might have been carried continuously to the mountainous Isle of Mull itself, where Ben More holds its own among the Western Highlands.

It was in the shoreland and mountain caves of western Inverness-shire that Bonnie Prince Charlie, together with many of the more intimate of his followers, sought refuge after defeat at Culloden. A small sign-post in the grounds of Arisaig House points in the direction of one such cave, the mouth of which looks out over a stretch of green shoreland to Loch nan Uamh, and to Ardnamurchan beyond. Another cave, also known as Prince Charlie's

47

INVERNESS CASTLE

The suspension bridge that crosses the River Ness, just above the point where it flows into Loch Beauly, and the castle are two of the most imposing structures in Inverness—a town that is a royal burgh and one of the great tourist centres of northern Scotland. The castle itself dates from only 1835 and is used as the sheriff's court, but it followed a much earlier building known as Macbeth's Castle, which, tradition relates, is where King Duncan was murdered by Macbeth in the eleventh century. Beside the entrance to the suspension bridge is Queen Mary's house, where Mary Queen of Scots stayed during her travels in Scotland after her return from exile in France.

Cave, lies in the hillside high above Loch Beoraid, one of the inland lochs of South Morar.

In 1745 the Prince, then so full of hope, came ashore at Loch nan Uamh, the Loch of the Caves, from a French frigate. The following year, after he had spent months as a fugitive in these inaccessible parts, another French vessel entered this same sea-loch to bear him away to France, never to return.

These mountains, and the lochs and valleys diversifying them, were so closely associated with the Prince's coming, with his seclusion, and with his final going, that they comprise the part of Scotland appropriately referred to as Prince Charlie's Country. Was it not at Glenfinnan, by the head of Loch Shiel, so near at hand, that the Jacobites, with the highland hills towering on three sides of them, raised their standard on that memorable day, 19 August, 1745, thus officially inaugurating "The Forty-five"?

Running diagonally through the county of Inverness, in a south-westerly and north-easterly direction, is the Great Glen of Scotland, with its three lengthy lochs, namely, Loch Lochy, Loch Oich, and Loch Ness. These three lochs, of course, are connected with one another and with the sea by the

48

Caledonian Canal. Mountains tower on both sides of the Great Glen throughout its entire length of sixty miles between Inverness and Fort William. To the east of it (that is to say, in the Lochaber and Badenoch regions of the county) three main mountain masses fall to be noted. They are the Ben Nevis group, the Monadhliath, and the Cairngorms. The more easterly peaks of the last mentioned are situated in Braemar, which lies to the east of Badenoch.

Where the Great North Road passes through Badenoch, one is truly in the heart of the Grampians, though even experts on the subject of highland mountains differ as to which should be included under this name and which should not. The term nowadays is loosely applied to all the mountainous country lying roughly between Loch Linnhe and the Moray Firth, and to the east of the Great Glen. Aviemore, on the main railway route to Inverness, is the best centre from which to reach most of them.

Of Ben Nevis one need not say a great deal here. Everybody knows it to be the highest peak in the British Isles, though few may know that Ben MacDhui, that great Cairngorm mountain, falls short of it by no more than 110 ft. Fort William is the most suitable base from which to explore Ben Nevis. The routes to the top of it, as also to the summits of its neighbours, the Carn Deargs, are as numerous as they can be dangerous.

FREQUENTED BY SKIERS

On the north side of the River Spey, almost from its source as far downstream as Kingussie, lie the Monadhliath—the Grey Moor, as its Gaelic derivatives indicate. This group is less interesting than many, though it should be observed that no fewer than eight of its summits exceed 3,000 ft., and that several others fall not far short of that height. The Monadhliath are frequented not so much by climbers as by skiers. Indeed, climbers will tell you that they are wholly devoid of "climbs."

Of much greater interest to the lover of the high places is the Corrieyarrick, lying but a few miles to the west. Over the Pass of Corrieyarrick, General Wade carried his famous road between Dalwhinnie and Fort Augustus, never imagining that a few years later it was to be of service to the rebelling Jacobites, whose activities the construction of such military roads was designed to curtail. When Sir John Cope learnt that Prince Charlie's army lay firmly entrenched in the Corrieyarrick, he decided not to pursue his original plan of crossing by the pass to Fort Augustus, but of marching north to Inverness. This left the lowland plains unprotected against invasion by the Jacobite forces, and with results which are well known.

Wade's mountain-road over the Corrieyarrick has long since fallen into disuse. In parts it seems to have disappeared. Yet the eye can follow its alignment easily; and the great traverses and buttresses, whereby it was carried in zigzag fashion up the steepest gradients, are still fairly well preserved after more than two centuries, though much overgrown. The old bridges bearing it across river and stream are also there. One of these, situated high among the mountains, carries the road over the stream known as the Yarrick. However, the largest and most imposing of them is the double-arched bridge at Garva,

PASTURES OF ARGYLLSHIRE
Kilchoan, shown in this picture, is within seven miles of Ardnamurchan Point, the most westerly part of Scotland. The water in the background is a broad inlet of the Atlantic Ocean, here seen at low tide. The cattle in the foreground are the stock-in-trade of the crofters. In the right background is seen a quite extensive area of field marked out and the land ploughed to grow corn crops, whilst there is fair pasturage on the hillside.

completed in 1732, the point at which the road crosses the Spey.

The Corrieyarrick offers one of the most fascinating mountain journeys in Britain to anyone sound in wind and limb, keen of eye, and sure of foot. It demands more fortitude and endurance than does a passage through the Lairig Ghru, that famous Cairngorm defile between Rothiemurchus and Braemar.

The Corrieyarrick is haunted—haunted not only by the grey ghosts of the ancient fighters, but also by that of a shepherd who accosts one in the Pass itself, and asks in the Gaelic: "*C'aite am bheil thu dol?*" "Where are you going?"

It is a solitary journey. For miles and miles one never sees a cottage or, indeed, any evidence of a habitation. It is seldom, too, that one meets even a shepherd or a gamekeeper. The hardy will attack it either from Laggan, which may be reached from Dalwhinnie, on the Great North Road, or from Fort Augustus, that peaceful town at the head of Loch Ness, easily reached by road from Inverness as from Fort William.

The Cairngorms, rising in majestic contours between the Spey and the Dee, are the largest group of high mountains in Britain. Ben MacDhui, as we have seen, is the second-highest mountain in the British Isles. In addition to it, three well-known Cairngorm mountain-peaks exceed 4,000 ft. They are Braeriach, Carn Toul, and Cairn Gorm, after which the group is named. A little to the east of these four lofty summits are two peaks, Ben Avon and Beinn a' Bhuird, both of which fall very little short of the 4,000 ft. contour.

The Cairngorms occupy an area of some three hundred square miles. This area includes not only the lofty parts already mentioned, but many square miles of foot-hills, of lochs and rivers, forests and moorland. Nowhere else in Britain, within similar limits as to area, is there such diversity, such natural magnificence. Heather abounds in astonishing profusion; and the dark-green pine-woods of Rothiemurchus, encircling Loch an Eilein and stretching eastward from it well up into the foot-hills, would seem to have no ending. Even after considerable fellings these forests appear but little reduced.

Unlike most mountain groups, the Cairngorms are set loftily in surroundings which, to a large extent, may be regarded as highly cultivated. Speyside, to the west and north-west of them, and Deeside, to the east, include some of the richest farming land in the country. There are few elevated regions from which one may scan so vast a panorama of agricultural land as can be seen from this point.

Although their approaches seem free from hazard, scarcely a year goes by without mishap among them. Even the most skilled mountaineers have been known to come to grief in their dark, sunless corries, in their lonely passes, on their storm-scarred summits, steep screes, or perpendicular precipices. If one cannot envisage such disasters from the gentler approaches to this stupendous mountain mass, one need penetrate but a little way into its higher altitudes to be confronted with dangers and pitfalls.

Perhaps the only other mountains presenting the climber with so many

THE ROAD TO INVERARAY

The main road to Inveraray, Argyllshire, here passes by the head of Loch Fyne, which reaches from the Sound of Bute forty miles into the heart of the Grampian mountains. The snow-clad slopes on the farther bank are those of Ben Vorlich, which rises 3,000 ft. above sea-level and lies between the head of Loch Fyne and Loch Lomond. Although the snow rarely disappears entirely from Ben Nevis, the highest peak, it is comparatively rare for the loch-side roads to be covered.

perils are the Coolins of Skye. The mountains of North Wales, the Cumberland Fells, the Southern Uplands, and the rest, are harmless and even benign by comparison. This explains how mountaineers, already sure-footed enough on hills less demanding, feel that their conquest of the Cairngorms or of the Coolins is the greatest thing they can achieve. But experience is no guarantee against fatality. Many a proficient mountaineer has come to grief in these two groups of mountains.

In olden times, when there existed no means of communication except by foot between, say, the people of Badenoch or of Rothiemurchus and those of Deeside, travellers often perished in the Cairngorms. Thus originated many an awe-inspiring legend of their being the abode of ghosts and monsters. If the actual mountains were not inhabited by fearsome creatures, their lochs and rivers assuredly were the haunt of the dreaded water-horse. The Valley of the Spey is as rich in folk-lore of this kind as is any part of the country.

PEAKS OF THE CAIRNGORMS

The Cairngorms are, indeed, immense; but one has to stand well back from them to appreciate this—back as far as Aviemore or Grantown-on-Spey, from either of which places the stranger may reach them comfortably. One is denied any idea of the even greater immensity of Ben Nevis because neither at Fort William nor at any place within reasonable distance of that West Highland town is one able to see it in proper perspective, even if it were free from mist and rain, which it so seldom is. The Cairngorms, on the other hand, occur in a part of Scotland where weather conditions are "east coast" rather than "west coast" and are, therefore, comparatively dry. On most days of the year the skyline is sharp and the peaks plainly visible.

So pleasing, so inspiring, is the prospect from almost any of the Cairngorm summits that one is spared that sense of desolation, and perhaps of futility, which is inclined to overshadow one when traversing Glen Sligachan or the Corrieyarrick. The welter of mountains seen to the westward of the latter, especially on a dull, foreboding day, can at times be oppressive and repellent. There is nothing like this about the Cairngorms. On every hand they are uplifting. Massive, and even treacherous, as they are, they remain free from any impression of their being god-forsaken. Their gentler foot-hills, largely covered with pines and birches and in places so ardently tilled, exalt them. Their great bulkiness, even when covered with snow, but emphasizes the plenteousness and prosperity of much of the territory impinging upon them.

Owing to their height, as also to their more easterly location, they are snowclad more often and for longer periods than are the other mountains of the Highlands. All through the summer, snow may be seen in the loftier corries and ravines. Indeed, it may also be said that patches of the Cairngorms are covered by perpetual snow. Thus, at any time of the year, the mountaineer may find use for his ice-axe.

To the mountaineer and cliff-climber, the Cairngorms offer unending challenge. The number of routes through them and over them is countless.

CHARMING PERTHSHIRE VILLAGE

North of a line drawn from the Forth to the Clyde there are few villages, except in coastal districts, that have real beauty of architecture and composition, but in Perthshire there are several exceptions. These thatched cottages at Fortingall make up one of the prettiest scenes in the Highland district. The village is beautifully situated at the foot of Glen Lyon, the longest of all the Highland glens. In the background is Carn Marig. The contrast between the rocky slopes of the mountain and the rich foliage of the valley is noticeable.

Their passes are as inviting to the adventurous as they are fraught with perils. If the traveller among them be superstitious or of a nervous disposition, he may also have to contend with an infinite variety of ghosts and spectres! The Spectre of the Brocken will assuredly terrify him; and, if he come by way of the Glen More pine-forests, he is pretty certain to be detained by the Lamhdearg, or the Bloody Hand, that fearsome goblin known to have scared even the stoutest.

The Lairig Ghru, it is generally conceded, is one of the most interesting crossings between major watersheds in Great Britain. This famous pass runs between two of the finest of Britain's possessions, namely, the Valley of the Dee and the Valley of the Spey. When walking through it from Aviemore to Braemar, one has Ben MacDhui on the left and Braeriach on the right, two very splendid mountains. Although the neighbourhood can supply any number of tales of misfortunes that have befallen travellers throughout the years,

ROCK-CLIMBING IN THE WESTERN HIGHLANDS

The Scottish Highlands in general afford fewer opportunities for rock-climbing than do the peaks of the Lake District of Cumberland or those of North Wales. Some of the finest rock climbs are in the south-western Highlands, within comparatively easy reach of Glasgow and the other industrial districts of Scotland. Ben Arthur, seen *above*, also known as The Cobbler, rises abruptly to almost 3,000 ft. at the head of Loch Long. This peak dominates the whole valley in which lies the loch, seen here in the background.

it can also supply many of great endurance and achievement. One hears about the prowess of an Aviemore mason who, while employed for several months in building houses at Braemar, always walked home across the Lairig Ghru for his Sunday dinner, and returned to Braemar the same evening—a distance of over twenty miles in each direction, even as the crow flies! He allowed himself one brief halt by the Pools of Dee, where he ate the snack he carried in his pocket.

Accidents to inexperienced travellers are as easy as they are frequent in this domain of the red deer, of the golden eagle, and the snowy ptarmigan. Indeed, they have been so numerous of late among the mountains of Inverness-shire, and have involved so many hazardous rescues, that warning notices have been issued by the county police.

In passing southward to Argyll we are still very much in the land of mountains. They tower over all its famous glens—Glen Lochy and Glen Orchy, Glen Strae and Glen Kinglas, Glen Etive and Glen Coe. About the marches of the three counties of Argyll, Perth, and Dumbarton, they are indeed dense and intricate. To the west of Loch Lomond, where that great inland sheet of water runs narrowly up toward Glen Falloch, lies the lovely group of Dumbarton mountains known as the Arrochar Hills. To Glasgow climbers and hikers its four principal peaks (Ben Arthur, or the Cobbler, Ben Ime, Ben Vane, and Ben Vorlich) are a paradise, since they are no great distance from that city. There can be few Sundays in the year on which the cliffy summit of the Cobbler is not assailed by youths from this, the second city of Scotland, travelling to it by way of Loch Lomond or Loch Long.

AMONG THE GRAMPIANS

When you move northward from Tyndrum you are confronted by Ben Doran, that noble peak which is the subject of so many Gaelic songs and poems. It forms one of the group of mountains overlooking Loch Tulla, the Black Mount, and the upper reaches of Glen Orchy. Here we are among the Grampians proper. This mighty range forms part of Drumalbain—part of the Ridge of Alba, of Scotland—to which the writers of old referred. On looking back at it from the road crossing the Black Mount on its way to Kingshouse and Glen Coe, one realizes how apt is the ancient name, Drumalbain.

Rising steeply behind the sheep-farm of Achallader, in upper Glen Orchy, is Beinn Achadh-fhaladair. Some twenty years ago, considerable interest was shown in this mountain, following upon the disappearance of a young mountaineer named Henderson, whose body was found after a protracted search and under eerie circumstances. The organizers of the search-parties received a number of anonymous letters, purporting to tell the exact spot on Beinn Achadh-fhaladair where the body would be found. The actual spot at which, eventually, it *was* found showed that many of the clues contained in these psychic communications were astonishingly accurate. Three weeks after Henderson was reported missing, and a radius of fifteen miles of mountainous country had been scoured, Duncan Smith, the sheep-farmer at Achallader, found the body at an altitude of about 3,000 ft., only 60 ft.

below the level indicated in the anonymous letters. It had slipped down that distance in the interval.

Some idea of the expanse of Drumalbain may be had when one realizes that it takes seven or eight shepherds, and twice as many dogs, an average of sixteen hours to gather the sheep on one hirsel of the 30,000 acres comprising merely the sheep-farm of Achallader. As there are several hirsels, the ingathering occupies several days, even in good weather, or weeks when it is misty.

Two well-known mountains border the Black Mount on the west; they are Stob Gabhair and the Clachlet. The latter is a recognized deer sanctuary. Beyond these lies Glen Etive, that glen of Celtic myth and legend. Here, they say, lived Deirdre of the Sorrows, at a spot near the present lodge at Dalness. Here she roamed in contentment with Naoise, until Fergus, Knight of the Red Branch, and emissary from King Conchobar, came to lure them away to Ireland, and indeed to sorrow.

WORLD-FAMOUS NAMES

Between Glen Etive and Glen Coe of gloomy memory lies that cluster of fine mountains which used to be known as the Royal Forest of Dalness. In 1937 it became the property of the National Trust for Scotland. It contains some of the finest mountain country in the Highlands.

A word or two in conclusion about the uplands of Perthshire, where the peaks bear names that, thanks to *The Lady of the Lake*, and perhaps also to *Rob Roy*, are known the world over. One has only to mention them to be reminded of familiar passages. *The Lady of the Lake* did much to enhance the Highlands throughout the English-speaking world, and to ensure for the Clan MacGregor the foremost place in the wild and romantic history of the northern kingdom. We recall "the antlered monarch of the waste" seeking the heath of Uamh Mhor (Uam-Var), that mountain near Callander notorious for its cave in which marauders and blackmailers hid in olden times. We recall, too, the echoes from Ben Vorlich, as hound and steed and huntsman pursued their quarry. And what of Ben Ledi, and the Fiery Cross it knew?

No great distance to the west lie the Trossachs, with Ben A'n and Ben Venue rising high above them. These lovely, wooded parts are so different from the barren localities with which we have been concerned up till now. Yet the sylvan beauties of Loch Achray and Loch Katrine in no way diminish the glory of these mountains. Callander is undoubtedly the place from which they are most accessible. In the height of the season, the narrow roads winding among them are always very busy, since they are much used by tourist charabancs from such centres of population as Edinburgh and Glasgow. In recent years the two principal towns in Scotland have made a great feature of their day trips to these romantic parts.

In the Trossachs, legend and folk-lore, romance and history, are inextricably commingled. The Goblin's Cave actually exists; and you may find it easily. Unless you have a row-boat at your disposal, you must needs climb over the Bealach nam Bo, the Pass of the Cattle, to reach Glasachoil, just as the clansmen were obliged to do in the days of Rob Roy MacGregor. There is

LOCH TAY, PERTHSHIRE

Loch Tay extends nearly twenty miles from Killin to Kenmore through the heart
of the southern Highlands. It is a countryside of many great castles and shooting
estates, picturesque alike in its barren uplands and in the woods and coppices
of the lowlands bordering on the loch. This view shows the Killin end of Loch
Tay, with the River Dochart in the right foreground, which flows out of it
and connects it with the village of Killin. The Dochart and the whole of Loch
Tay are famous the world over for their salmon-fishing.

many a remote place about Loch Katrine, but none more so than the sheep-
farm of Glasachoil, where Mrs. MacDougall, the shepherd's wife, often does
not see another woman for three or four years. If the shepherd and his wife
cannot have the use of a boat, in which to row themselves to the Trossachs
end of Loch Katrine, only by tramping over the hills by way of the Tinkers'
Loch to Ledard, on Loch Ard, can they reach the world inhabited by other
human beings.

For all the improvements in the means of communication elsewhere,
many of the dwellers among the highland mountains still live remotely. They
live contentedly, too. The ancient ways are still with them, and none more
persistently than the hospitality for which the Highlands have always been so
famous. Furthermore, they are inclined to be a solemn people, these mountain-dwellers. In the narrow, conventional sense, they are inclined to be
extremely pious, especially on Sundays. The more isolated they are from one
another, the more tenaciously do they cling to the old custom of church-going,
which often affords them the few opportunities they have of seeing relatives
and friends. Their hardiness is shown by the distances they travel comfortably on foot to church, even in the wildest weather.

57

The Scottish
Lowlands and Uplands

BROADLY speaking, the Lowlands and Uplands of Scotland occupy that part of the country lying to the south of the Highland Line. In olden times, when the great mountain masses of the Grampians formed a natural boundary between the Highlands and the Lowlands, this line could be drawn more accurately than is possible today, when one finds it increasingly difficult to fix any such hard and fast boundary. In the days when the language of the Highlands was entirely Gaelic, and that of most of the remainder of Scotland the ancient Scots tongue, the demarcation was more obvious. Gaelic is gradually dying out, though efforts are being made, as in Ireland, to resuscitate it; and the Lowlands would appear to be encroaching upon the more southerly fringes of Gaeldom. Moreover, much territory which formerly was highland wasteland and moorland has for centuries been highly cultivated under lowland influence, rather than under the more primitive system still obtaining in much of Celtic Scotland.

Yet one must be careful, even when using language as the basis for differentiation, since it should be remembered that the ancient kingdom of Strathclyde, which included Galloway, the south-western corner of Scotland, was also Gaelic-speaking. The Goidelic Celts of Galloway and the Britons of Strathclyde spoke a language similar to that spoken in the Highlands proper. The etymologist need not be surprised, therefore, at finding, in these parts, many place-names of purely Gaelic origin.

A glance at the map of Scotland readily shows how impossible it is to separate precisely the Lowlands from the Highlands. Even those seeking to do so by reference to the territories occupied by the clans are in danger of error, for the Lowlands and Uplands also had their clans. Indeed, much of their early history is concerned with clan rivalry. This is certainly true of the Borders, where the Scotts, the Elliotts, the Douglases, and the Armstrongs conducted bitter and protracted feuds.

When one realizes that the Mull of Kintyre, the southernmost tip of the ancient Gaelic-speaking kingdom of Dalriada, lies well to the south of Berwick-on-Tweed, and that the Mull of Galloway is south of Durham, one sees how impracticable it is to say that to the north or to the south of such-and-such a line lay this or that place or region.

SOUTHERN
SCOTLAND

Generally speaking, then, the area under review embraces the whole of
the central valley of Scotland (that is to say, the rich industrial belt lying
approximately between the Forth and the Clyde), the whole of Strathclyde
(roughly Ayrshire), the southern counties of Galloway, Kirkcudbright, and
Dumfries, the pastoral lands separated from England by the Cheviot hills,
and, of course, the fertile Lothians. It also includes what is usually referred
to as the north-east of Scotland, the counties of Fife, Angus, Kincardine, and
Aberdeen. One would be justified in adding the lower part of Speyside. In
natural resources, both as regards fertility and mineral deposits, the Lowlands
are as rich as the Highlands are poor.

It cannot be claimed for the Lowlands and southern Uplands that they
possess anything of the scenic beauty and grandeur of the Highlands, especially of the western Highlands. Their seaboard is not penetrated by sea-lochs, as
is that of Argyllshire, and of the highland counties lying beyond it. They can
boast nothing as fine as the fiords of Knoydart, of Wester Ross, or of Sutherland, where such magnificent mountains rise steeply from the water's edge.
Nevertheless, they have a beauty of their own—a quieter beauty, a beauty of
rounded hills and smooth-flowing rivers, rather than of jagged peaks and
tumbling cataracts.

They are by no means without their high points, however, though none

59

CHEVIOT COUNTRY

This view typifies the upland country of southern Scotland near the English border. It shows the valley of the Bowmont Water from the road to Mindrum Mill against the background of the Cheviot Hills. There is the same contrast here between the ploughed fields of the valley and the bare grassy slopes of the uplands that characterizes almost the whole of southern Scotland. Farmhouses and village dwellings are half hidden among the trees. Hedges divide the lowland fields, while the upper slopes of the hill are open and unfenced. The flood plain of the stream is uncultivated, because after heavy rain a great weight of water rushes down the valley and often floods it.

of them compares either in altitude or in bulk with, let us say, the Cairngorms, or the Grampians. They are in every way tamer; and their waters are gathered straight into rivers rather than into lochs, which explains how their rivers are longer and more voluminous.

Among the more important of the heights may be mentioned the Campsies, the Ochils, the Pentlands, Moorfoots, and Lammermuirs, the Tweedsmuir hills, the hills of Galloway, and such of the Cheviots as lie north of the Border.

When considering mountains, the southern Uplands are usually treated by themselves. They attain their highest points in Merrick, Rinns of Kells, and Cairnsmuir of Carsphairn in Kirkcudbright, Hartfell in Dumfries, and Whitecombe in Peeblesshire. All these attain an altitude of between 2,500 and 3,000 ft.

Lowland topography is less complicated than highland. Yet it is not lacking in interest. The first writer of importance to exploit this field to any appreciable extent was that most illustrious of Lowlanders, Sir Walter Scott. His writings did for the south of Scotland what many earlier writers had already done for the north. Still, it is curious that, lovely and historical as are the Lowlands and Borders, and so much more accessible than the Highlands, the number of topographical books written about them is comparatively small. This is due to their lacking, in the mind of the reading public at any rate, that romantic elusive quality with which so many associate the Highlands. It is only during the last decade or two that authors have been attracted to this field, the field in which Scott was the pioneer.

The Lowlands and Uplands are lovely and romantic, too; and one cannot but wonder on what sort of day, and in what mood, Washington Irving wrote of them so disparagingly. It was with mute surprise, if not also with disappointment, that he gazed at "a mere succession of grey, waving hills, line beyond line, as far as the eye could reach, monotonous in their aspect, and so destitute of trees that one could almost see a stout fly walking along their profile; and far-famed Tweed appeared a naked stream, flowing between bare hills, without tree or thicket upon its banks."

To Geikie, who wrote so authoritatively on the scenery of Scotland, tne Lowland scene made a very different appeal. Nowhere else in Scotland, he writes, can the exquisite modelling of flowing curves in hill-forms be seen so conspicuously, and to more pleasing advantage. "From the skyline on either side," he wrote of the southern Uplands, "gentle but boldly drawn curves of bent-covered moorland sweep down into the grassy meadow on the floor of the valley. There are architectural forms, which remain distinct at all seasons

THE OCHIL HILLS FROM STIRLING CASTLE

The valley of the Forth lies between Stirling and the Ochil Hills, which mark the most south-easterly extension of the Highlands of Scotland. In this photograph there is clearly seen the sharp distinction between the Lowlands and the Highlands that rise from the plain like a cliff, bare, rocky, and windswept. On the left, immediately in front of the Ochil Hills, is the memorial to Sir William Wallace, the Scottish national hero, who as chief of a band of outlaws defied the authority of Edward I and later took the lead in a general revolt. After the Battle of Stirling Bridge in 1297, Scotland was free from English rule for a year, and it is this victory the monument commemorates.

of the year. But their beauty and impressiveness vary from month to month, almost from hour to hour."

Few writers fail to comment on the colouring of the Lowland hills—the tones of heather and bracken, of moor-grass, of woodland and dene, and of the variegated farm-lands for which so much of the Lowlands are renowned. Anything lovelier than the spring and autumn tintings of Tweedside or of the Border fells of Roxburghshire would be difficult to imagine.

The Borders, which are usually regarded as comprising the counties of Roxburgh, Selkirk, Berwick, and at least part of Dumfries, are a land of hills and rivers and fertile valleys. The hills are scarcely lofty enough to be termed mountains. Yet they have provided this countryside with the basis upon which so much of its prosperity has depended, namely, sheep-farming. Among the more conspicuous of them, though by no means the highest, are the Eildons, which are easily accessible from Melrose. From this ancient Border town, a resolute walker can reach their base in twenty minutes, and ascend any of their three peaks in another twenty. And what a view therefrom! At one's feet lies the land immortalized by Sir Walter Scott, the Wizard of the North—a land now known far and wide as the Scott Country. There is hardly a place-name within a radius of thirty miles which he has not rendered memorable in prose or in verse. No historic incident relating to this region, no folk-tale, no fragment of folk-lore evaded his scrutiny. At the farm of Sandyknowe, in

KELSO, ROXBURGHSHIRE

This lovely bridge over the Tweed was designed by the architect John Rennie, who used it as a model for his masterpiece, the old Waterloo Bridge over the Thames at London. Near the bridge are the ruins of the abbey which was founded early in the twelfth century by David I. Built in the Norman and Early English styles it was pillaged by the Earl of Shrewsbury in 1522 and again by the Earl of Hertford in 1545.

MELROSE ABBEY

There is a close link between Melrose Abbey and Rievaulx Abbey in Yorkshire, for Melrose was set up in 1136 in the reign of David I by emigrants from Rievaulx. It was twice destroyed in the wars between England and Scotland, and was finally rebuilt at the beginning of the fifteenth century. So the ruins represent a more ornate and developed form of architecture than most of those of the Scottish abbeys. The curvilinear tracery of the windows, and the buttresses with niches for figures, are characteristic of the late Decorated style. Tradition says the heart of Robert Bruce was buried near the altar.

the shadow of Smailholm Tower, you will see the place where he romped as a delicate child. In Selkirk you will find the town where he officiated as sheriff. At Abbotsford, close to his belovèd Tweed, you will find his "romance in stone and lime," a shrine, as it were, to which people come from all over the world. Indeed, one can scarcely move a step in the Borderland without running into scenes and associations from which time itself could never disentangle him.

On the slopes of the Eildon Hills, they say, King Arthur and his Knights of the Round Table lie a-slumbering, awaiting the call that one day will release them from "the bondage of enchantment." Just where they lie, the Lowland Scot cannot tell one with any precision; but a farmer, in whose company the writer trod these hills some years ago, told him that he thought it was probably on the north side of the central peak! (Giants and faeries and the like, one must bear in mind, are firmly believed in by Lowlanders, as well as by the Highlanders.) "Three peaks comprise the Eildons, you see," the farmer continued as one sat with him on the highest of them, contemplating the grandest and most expansive prospect in the Lowlands. "Ay, three peaks.

Nae doot, ye'll hae heard tell o' Michael Scot. He it was who divided the Eildons in three by nae mair nor the utterance o' a magic word." As Sir Walter puts it in *The Lay of the Last Minstrel*:

> "*And, Warrior, I could say to thee*
> *The word(s) that cleft Eildon hills in three.*"

So spake the monk of St. Mary's Aisle while watching with Deloraine by Michael's grave at midnight.

Michael Scot, one should explain, was a wizard of great renown in medieval Scotland; and popular tradition has it that the Eildons were by no means the only topographical feature of this countryside owing their origin to his magical powers.

One of the finest distant views of the Eildons is that to be had from a spot on the road between the two Border towns of Galashiels and Melrose, marked by a tablet set in the wall fringing one side of the highway hereabouts. The inscription on the tablet commemorates that passage from Lockhart's biography of his illustrious father-in-law, describing the latter's returning home to Abbotsford from Italy, and gazing upon this scene for the last time. "As we rounded the hill at Ladhope," wrote Lockhart, "and the outline of the Eildons burst on him, he became greatly excited; and, when turning himself on his couch, his eye caught at length his own towers at the distance of a mile, he sprang up with a cry of delight." The Wizard of the North had come home to die. There, at Abbotsford, he breathed his last on 21 September, 1832, in the presence of all his children. "It was a beautiful day—so warm that every window was wide open—and so perfectly still, that the sound of all others most delicious to his ear, the gentle ripple of the Tweed over its pebbles, was distinctly audible as we knelt around the bed, and his eldest son kissed and closed his eyes. No sculptor ever modelled a more majestic image of repose."

Scott's favourite Borderland view, however, was that from the summit of Bemersyde Hill. Here he always reined up his horses, that he might imbibe yet again of this wonderful panorama. On the dark, windy, and lowering day his funeral passed by, on its way to Dryburgh Abbey, the hearse, owing to some temporary delay, stood for several minutes at this very spot.

THE COUNTRY OF THE COVENANTERS

From the high lands of the region under review one cannot pass without a word or two about the Covenanters, for the hills were their refuge in time of stress. What Scot, worthy of his race, does not know something about the Pentland Rising, about Drumclog, where the Covenanters defeated Claverhouse, or "Bonnie Dundee," in 1679, about Bothwell Brig, where, later that same year, they were routed? It was among these hills that were held the conventicles, those field-preachings to which the Cameronians—the hunted Covenanters—were forced to resort. Galloway and Ayrshire and part of Lanarkshire are sometimes spoken of as the Covenanters' Country, for it was as fugitives among its lone and remote places that those stout defenders of the Presbyterian faith took refuge, and pursued their own religious ways.

VALLEY OF THE TWEED

Seen across the valley of the Tweed from Bemersyde, this estate, which was presented by public subscription to Earl Haig after the First World War, was picked out by Sir Walter Scott as his favourite view in all the southern Uplands.

Not in all the history of mankind has there been a persecution more ruthless than that which is commemorated in the Martyrs' Monuments and the graves of solitary Covenanters to be found among these hills, more especially, perhaps, in the southern Uplands. The ratification of the National Covenant, with its solemn obligation to defend Presbyterianism, precipitated for Scotland half a century of woe, as Greyfriars' Kirkyard, Edinburgh, so truly testifies. There, in the oblong enclosure at the south-west corner, stands the Covenanters' prison, where some twelve hundred of those rounded up by Royalist cavalry, after their defeat at Bothwell Brig, were herded together for five wintry months, with no canopy but the cold, cloudy sky. In the most appalling misery, they were detained by a guard of soldiery charged, under pain of death, to allow no one to escape. Hundreds perished of exposure, and of brutal treatment received at the hands of those placed in authority over them. A few were given their freedom on swearing to a bond never again to take up arms against the king, or without his permission. More than four hundred declined this avenue of release, "not accepting deliverance, that they might obtain a better resurrection." Two hundred and fifty perished when the vessel transporting them from Leith to the Barbados slave plantations was wrecked off the Orkneys, and only forty of their number were saved.

The Covenanters are still revered in Scotland, especially throughout the Lowlands and those parts of the south-west of the country where, at one moment, they triumphed, and at another they suffered so grievously. Each year in May, in commemoration of their stand, armed sentries are posted on the surrounding hills, guarding the approaches to the field, when the annual conventicle is held near Douglas, Lanarkshire, to mark the anniversary of the Cameronians, or Scottish Rifles. It was on 14 May, 1689, that the disbanded Covenanters assembled at Douglas, and enlisted to form this famous regiment. A detachment from the depot, with Territorials and cadets under their respective leaders, is usually present at these anniversary services, as well as a large deputation of the Regimental Association.

The Cameronians exercise their privilege of appearing at divine worship armed with rifles. After the service, a soldier of renown, acting on behalf of the Regimental Association, lays a wreath at the base of the statue near-by— the statue of the first commander, the eighteen-year-old Earl of Angus, who was killed in 1692.

Why relate all this in the middle of a chapter of this kind? Simply because there is no country in the world where the national history is kept so evergreen, where the deeds of past centuries are re-enacted so faithfully, so

JEDBURGH ABBEY
Beside the little River Jed, a tributary of the Teviot, the roofless abbey church of Jedburgh is a ruin of unusual beauty and historic interest. The abbey was founded in the twelfth century by David I. The lower part of the present building is little changed since it was built. The rounded arches and their subdivisions belong to the best traditions of late Norman architecture. The elaborate arcade was added later. Apart from these lovely ruins of the church, little has survived except fragments of the cloisters.

THE CAMPSIE FELLS

The Lennox Hills extend through the county of Stirling from the neighbourhood of Dumbarton north-eastward toward Stirling itself. They belong to the lowlands of Scotland rather than to the highlands, which rise a few miles to the north beyond the valley of the Forth. The Campsie Fells, almost 2,000 ft. above sea-level, form the most outstanding hills in the Lennox range. Here they are seen from the fertile valley of the Endrick Water, which, rising in Stirlingshire, flows westward into Loch Lomond.

lovingly, and with such fervour. History and geography are very closely linked together in the Lowlands and southern Uplands of Scotland.

Eight miles to the south of Edinburgh, on the eastern slope of Turnhouse Hill, one of the Pentlands, is the spot called Rullion Green. There, in 1666, was fought the battle in which the Covenanters, led by Colonel James Wallace, were routed by the king's troops under General Sir Thomas Dalyell of the Binns, their commander-in-chief in Scotland. Dalyell, who refused to cut his beard after the execution of King Charles, had seen service in Russia and Poland, and against Turk and Tartar. In 1681 he raised the Scots Greys.

At Rullion Green over fifty Covenanters are said to have been killed. Several of those who escaped with their lives, not a few of whom had been wounded, were brought in afterwards by the country folk; and it is believed

THE LAMMERMUIR HILLS

Most easterly of the southern uplands of Scotland, the Lammermuir Hills form the boundary between Berwickshire and East Lothian. This viewpoint from near the village of Preston looks toward Cockburn Moor across the valley of the River Whiteadder. In the panorama of wooded fertile valley and rolling grass-covered hills there is a strong resemblance which is maintained over much of the southern uplands, especially in those parts where the land is less than 1,500 ft. above sea-level.

that, in addition to these, numbers of others were shot or slain in flight from the scene of their disaster, and were buried in neighbouring churchyards. Many are said to lie at Penicuik and at Glencorse, not far from Edinburgh. In the kirk-session records at Penicuik one finds the following minute: "9 December 1666. Disbursed to John Brown belman for making westland-men's graves, 3s. 4d." Rullion Green was fought ten days earlier. On the Pentland hillside, by the fringe of a sparse woodland overlooking the battle-field, with the rich tilth of East Lothian stretching beyond, as far as the foot-hills of the Lammermuirs, may be found the martyrs' tomb. Here were interred most of the slain Covenanters.

Ever since that fateful day in the fall of 1666, much of the Pentland country would appear to have remained sacred to the memory of the Covenanters. Here and there about it, from time to time, were found the remains of some fugitive from Rullion Green. Many a wounded trooper is believed to have succumbed in the Pentland bogs, when endeavouring to reach the West Land, whence most of them had come to join issue with Dalyell's army. They were, for the most part, Covenanters from Lanarkshire and Ayrshire, and from distant Galloway, where, among the remote hills, they held their conventicles in defiance, until the dragoons put them to the sword or to flight.

Everyone who knows anything of the hills of the Lowlands and Uplands knows of the Covenanters' graves scattered about them. One of the best-known of such graves among the Pentland Hills is that of the nameless fugitive who died at Oaken Bush the day after Rullion Green, and was buried by Adam Sanderson, of Blackhill, a small farm that once existed near Dunsyre, in Lanarkshire. The grave is marked by a stone standing on the moorland slope of the hill known as Black Law. Tradition has it that a Covenanter, sorely wounded, and striving to reach his native Ayrshire, came to Adam Sanderson's threshold in the dead of night, and asked that he might be given some temporary relief. He declined to tarry long, however, explaining that his so doing might endanger those upon whose mercy he had cast himself. Early the following day, Sanderson set out with him on the first stage of his hopeless journey homeward. Soon his strength failed him; and he lay down to

THE BERWICKSHIRE COAST

The eastern coastline of southern Scotland is less varied and less indented than the western, but contains several rocky headlands and a number of fishing villages situated in the many small bays of East Lothian and Berwickshire. The photograph shows St. Abb's, a small straggling place, with its fishermen's cottages alongside the wall of the tiny harbour and the few fishing boats drawn up precariously on the rocky beach. In the background is the abrupt cliff-face of St. Abb's Head, a bold rocky promontory which rises over 300 ft. above sea-level and which has a lighthouse 200 ft. above high-water mark.

die. "Bury me in sight of the Ayrshire hills!" was his dying request. So Sanderson bore his corpse from Oaken Bush to the heathery spot on the slope of the Black Law, where stands the tombstone erected to his memory many years later, and wherefrom, on a clear day, one gets a glimpse of Ayrshire, some twenty miles away.

Under the auspices of the Reformed Presbyterian Church at Loanhead, and for many years now, it has been customary to hold, in the preaching-field at Flotterstane, almost within earshot of Rullion Green, a memorial service after the manner of the Covenanters' conventicles. Though the battle was fought in the month of November, June is the month during which this commemoration takes place because usually at that time of the year one may be assured of better weather, and consequently of an encouraging attendance, not only from Edinburgh but also from several of the towns, villages, and remote homesteads of the Lothians.

The historic associations of Galloway go very much farther back than Covenanting times, as is shown by the huge boulder set upon a plinth on an eminence by the roadside overlooking Trool, one of Galloway's lovely lochs. On the plinth is an inscription in memory of Robert Bruce "whose

THE OLD TOWN OF KIRKCUDBRIGHT

Kirkcudbright is a royal burgh, the county town of the county of the same name, and one of the most important places in a little-known south-west corner of Scotland. Yet in spite of its importance it has a population of fewer than three thousand. Among its houses are many old cottages, some whitewashed or colour-washed like those shown in the photograph. The river is the Dee, here seen at low tide flowing between extensive mudbanks.

HOME OF SIR WALTER SCOTT

This is Abbotsford, the home of Sir Walter Scott from 1811 until his death. It lies in the valley of the Tweed, about three miles from the centre of Melrose, in a setting dignified by the bare outline of the Uplands rising above the wooded valley. The house itself was built for the novelist to the design of Edward Blore and shows well the beginning of the country-house style known as Victorian. The irregular shape and disjointed turrets are reminiscent of some of the Deeside mansions such as Balmoral. The wooded park in which Abbotsford lies was also designed for Sir Walter Scott.

victory in this glen over an English force in March, 1307, opened the campaign of independence which he brought to a decisive close at Bannockburn on 24 June, 1314."

This monument stands appropriately in the land where Bruce, during his fugitive days, wandered after the spider on Rathlin Isle urged him to try again. Thus the name of Bruce means to the Gallovidians what that of Prince Charles Edward means to so many of the Highlanders.

Galloway occupies the south-western extremity of Scotland, and consists of the counties of Wigtown and Kirkcudbright. It is famous for its "belties," those jet-black cattle having a wide band of white round their middles. It is also famous for its dairying and creameries. Scattered at intervals along the roads threading through its farm-lands are scores of those wooden platforms upon which, in the early hours of the morning, the dairy-farmers place the great milk-cans collected by itinerant motor-lorries, and whipped off with speed and efficiency to the Galloway creameries.

Two things the stranger to Kirkcudbright must learn speedily if he wishes to ingratiate himself with the inhabitants. The first thing is how to pronounce the name. Strange as it may seem, it is pronounced *kir-coó-bree*.

THE COUNTRY OF THE FORTH BRIDGE

It is harvest-time in the fertile fields that line the Firth of Forth, as viewed from Dalmeny, near Edinburgh. The Forth Bridge in the background carries the main railway line northward from Edinburgh. It was built in the eighties of the last century, and from an engineering point of view is one of the wonders of the world. Its main spans are 1,700 ft. in length and are exceeded only by the spans of the Golden Gate, the Hudson, and the Quebec Bridges.

The other is never to affix "shire" to it, any more than one would to, say, Cornwall, although the Post Office does so for official purposes, in order to differentiate between the county and the county town. One may talk of Wigtownshire, but never of Kircudbrightshire. Indeed, if one desire to show oneself *au fait*, one will refer to it, rather, as "The Stewartry," the old name in the employment of which so many of the natives still take pride. But why, one may ask, should this county be known by such a name? The answer is to be found in the fact that during the fourteenth century the lord of Galloway appointed a bailiff or steward to collect, in Kircudbright, the rents and dues payable to him. This office became hereditary; and the region over which the steward's jurisdiction extended thus became known as "The Stewartry."

Of all the regions of Scotland—and many of them are, indeed, remote— Galloway probably remains the least known. Its situation isolates it from the stream of traffic constantly passing by the west-coast route between England and Scotland. The main railway line on the west side of Britain runs into Scotland from Carlisle, by way of Carstairs, by-passing Galloway at a goodly distance. Moreover, the railway was later in reaching Galloway. When, eventually, it did penetrate those parts, it provided the theme for much satirical verse. Hitherto Ayr, to the north, and Dumfries, to the east, had been the nearest railway stations.

Gaelic was spoken in Galloway well into the seventeenth century; and

72

the Gaelic flavour of this land is maintained not only in its place-names, but also in many of its surnames. Macs galore are to be found there—MacWhirters, MacCubbins, MacHarries, MacCutcheons, MacCrindles, and MacSkimmings, to mention but a few of them. These Mac surnames are quite different from those of the rest of Celtic Scotland.

Galloway has its memories of the Picts, of the Romans, of the early Christian missionaries, of William Wallace and of Robert the Bruce, and of Devorguilla, the saintly wife of John Balliol, with whom Gallovidians the world over instantly associate the lovely Sweetheart Abbey, which she founded there in 1275. But more poignant, more evergreen than any are those memories to which reference has already been made, namely, memories of the Covenanters. There is not a kirkyard in Galloway but has its graves of those martyrs for the Covenant.

It also has proud memories of a distinguished native, John Paul Jones, reputed to have been the founder of the American Navy. Paul Jones was born in the village of Arbigland. American citizens are now raising a large sum of money in order to convert its old Tolbooth (the prison in olden times) into an American museum in Paul's honour.

If the hills and valleys of the Pentlands, of Ayrshire, of Lanarkshire, and of Galloway have their associations of the Covenanters, those of the Borderland have theirs of the feuds and forays belonging to the centuries

SWEETHEART ABBEY, KIRKCUDBRIGHT

Beautifully situated and beautifully named, Sweetheart Abbey lies in Kirkcudbright, near the estuary of the Nith. More properly its name is New Abbey, founded towards the end of the thirteenth century, nearly a century later than most of the abbeys of southern Scotland. The beautiful tracery of the "wheel" window and the graceful Gothic arches of the nave belong to the late thirteenth-century style of architecture. The romantic name Sweetheart derives from a legend that the traditional foundress of the abbey, Devorguilla, brought to it, as soon as the church was built, the tomb in which the heart of her husband, John Balliol, was interred.

when Scotland and England were perpetually at loggerheads. They also have associations with illicit stills and with smuggling. Tales of such unlawful enterprises are as numerous as are those of the Border raids.

It was in the first half of the sixteenth century, during the reign of King James V of Scotland (the Poor Man's King, as the history-books describe him) that serious attempts were first made to curb the lawless border clans, whose chiefs, when not invading England, were constantly at strife with one another, ravaging one another's territories. As soon as James was old enough to be entrusted with the powers of a ruler, he made a beginning with the Douglases, with whom the Crown had many an old score to pay off. The history-book tells the Scottish schoolboy that one day, in revengeful mood, the king declared: "I vow that Scotland will not hold us both!" He acted promptly upon his vow, firstly by banishing the Douglases beyond the River Spey, and forbidding any of them to approach within six miles of him, wherever he might be. He then got Parliament to pass a measure depriving them of their estates, and banishing them from Scotland. Having settled the Douglases, at any rate for a time, he turned his attention to Johnnie Arm-

BY THE BANKS OF THE TWEED

Most gracious of the rivers of southern Scotland, the Tweed in its long course includes almost every type of river scenery. For the first thirty miles of its course northward from Hart Fell it is a moorland stream running over a rocky bed between bare windswept ridges. Lower down, where it turns east, it has carved for itself a broad quiet valley which is singularly well wooded and fertile, with many large farms and country estates near the river banks. It passes through Peebles, and between that town and Melrose, where this photograph was taken, are some of its loveliest reaches.

strong, chief of the clan of that name. The Armstrongs had been particularly troublesome. They kept the Borderland in a continual ferment. Within a short space of time, they destroyed more than fifty churches in Scotland, and carried off from England an enormous amount of booty. Their cattle-thievings were unequalled except, perhaps, by those of the West Highland clans. It was their boast that they ignored, alike, the edicts of the king of Scotland and of the king of England.

One of the several ballads for which the Borderland is so famous tells how King James punished Johnnie Armstrong and his murderous tribe. When riding through the Borders at the head of a band of armed men, Johnnie, gaily attired, and attended by four-and-twenty of his jolliest gentlemen, came out to meet him. "What lacks this knave that a king should have?" James exclaimed, and immediately ordered that Johnnie and his jolly gentlemen should be hanged on the spot! And hanged they were!

All this land is haunted by its past. Every wind that blows would seem to bear some memory of old hatred and old vengeance, of bloody fray and foray, for these were no less common among the southern clans of Scotland than among the northern. Nothing in the nature of immovable property was safe from the vengeance or caprice of the destroyer. Nothing movable was safe from the raider. "If ye had four legs on ye," a Scots cattle-lifter is said to have remarked to a haystack, "ye wouldna be standin' there sae lang!"

As for romance, it is there in plenty, too. Who, in crossing into Scotland at Gretna, has failed to observe the notice-board erected in a garden, and bearing the legend, "This is the House Famous for Gretna Green Marriages"? Over the doorway of that little house may still be seen the words everyone pauses to read and consider: "Over Ten Thousand Marriages

Performed in this Marriage Room." For sixpence one may step inside and have a peep at this little front apartment, so chock-full of relics.

The Borders were renowned for their gypsies. Indeed, the quiet hamlet of Kirk-Yetholm, situated among pastoral fells in the Vale of Bowmont, in the shadow of Staerough, a spur of the Cheviots, was for centuries the headquarters of all the Scottish tribes. "Alike inaccessible from without, and not to be left from within," was the apt phrase used by Dr. Robert Chambers (the younger of the brothers, who founded the famous publishing house of W. and R. Chambers), to describe Yetholm, after it had elapsed into a dreamy forgetfulness demanded by a quieter and more orderly era than it had known in the days of the Border raids. At Kirk-Yetholm may still be seen the palace occupied by the gypsy "royal family"—the place of residence of the kings and queens, princes and princesses, of gypsydom. To this day, one is able to recognize about the parish of Yetholm the dark eyes and swarthy countenance of the Romany, although half a century has passed since the coronation on the Green o' Kirk-Yetholm of the last king of the gypsies. When Borrow visited the Scottish gypsies, he was told by one of them that Kirk-Yetholm had been their centre "beyond the memory of man."

ROMANY TRIBES

The gypsies are believed to have come to these parts about the middle of the fifteenth century. At that time, and for a considerable period thereafter, they were known throughout the land as the Saracens. Tradition asserts that a band of them had committed extensive depredations in Galloway during the reign of James II of Scotland, who, as one may remember, was killed at the siege of Roxburgh Castle in 1460.

The earliest record of these wandering tribes within the realm would appear to be an entry in the book of the Lord High Treasurer, which runs as follows: "22 April, 1505—Item to the Egyptianis be the Kingis command, vij. lib." In July of the ensuing year Anthonius Gawino, who is described as the Earl of Little Egypt, received from James IV (he whose army the English defeated at Flodden Field, but a few miles from Yetholm) letters commending him to the king of Denmark, for which country this gypsy chief was on the point of taking ship. In 1540, James V, father of the luckless Mary, Queen of Scots, entered into some sort of bargain with the gypsy potentate, John Faa, when he subscribed a letter, under the Privy Seal of Scotland, in favour of "oure louit Johnne Faw, Lord and Erle of Littill Egipt." The Faws, or Faas, were among the earliest and most powerful gypsy settlers at Kirk-Yetholm. They were, moreover, the Royal House among the Scottish Romany.

The last of the Faas, in the direct succession, to rule over Gypsydom was King William Faa II. He died in 1847, at the age of ninety-six, and was succeeded by his brother-in-law, Charlie Blythe. There were few in all the Borderland so well versed in its ballads as was King Charlie. He numbered among the friends of his earlier years Sir Walter Scott, with whom he frequently conversed. Scott often sauntered along to visit him when he pitched tent at a certain spot near Abbotsford, during his seasonal wanderings. It

ROXBURGH LANDSCAPE

The village of Kirk-Yetholm, seen here from the slopes of Staerough on the Cheviot Hills, lies in Roxburghshire, less than five miles from the English border, where the Cheviot range falls away to the valley of the Tweed dividing England from Scotland. This area was one of the "cockpits" of fighting in the wars between England and Scotland; the village was for many years the head-quarters of the gypsy people whose happy hunting ground, until comparatively recent times, was the Border country.

ought to be mentioned in this connexion that Scott derived much material for his writings from the contacts he had made with the Yetholm gypsies. Indeed, Jean Gordon, a gypsy born at Yetholm about 1670, is believed to have been the prototype of Meg Merrilees, of whom we read in *Guy Mannering*.

King Charlie died at Yetholm in 1861, after a peaceful reign of fourteen years. His two daughters, Princess Helen and Princess Esther Faa, were claimants to the throne; and in the long quarrel that ensued, Esther, one of the best known of the Border gypsies, succeeded as Queen. She reigned over Little Egypt until 1883. Her funeral was one of the largest ever seen in the Borderland. With her passing, the throne became vacant. It was not until Whit-Monday, 1898, that her eldest son, Prince Charles—Charles Faa Blythe, to give him his full name—was crowned Charles II, King of the Gypsies. He did not reign long, however. Death bore him away in 1902; and the throne of the Romany Kingdom has been without an occupant ever since. He was the last of the gypsy hierarchy to wear the tin crown, and to wield the gypsy sword of state.

This part of the Borderland is indeed beautiful. It is typical of the kind of country in which the Scottish gypsies have been located for centuries. These tribes of wanderers seem to have had a partiality for settling on the fringe of low, fertile, populous country with a background of inaccessible hills and valleys, or of moorland or impenetrable swamp, to which they might readily retire out of reach when harassed or pursued by the authorities. In such respects all the well-known gypsy haunts in the Lowlands and southern Uplands bear a resemblance to one another—Biggar, in Lanarkshire, for example; Lochmaben, in Dumfries; Lochgelly, in Fife; Greenlaw and Gordon, in Berwickshire; and Middleton, in Midlothian.

The Borders are particularly lovely at the time of the Teuchat Storm, or Peesweeps' Blast, as the folks of Ettrick and Teviotdale term the erratic snows falling in March and April, at lambing time, since they are associated in these parts with the arrival of the green plover.

If the glory of the Highlands be their mountains, the glory of the Lowlands and of the Borders is their rivers. Scotland's principal river, of course, is the Clyde. The lower part of the river, together with its estuary, forms one of the most important commercial highways in the world.

THE RIVER CLYDE AND ITS VALLEY

The Clyde, on its course to the sea, passes over four well-known falls— Eonnington Linn (30 ft.), Corra Linn (84 ft.), Dundaff Linn (10 ft.), and Stonebyres Linn (80 ft.), the lowest of them, occurring below the town of Lanark. Though there is much disagreement as to where the river begins and ends, its total length, taking into consideration all its windings, is usually given as 106 miles. The infant Clyde at Crawford, where one of Telford's famous bridges carries the highroad over it, gives little indication of its greatness by the time it passes through the city of Glasgow to furnish so amply its huge docks and the great shipbuilding yards at Dalmuir, Partick, Clydebank, and Dumbarton. Much of that part of the river which, for many a year now, has been navigable by the largest of vessels, was little more than a muddy stream when, at the beginning of the nineteenth century, Glasgow, largely influenced by the Tobacco Lords and the prospect of increasing trade with America and the West Indies, set itself the formidable task of converting it into the spacious channel we know today.

The upper part of the Clyde Valley is an enormous orchard; and how very different are the river's lower reaches, among one of the most densely populated and highly industrialized regions of the world!

The Tweed, rising in the heart of the southern Uplands, is 96 miles long. This river, with its many notable tributaries, is perhaps more enshrined in the song and story of Scotland than is any other. Countless poets and writers have sung its praises. It is famous for its salmon-fishings and, also, for the woollen mills by its banks, producing the tweeds to which it gave its name. The countryside hereabouts is renowned for its sheep-farming. This means wool; and wool means woollens. In this connexion one instantly recalls the towns of Hawick and Galashiels. The valley of the Tweed is noted for its thriving towns and villages. Besides Galashiels, one might mention Peebles, Innerleithen, Walkerburn, Melrose, Kelso, Newton, Roxburgh, and Coldstream, the little town where General Monk raised the Coldstream Guards in 1660, and which, until roughly the middle of last century, was nigh as famous for runaway marriages as Gretna. At its estuary lies historic Berwick-on-Tweed, the town which, in the centuries of Scottish and English warfare,

A LANARKSHIRE VILLAGE

The valley of the upper Clyde, from its source in the midst of the southern
Uplands to the point where it enters the central plain of Scotland, is justly
famous for the beauty of its scenery and the charm of its many villages. Of
these Kirkfieldbank, shown above, in spite of being very near the outskirts of
the town of Lanark, which is a place of considerable industrial importance,
retains its rural appearance.

changed hands so repeatedly that, even at the present day, one is never quite
certain to which of the two countries it belongs. Few towns in Great Britain
have had so chequered a history.

Most important of the Tweed's tributaries is the Teviot, flanked by the
rich farm-lands of Teviot-dale; and one must not omit mention of the Till,
for it was over the Till by way of Twizel Bridge that, in 1514, James IV of
Scotland, in a moment of excessive foolhardiness, allowed the English army,
under the Earl of Surrey, to march without molestation. So soon thereafter,
this army defeated the Scots at Flodden Field.

Another river of note is the Tay, the longest of Scottish rivers. It is 117
miles in length. At its estuary, which is spanned by the Tay Bridge (opened
in 1887 to replace the structure destroyed with considerable loss of life by the
gale of 1879, and measuring over two miles in length), lies the manufacturing

THE FIRTH OF TAY

In the foreground of this picture showing both banks of the Firth of Tay is Newburgh, Fifeshire; on the farther bank the Carse of Gowrie, one of the richest areas of farm-land in Scotland. The Sidlaw Hills rise sharply in the extreme background. Ploughed fields are numerous on the Fifeshire bank, and, together with rich pastures on the higher slopes, yield a good return of oats and most other kinds of corn crops.

town of Dundee. The Tay also is noted for its salmon-fishing, as well as for its pearl-fishing.

Pearls have been fished out of the Tay for centuries. In fact, the pearl-fishing industry was once a remunerative one in Scotland, especially in Perthshire, where the Teith and the Earn, as well as the Tay, still yield pearls of quite considerable value. In the latter half of the eighteenth century, pearls to the value of £100,000 were exported from Scotland to France.

The Tay Bridge recalls that marvellous achievement of last century, the Forth Bridge, constructed between 1882 and 1889 at a cost of roughly £3,000,000, and spanning, together with its approaches, 8,295 ft. of the Forth's estuary. The length of the actual bridge is 5,330 ft.

The Forth, though only 66 miles long, is full of interest, industry, and charm. It is navigable as far inland as Stirling, beyond which its character is highland, rather than lowland.

Among the rivers of the north-east which should at least receive mention are the Dee, the Don, the Deveron, the Findhorn, and, of course, the Spey, swiftest and most impetuous of all Britain's rivers. The Spey, rising among the Grampians, is 110 miles long. Its incontinence in time of flood has wrought much havoc during the centuries. How often must it have changed its course within historic times! The Great Moray Floods of the early nineteenth century are still spoken of in the north-east of Scotland as a disaster that might have occurred but a few years ago.

The Findhorn is another river which has altered its course much. Spey and Findhorn together have bequeathed to Morayshire, particularly, those farm-lands which are as fertile as any in Britain.

The Findhorn immediately recalls that great desert known as the Culbin Sands. It fringes the Moray Firth from Mavistown, in the west, to the river's mouth, in the east. Here, in olden days, were the villages and churches, farm buildings and farm-lands, which the sands buried. The efforts of the Forestry Commission during the last half-century to reclaim much of the Culbin by the scientific planting of marram-grass, and later of pine trees, have been so successful that Britain's only desert is gradually disappearing.

In the ruins of ancient castles and keeps, the Lowlands and Uplands truly abound. Space will permit of but a few of them being named. In

CULBIN SAND-DUNES

The Culbin Sands, bordering on the Moray Firth, form the largest single area of sand-dune in Britain. They are shifting sands, which even within living memory have advanced appreciably inland. Many legends centre round them, relating to the farms and homesteads they have engulfed in times past. There is evidence that in a great storm during the later Middle Ages a whole village was swallowed up and finally buried. During the last fifty years many experiments have been made with a view to binding the sands by planting rank grass and conifers—a policy that seems to promise success.

Liddesdale stand the gaunt ruins of Hermitage Castle, the Douglases' chief stronghold. In Berwickshire, not far from St. Abb's Head, is Fast Castle (the "Wolf Crag" of Scott's *Bride of Lammermuir*), where the Gowrie conspirators laid their plan to imprison James VI of Scotland and I of England because of the endeavour to rid Scotland of "a young and insolent company of papists, atheists, and furtherers of the bloody Council of Trent."

Perched on the sea-cliffs, near the golfing centre of North Berwick, one finds Tantallon Castle, which General Monk reduced to ruins during the Civil War. On an islet in the River Dee, in Kirkcudbright, not far from Castle Douglas, stands Threave, the great stronghold of the Black Douglas. In Dumfriesshire, by the north shore of the Solway Firth, are the ruins of Caerlaverock, Scott's "Ellangowan." Today they appear much as they did in 1640, the year in which, during the famous three months' siege by the Covenanters, the castle was so largely destroyed. On the outskirts of Edinburgh is Craigmillar Castle, so intimately linked with Mary, Queen of Scots. To Craigmillar went Mary after Rizzio's assassination; and it was within the walls of this old keep that the Confederate Lords assembled to discuss what should be done with that "young fool and tyrant," Darnley. To Craigmillar Mary hastened, followed by Bothwell, after the affair at Kirk o' Field. In Edinburgh Castle is enshrined not merely the history of the Lothians, but that of all Scotland, in the days when she was a separate kingdom, and Edinburgh was her capital in the fullest sense.

This list of ancient castles and keeps one could extend indefinitely. There must be a hundred of them, each with a lengthy history.

BEAUTIFUL BORDER ABBEYS

Ancient religious houses are numerous, too. Dunfermline has its abbey, where the Scottish kings used to be crowned. Paisley has its abbey; and so has Balmerino. Among the fertile fields of Morayshire are situated the ruins of Kinloss Abbey, which must have been an enormous place in its splendid days. At Coldingham, Dundrennan, and Lesmahagow stand the ruins of priories.

Scotland, of course, is not so well endowed with abbeys as is England. Yet, in her Border abbeys—Kelso, Dryburgh, Melrose, and Jedburgh—she possesses four of the loveliest structures of their kind, though now in so ruined a condition. They suffered repeatedly at the hands of the marauding English, who came north to assail them, just as the Scots marched south to pillage and to burn in Northumbria.

The finest and largest, as well as the most complete, of the Border abbeys is Melrose, founded in 1136 by David I, "the sair sanct." How often it was sacked and burned during the centuries of Border strife it would be impossible to say. So greatly did it suffer at the hands of Edward II in 1322 that it had to be rebuilt almost from its foundations. Under the high altar of this abbey, it is said, the heart of Robert the Bruce lies buried.

Of Kelso Abbey little remains except the tower and part of the east wall. Fire and pillage were its portion also. In its heyday it was liberally endowed, and its privileges were considerable. Many a Scots monarch bestowed royal

CRAIGMILLAR CASTLE

Edinburgh is hemmed in on the south by a line of hills which are an extension of the Pentland Hills, and which run north-eastward to within three or four miles of the Firth of Forth. On one of the isolated hills at the end of this range stands Craigmillar Castle, now in ruins but still showing much of the beauty and craftsmanship of Scottish late medieval architecture. Because of the danger of flying arrows the window spaces in the lower storeys are small rectangular openings, little more than slits. This castle, perhaps on account of its proximity to Edinburgh, was one of the palaces where Mary, Queen of Scots, spent much of her time.

favours upon it; and it waxed rich in consequence. As in the case of a great number of ecclesiastical buildings in Scotland, its final devastation is wrongly attributed to what is loosely termed "the zeal of the reformers at the time of the Reformation."

Jedburgh Abbey, according to H. Drummond Gauld's great work, *Brave Borderland*, is the most perfect and beautiful example of Saxon and early Gothic architecture in Scotland. In 1118, King David I founded on the Jed a priory, which he placed in the possession of canons regular from the Abbey of St. Quentin, at Beauvais, raised to the dignity of an abbey in 1147. It was endowed with a number of profitable tithes. With the other abbeys of the Borderland, it shared in the pillage and destruction of the fifteenth and sixteenth centuries. In 1522 the Earl of Surrey played havoc with it and with the town of Jedburgh also; and in 1544 Hertford's destructive hand fell all too heavily upon it. Fifteen years later the abbey was suppressed, and its revenues forfeited to the Crown. Nevertheless much of it remains. Though treasury,

83

library, scriptorium, and refectory have all gone, the centre of the nave, the central tower, and the north transept are still extant.

The town of Jedburgh, perhaps more than any other in the Borders, has intimate associations with the ill-fated Mary, Queen of Scots. It was from Jedburgh that she rode out to distant Hermitage to see the Earl of Bothwell, as he lay in his fortress, seriously wounded by Little Jock Elliott, a noted Border raider. The house in Jedburgh where Mary herself afterwards lay so ill still stands in the centre of the town. It dates from about 1523. In 1928 this historic place was acquired by the town, and, after restoration, was formally opened to the public by J. M. Barrie. It holds many of the queen's relics, but none so interesting as her watch. When Mary was on her way to Hermitage, her horse stumbled in the bog known ever since as the Queen's Mire. In the bog she lost her watch, while endeavouring to reach terra firma. At the close of the eighteenth century, some little time after the bog had been drained away, the watch, thrown up to daylight by burrowing rabbits, was picked up by a shepherd. It may now be seen in the old house at Jedburgh, whence Mary set out with it for Hermitage, nearly four centuries ago.

In the year 1150, David I, and not Hugh de Morville as commonly

DRYBURGH ABBEY

This photograph shows the ruins of the abbey church and chapter house, an abbey which, tradition relates, was founded by David I in 1150. The ruins show that it cannot have been much later in foundation than that, for the beautiful rounded arches shown on the right are definitely Norman in style. The abbey was rebuilt and enlarged in the thirteenth and fourteenth centuries. The window in the background with the graceful tracery is typical of the fifteenth century.

THE OLD HARBOUR, STONEHAVEN

Stonehaven is one of a number of old-world fishing towns along the east coast of Scotland. It has been a flourishing centre of the industry since the fourteenth century and is the county town of Kincardineshire. The old harbour, fringed by dwellings, some of which are two hundred years old, is just as quiet and secluded a backwater as ever it was. In the background can be seen the bold cliffs that hem in Stonehaven on either side.

stated, founded Dryburgh Abbey. Drummond Gauld reminds his readers that its monks, or canons regular, were of the Premonstratensian Order (the Norbertine Order of Augustinians) introduced from Alnwick. They were designated White Friars because of the white, woollen copes covering their black cassocks.

In 1322, Edward II set Dryburgh Abbey on fire, and in the years 1544 and 1545 it shared in the worst devastation the Borderland has experienced.

Among the ruins of St. Mary's Aisle at Dryburgh sleeps the greatest of all Borderers—indeed, one of the greatest of all Scotsmen—Sir Walter Scott. There also lies Douglas Haig—Earl Haig of Bemersyde.

Dumfriesshire and the West Land likewise have their abbeys. One remembers Lincluden, situated on a grassy mound by the banks of the Cluden Water, not far from Dumfries—situated in a part of Scotland so intimately associated with Robert Burns as to be known as the Burns Country.

One also recalls Glenluce, in Wigtownshire, and Sweetheart Abbey, in Kirkcudbright. Today they are all lovely in their very ruins.

All but one of Scotland's principal burghs (Perth, which must be regarded as Highland) are situated in the Lowlands, where resides the great bulk of the country's population. Every form of activity, other than agriculture and fishing, is represented by these burghs. Most of them are highly industrial. Those in the central valley, in Lanarkshire, and in Fife are engaged,

85

for the most part, in coalmining and in the heavy industries associated therewith. Glasgow, Greenock (or Port Glasgow, near-by), Clydebank, and Dumbarton have their shipyards and engineering establishments. Dundee also builds ships, though of lesser tonnage. With Aberdeen, as with so many of the towns and villages situated on the east and north-east coast, we associate the fishing industry. The small ports of the Moray Firth and of Aberdeenshire —Buckie, Banff, Macduff, Portsoy, Cullen, Lossiemouth, Peterhead, Fraserburgh—are very much the backbone of the Scottish herring industry, which has been declining somewhat rapidly in recent years. Aberdeen deals in fish of every kind. It is the base from which trawlers operate over a wide area, many of them steaming as far north as Greenland and Icelandic waters. All down the east coast, roughly from Port Gordon, in Banffshire, to Berwick-on-Tweed, are to be found long-established fishing communities.

If West Fife has its coal-mining, East Fife has its fishings. The Lothians have their agriculture—their rich grain-growing acres. The Borders have their sheep-farming, their woollen industries, and their stock-raising.

GARDENSTOWN, BANFFSHIRE

The hardihood of those who man the fishing fleets of Britain is exemplified by the fishermen of Gardenstown, fifty miles to the north-east of Aberdeen. The village came into existence on account of the easily accessible fishing grounds in the Milch. Today erosion by the sea is eating away the very soil on which the village stands and a ban has been placed on the Milch to prevent over-fishing. Yet the hard-working fishermen of this little place are so wedded to the sea that they continue to ply this trade in the face of all difficulties, concentrating now on the east-coast herring season.

HISTORIC EDINBURGH

This unusual view is taken from the Scott Monument in Princes Street. It shows in the foreground the famous Princes Street Gardens, the classical architecture of the Royal Academy of Scotland, and the Castle Rock surmounted by its historic fortifications. For many hundreds of years the whole history of Edinburgh was the history of its castle. There is a tradition that the first castle was built in the seventh century by Edwin, King of Northumbria. Certainly the Castle Rock is a perfect natural defensive position; it has been fortified almost continuously through the ages and has suffered many sieges and battles. One of the proudest phases of its history was in 1545, during one of the wars between the English and the Scots, when Edinburgh Castle was one of few strong-points that held out against the English.

Ayrshire has its dairy-farms and its potatoes. Galloway boasts its cattle, its granite quarries, and its memories of raiders, smugglers, and pirates. Otherwise, it would seem to be largely a territory by itself, still somewhat inaccessible, but offering wonderful scope for the artists who habitually find their way there. It is the country which is the scene of *Guy Mannering*, and the country about which S. R. Crockett wrote so intimately; and, as one has already seen, it is very much the Covenanters' land. It is also Paul Jones's country, more especially that part of it lying between the Criffell Hills and the Solway. This celebrated admiral, who, as we have already seen, was founder of the American Navy, was born in 1747, at the village of Arbigland, in Kirkcudbright.

Of the industrial prowess of Glasgow and Clydeside everyone is aware. Edinburgh, fairest of cities, one likes to remember principally for her contribution to learning and scholarship. There exists nowhere in the world a city more handsomely endowed by Nature, more beautifully fashioned by man.

WALES AND THE WELSH MARCHES

South Stack Lighthouse

Holyhead

ANGLESEY BEAUMARIS

Menai Strait

Nevin

Criccieth Castle

Conway Castle Llandudno Rhyl

CAERNARVON
CAERNARVON
SNOWDON 3,560 ft.

Llanrwst

Ffestiniog

Harlech Castle Lake Bala

MERIONETH

Barmouth DOLGELLEY
CADER IDRIS 2927 ft.

Towyn
Aberdovey Dove

Cardigan

Bay

Aberystwyth
Ystwyth

Aberayron

Tregaron
CARDIGAN

Lampeter
Teifi

CARDIGAN

Cenarth

Fishguard Newport Castle

PEMBROKE

HAVERFORDWEST

Pembroke Carew Castle

Llanstephan Castle

Llandovery Castle

CARMARTHEN
Towy Carrig Cennen Castle
CARMARTHEN

Kidwelly Castle

Swansea

Neath Abbey Caerphilly

GLAMORGAN

St. Donat's Castle CARDIFF

BRISTOL CHANNEL

St. Asaph

DENBIGH

Ruthin

DENBIGH

Valle Crucis Abbey
Chirk

Wallasey

Birkenhead

Ellesmere Port

FLINT

MOLD

Wrexham

Llandrindod

Lake Vyrnwy

Powis Castle

MONTGOMERY
MONTGOMERY

PLINLIMMON 2469 ft.

Rhayader PRESTEIGNE

RADNOR

New Radnor

Builth Wells

BERWYN MTS.

Dee

Oswestry

Ellesmere

SHREWSBURY

Pitchford

SHROPSHIRE

LONG MYND 1696 ft.

Stokesay Castle

Hopton Castle

Ludlow Castle

Leominster

Weobley
Broadfield Court

HEREFORD

Talgarth BLACK MOUNTAINS

BRECON

BRECON
Usk

Llandovery Castle

BRECON BEACONS 2907 ft. SUGAR LOAF

Ebbw Vale Raglan Castle

MONMOUTH

MONMOUTH

Caerleon Chepstow Castle
Newport

R. Severn Severn Tunnel

Wallasey

Lymm Stockport

Mersey Northwich Chorley Hall

CHESHIRE

CHESTER Moreton Old Hall
Crewe

Combermere Abbey Doddington

FLINT

Market Drayton

Newport

Boscobel House

THE WREKIN 1335 ft.

Bridgnorth Castle
BROWN CLEE 1792 ft.
WYRE FOREST

Tenn

Severn

HEREFORD
Abbey Dore

Wye

Ledbury

MALVERN HILLS

Ross

Tintern Abbey

Llanddewi-Brefi

Brecon

Neath

Hawe

S. J. Turner, F.R.G.S.

Scale of Miles
0 5 10 15 20 25

88

North Wales

"THE charm of North Wales," said Matthew Arnold, writing from Llandudno in 1864, "is the extent of the country, which gives you untouched masses which the tourists do not reach; and then the new race, language, and literature give it a charm and novelty which the Lake country can never have. Wales is as full of traditions and associations as Cumberland and Westmorland are devoid of them." In so devout a Wordsworthian this may sound like sad heresy, but although there are today few places which the tourists do not reach, the essential things that give North Wales character remain.

The region includes six counties, Flint, Denbigh, Caernarvon, Anglesey, Merioneth, and Montgomery. In medieval times Anglesey and Caernarvon, with portions of the modern counties of Denbigh, Merioneth, and Flint, formed the principality of Gwynedd. Portions of the three latter counties and the whole of Montgomery were in the principality of Powys, which also included Radnorshire in South Wales. In the course of time Gwynedd came to occupy the paramount position in Wales and its rulers claimed the title of Prince of Wales. It was as Prince of Wales that Llywelyn ap Gruffydd, the last of the independent line of Welsh princes, waged war against Edward I.

Tide after tide of invasion, conquest, and settlement has swept over North Wales. The Romans, although they established there no towns such as Uriconium or Caerwent, had important military stations at Segontium, the modern Caernarvon, where the foundations of their buildings are still to be seen, at Tomen-y-Mur, in the Trawsfynydd district of Merioneth, and at other places. "The legions thundered past," leaving not only their roads and masonry to commemorate them but many of their words as well, words that have a place in the language spoken in North Wales today. Two distinct sections of Celts, the Brythons and the Goidels, reached the British Isles from the Continent. The Brythons, who were the ancestors of the modern Welsh people, established themselves in England and Wales. On the other hand, the Goidels crossed direct to Ireland from the mouth of the Loire, later penetrating to the western coast of the British Isles.

The Goidelic Celts left a few place-names, and inscriptions cut on stone in the peculiar script that is known as Ogam. There is a field in Anglesey that still bears the name of a Goidelic chieftain of some fifteen centuries ago. But it is as the Brythonic Celts come on the scene, probably some time in the fifth century, that Wales begins to assume some likeness, however remote, to the Wales of today. The struggles with the pagan Saxons, the pirate Scandinavians who raided the long coastline, and the formidable Normans left, during the centuries that followed, abiding marks upon the country but did not radically change the national characteristics.

The traveller who enters North Wales by road from Chester may not at once realize that he is in a new country. He will hear English spoken, and along Dee-side, at such places as Connah's Quay, Point of Ayr, Shotton, and Mostyn, he will see the signs of an industrialism common to all countries. Mary may still go calling the cattle home across the sands of Dee, but if she does so she will never be out of the sight of tall chimney stacks and factory buildings. Even in Flint, where the ruins of the castle, in which Richard II was prisoner and which has the distinction of figuring in Shakespeare, overlook the little harbour, the industrial developments of today stand shoulder to shoulder with the defences of the Middle Ages.

On the Flintshire uplands, from which a bird's-eye view is obtained of the low-lying strip on Dee-side, the wide, sandy estuary of the Dee and the Wirral peninsula in Cheshire, however, one is almost immediately aware of a difference. One may not hear much Welsh spoken in the streets of Holywell or even in Mold, the home of Daniel Owen, Wales's most famous novelist, but there is some subtle difference in the look of the country and the people.

Presently, too, the traveller will hear a new language spoken in the villages and on the farms, while in front of him rise the hills—the experienced mountaineer will allow them no grander name—of the Clwydian range; the round summit of Moel Fammau can be seen from the streets of Liverpool as well as from some of the Anglesey headlands, so that, although it is under 2,000 ft. high, it is yet a mountain of some importance. Once Moel Fammau is passed you have said farewell to the Border and are well into North Wales.

Y GOROR—THE WELSH BORDER COUNTRY

Before exploring North Wales let us look at the Border Country, Y Goror as Welsh people call it. Three of the North Wales counties have an English frontier. Flintshire and Cheshire are neighbours; Denbighshire touches both Cheshire and Shropshire; and Montgomeryshire, the only inland county in the region, has a long Shropshire frontier. In the eighth century Offa, King of Mercia, built the great earthwork, still known as Offa's Dyke, from the Dee to the Severn to protect his dominions from the Welsh. That wall may still be traced all along its line, although there are many gaps, but from time to time the border has advanced or receded according to the fortunes of war. Prestatyn, a name that sounds so Welsh to its many English visitors, is a Welsh adaptation of an English name given to that settlement when it was a part of England.

There is great variation in different parts of the Border Country, a variation even more apparent in language and people than in scenery. In places like Rossett, near the point where Denbighshire and Cheshire fade almost imperceptibly into one another in field and woodland, the Welsh language has practically disappeared; the same thing is true of places on the Montgomeryshire border. English is the predominant language in towns like Montgomery and Newtown. The natural tendency of that part of the country

THE GANLLWYD VALLEY, MERIONETHSHIRE

One of the best-known beauty spots of the Dolgelley area of North Wales, the
Ganllwyd Valley runs up from the valley of the Mawddach by Llanelltyd into
the heart of the mountain area of northern Merionethshire. It reveals the
contrast between the densely wooded slopes of the lower ground near the river
valley and the bare slopes of the higher ground on which nothing grows except
rank grass. The narrow twisting road follows the banks of the river closely.

is to look towards Shrewsbury as the principal town, and although Shrewsbury was once Welsh and known as Pengwern, that was a very long time ago.

On the other hand, there are places only a few miles from England where the Welsh language and the Welsh way of life flourish. That is the case in Llansilin, which is almost in sight of Oswestry; Rhos Llanerchrugog, the large mining village near Wrexham and within less than ten miles of the English border, is essentially Welsh in every respect. In a town like Llanidloes, in Montgomeryshire, once famous for its woollen industry, the traveller is close to another border, that of the South Wales county of Radnorshire, which has been English-speaking for two centuries. But Llanidloes, like many other places along the Border, retains much of its Welsh language and its Welsh outlook.

THE PEOPLE OF THE BORDER

Whether English-speaking or Welsh-speaking, the people of the Border are in the main Welsh both in outlook and characteristics. One might go further and suggest that the people on the English side of the Border have many Welsh traits; the Welshman who reads the novels of that typical Border writer, Mary Webb, finds himself on familiar ground. The principal industry there, as in most other parts of Wales, is agriculture. There is rich arable land in some parts, especially towards the Cheshire plain, but along the greater part of the Border the hills rise like a low rampart and the farming is in the main the usual mixed farming of Wales. Dairy farming is carried on on a large scale in some parts and on the Montgomeryshire border there is some wheat-growing country. On market-days the typical soft speech of the hill people may be heard in the little towns—Wrexham is the only considerable town on the Welsh border—and one seems to come into touch with a more leisurely life than is usual in our own day. But the Border people are shrewd as well as kindly, good farmers as well as good business people.

Border scenery varies. There are the not very picturesque flats of Deeside, the woodland and arable of some parts of the Denbighshire and Montgomeryshire border, the moorland of other parts of Denbighshire and the Kerry hills of Montgomeryshire—the home of the famous Kerry sheep—facing toward Clun Forest in Shropshire. Much of it is very pleasant country, although not spectacular, even if Llangollen is called a Border town, and that is a matter for argument. Llangollen is certainly impressive, with the "sacred Dee" rushing under the old arched bridge and the gaunt ruin of Dinas Brân Castle on the hill. Today Llangollen is the scene of the International Eisteddfod, which attracts competing choirs from many parts of the world.

Let us return to our starting point in Flintshire, within sight of Moel Fammau on one hand and chimney-stacks of Connah's Quay and Flint on the other. We may wish to inspect St. Winifred's Well, the holy well which gives its name to Holywell, but after that we have only to move a little down the coast, past the industrial region, to come to Prestatyn. Here what is usually referred to as the North Wales coast may be said to begin. It is, of course, to some extent a misleading term, for it is usually confined to that strip of the

SHEEP-DIPPING IN NORTH WALES

In a country that has so much mountain pasture and so little rich agricultural land as Wales, sheep of necessity contribute in large measure to the rural economy. Vast flocks find pasture on the middle slopes of the hills, especially in Denbighshire and in the upland country adjoining the Berwyn mountains on the borders of Merioneth and Montgomery. The flocks range with their shepherds over vast areas of countryside and are brought down from the hills only in winter weather and for the annual sheep-dipping, when they are dipped in a mixture of arsenic and sulphur to protect them against maggots.

North Wales coastline between Prestatyn, near the mouth of the Dee, and Penmaenmawr and Llanfairfechan, near the mouth of the Conway. North Wales has considerably more sea-coast than that.

In this part of the country there has been a remarkable development. Some of the towns are old; some of them were popular as "bathing places" over a century and a half ago. Prestatyn, for instance, has a long history and still retains some of its former village air. Abergele, farther down the coast in Denbighshire, was a fashionable watering-place at the end of the eighteenth century. Another old town, Flint, had its patrons at that period, but was never fashionable. Penmaenmawr, in Caernarvonshire, has its great granite quarry

LLANDUDNO AND GREAT ORME'S HEAD

Along the north coast of Wales, in a position sheltered from the Atlantic storms by the Snowdon range, a number of holiday towns have grown up during the past hundred years. From east to west these include Rhyl, Colwyn Bay, and Llandudno. The last has a population of 21,000, and this view of the promenade shows how the town is dominated by the Great Orme's Head, which rises. abruptly to a height of nearly 700 ft. and is composed entirely of limestone Conway Bay lies on the farther side of the headland, which forms a promontory effectively dividing the north coast of Wales from the west.

and would have been a place of some importance for that reason, even had Mr. Gladstone, the Victorian statesman, not helped to make it popular as a resort in the nineteenth century.

Rhyl, Colwyn Bay, and Llandudno are all comparatively new towns, called into being to meet the demands of the tourist traffic that began to come in a flood some time after the opening of the Chester-Holyhead railway in 1848. Even as late as 1874 an Abergele newspaper could refer to Colwyn Bay as "a rapidly improving bathing village." Today it is the largest town in North Wales. In a guide to North Wales published in the eighteen-thirties, Rhyl is not even mentioned; today it is not only one of the favourite resorts of the Lancashire worker on holiday bent, but also the Mecca of children's day trips from many parts of North Wales. Up to 1850 Llandudno was a village, inland from the sea, housing a few copper-mine workers. Today the place is an excellent example of controlled and enlightened town-planning.

Llanfairfechan and Penmaenmawr are across the estuary of the Conway and, strictly speaking, should be referred to in another chapter. But they, with Deganwy, on the Llandudno side of the Conway, are now regarded as a part of the North Wales coast. Anglesey is a place apart and must be treated as such, and something will be said about other parts of the sea-coast as we travel southward. The impact on the life of Wales of the visitors, and of the permanent residents who have been attracted by the tourist traffic, has made considerable changes in some of these coast places. At first glance one might be inclined to think that there was little that was notably Welsh in some of them, and this, within certain limits, would be a correct impression.

The coast towns have been anglicized to a very considerable extent. At the same time, there is in all of them a quite active Welsh life, and Colwyn Bay welcomed the National Eisteddfod, the great Welsh annual gathering which brings together Welsh people from all over the world, in 1947, making a great success of it. But there are those who believe that the resorts would be even more popular were they more Welsh, giving visitors the impression that they were having a holiday in a foreign country without crossing the sea.

HIRAETHOG AND HISTORIC DENBIGH

The Clwydian hills overlook the pastoral valley of the River Clwyd, famous in Welsh song and story as Dyffryn Clwyd, a river that flows to the sea past a mingling of ancient and modern, Rhuddlan with its Edwardian castle on one side, St. Asaph with its ancient cathedral on the other, and Rhyl, with its marine lake and other seaside attractions, where it reaches the sea. On the other side of the valley, richly agricultural and one of the wheat-raising districts of North Wales, rises the great central moorland of Hiraethog. A part of this country sometimes goes by the name of the Denbigh Moors, but Hiraethog is not only the correct name but is also historic. The word moorland should not mislead us; Hiraethog, and the country around it, is not all heather and gorse or even bare upland. There are little green valleys here and there, glens in which little villages nestle; here, too, is historic Denbigh with its castled rock.

Market-day in Denbigh gives one a good idea of the resources of the country, when the Vale of Clwyd, the glens of Uwch Aled and Hiraethog, and the villages of the Merioneth border are all represented. Here will be the hill-farmers, tall and wiry, with the characteristic moorland stride, in every particular unlike the townsman's beefy idea of a farmer, with their wives, partners in every sense, kindly, responsible and business-like, usually with a highly efficient sense of humour and very ready tongues. These people are honest and generous, but anyone who sought to do business with them on the supposition that they were "dreamy"—as has sometimes been said—would soon be disillusioned. Poetical, which is not the same thing as being dreamy, they often are, and poetry is still a communal thing in Wales, a natural mode of expression, used to chronicle and commemorate everyday happenings.

The road which crosses Hiraethog from Denbigh to Pentre Voelas and so down to Bettws-y-Coed takes you through the heart of some of the most glorious moorland scenery in Wales. It is a great solitude, mile after mile of lonely country with no house in sight. The folded hills and the wide moor are all about you; here and there you may catch sight of a shining tarn—the Alwen reservoir from which Birkenhead draws its water supply is not far— and in the distance rise the blue summits of the Snowdonian mountains. The air is like wine and the panorama of wide sky and cloud overhead is something to remember. But contact with the people must be sought for in the solitary farms and in the little villages.

Upland farming in Wales, like much else, has changed and is changing. Welsh farming generally is on a comparatively small scale; the average holding in North Wales is under fifty acres, except in Montgomeryshire, where the average is slightly higher. It is true that some of the mountain sheep-farms count their acres in hundreds and even in thousands, but those acres include moor and fen, crag and torrent, the happy hunting ground of the agile hill sheep and the rough-coated cattle. The mountain-walker, by the way, would be well advised to keep an eye on any mountain rams he may happen to meet;

HARVEST-TIME NEAR LLANGOLLEN

Where the mountains fall away to the relatively low ground of the Marcher counties, Welsh farmers have made the most of the rich land that is their heritage. Long before a national crisis had compelled farmers all over Britain to bring more land under the plough, such valleys of Wales as this were yielding their harvest of wheat, barley or, as here, oats, which flourish in the relatively moist climate with little hot sunshine. Though Britain is one of the most highly mechanized agricultural countries in the world, the horse-drawn plough and harvester still hold their own in a land where the farms are rarely large enough to justify complete mechanization or to make it economical.

IV. A MOUNTAIN STREAM IN THE SNOWDON RANGE, NORTH WALES

V. RIVER CONWAY, BELOW BETTWS-Y-COED, CAERNARVONSHIRE

VI. CLATTERINGSHAWS DAM, GALLOWAY, SCOTLAND

CADER IDRIS

This view, looking south-west, shows one of the main peaks of the Cader Idris range on the left and the tumbled hill country which radiates from it in the middle distance. The valley is well wooded, watered by one of the many streams that rise near Cader Idris, and divided by trim hedges into numerous pasture fields. Cader Idris, almost 3,000 ft. high, is one of the most impressive mountains in Britain. Its name means "Chair of Idris," a legendary giant. Its slopes are precipitous and the gullies and ravines were deeply eroded by the action of glaciers many centuries ago.

a Welsh hill ram can be a formidable and aggressive animal, intolerant of trespassers on what Welsh people call the *cynefin*, the unfenced but well-defined area to which the sheep of one flock usually confine themselves.

Sheep-farming has its far-flung operations, which may include the gathering of the flocks from the upper slopes of Snowdon or Cader Idris and from the solitudes of the Berwyn or Hiraethog. These great drives, that begin before sunrise, with their background of hill and moor, the practised skill of the men taking part in them, and the almost human intuition of the dogs—not to speak of the wiles of the sheep—are well worth seeing and taking part in, but the visitor must be both a good walker and amenable to hill discipline if he is to be a welcome guest. To the farmer, of course, these drives are matters of routine, and, being Welsh and reticent, he will not readily admit that the smell of bog-myrtle and peat, the voice of the mountain stream, the bleating of his sheep and the barking of his dogs combine, with many other things, to make a way of life that has for him much more than an economic appeal.

That is just what farming on these uplands is for the people who are engaged in it—a way of life. It changes in many things from one generation to another, but in essentials the life in the square-built stone houses on the hillsides remains much the same. In the great kitchens there is furniture, much of it the work of local craftsmen, that has come down from father to son for perhaps a hundred years or more. There is usually a cupboard full of books, both Welsh and English, many of them modern and of a fairly wide range. In the remoter farms in years gone by there were musical instruments —a cornet, a fiddle, an accordion or an American organ—with which to while away the tedium of the winter evenings, and although the radio today has to a great extent taken the place of these things one may still find a *côr aelwyd*—a "hearth choir"—in many a farm. In some farms there are skilled harpists, and the *noson lawen*, when neighbours forgather in some farm kitchen, each contributing something to the entertainment by way of story, recitation or song, is still popular. In all these districts the chapels and churches are centres of social, as well as of religious life, and Workers' Educational Association and University Extension classes are extremely popular.

CONWAY—GATEWAY TO THE CENTRAL HIGHLANDS

It is when the traveller, whether by rail or road, comes to the wide estuary of the Conway that he comes to the gateway of the great central highland of North Wales. There is immediately a sense of difference, not accounted for alone by the medieval picture of Conway Castle and the town walls as seen across the river. That has something to do with it, but the chief thing is the glimpse which we catch here of the cloud-capped summits of Eryri, the high mountains that cluster around Snowdon.

Something has been said about spectacular scenery; in this central portion there is plenty to which that adjective might be applied. There are famous castles at Conway, Beaumaris, Caernarvon, Criccieth, Harlech, Dolbadarn, and Dolwyddelan; two of them, Conway and Caernarvon, being amongst the largest in Britain. More modern, but equally well worth seeing, are the two bridges spanning the Menai Straits, that narrow arm of the sea dividing Caernarvonshire from Anglesey—Telford's graceful suspension bridge, built in 1826 and still the only roadway into Anglesey, and Stephenson's massive tubular bridge, built in 1849, through which pass the trains on the main line from London to Holyhead and Ireland.

There are many lakes, some smiling and pastoral, others rockbound and gloomy. Passes, impressive by their grimness or notable for their beauty, penetrate the mountain country and there are wide estuaries along which is some of the finest river and mountain scenery. Traeth Mawr divides Caernarvonshire from Merioneth; the Mawddach Estuary, which has been called the loveliest in Britain, runs far inland in Merioneth; and beyond, to the south, are the waters of the Rivers Dysynni and Dovey, the latter reaching the sea by the Cardiganshire border, and thus close to South Wales.

There are mountains everywhere. Some would except Anglesey and the Lleyn peninsula, but the former has Y Garn and one or two other heights that, in another country, might be called mountains, and anyone who has seen the long outline of Lleyn across the bay from the Merioneth coast, with Garnfadryn in the centre of the picture, will hesitate to say there are no mountains in Lleyn. Strictly speaking, Cader Idris, Snowdon's rival in altitude and fame, is a part of the Berwyn, the range which runs from Merioneth and along the Denbighshire and Montgomeryshire border until it dwindles within sight of England, but Cader Idris, with the Ardudwy range which runs from behind

CONWAY CASTLE

Like Caernarvon, Conway Castle was one of the fortresses built in the reign of Edward I. Almost as soon as its building was completed the king was trapped here by an insurgent Welsh force and suffered a long siege before the royal army arrived to disperse the rebels. The natural strength of the walls and battlements is reinforced by the position of the castle on a rock rising abruptly from the River Conway. During the Civil Wars this part of Wales was loyal to the king and Conway was subdued only after another long siege. By order of Oliver Cromwell it was dismantled, like most of the other great castles, but the ruins are enough to show its great strength and the skill of its builders.

Harlech to the Barmouth hinterland (it has two famous passes, Drws Ardudwy and Bwlch-y-Tyddiad, the latter better known as the Roman Steps), and the Arenig mountains in the Bala country, must be considered together as a part of this central highland, the paradise of the mountain-lover and the climber.

Many travellers have written about these mountains from the days of John Leland, the English antiquary who journeyed through Wales in the sixteenth century and who thought Snowdon "horrible with the sighte of bare stones." Most of the earlier ones were more frightened than charmed by the mountains. Even the eighteenth-century Pennant, perhaps the most famous of travellers in Wales, and himself a Welshman, thought Cwm Idwal, at the foot of the Glyders, in Caernarvonshire, "a fit place to inspire murderous thoughts."

In more recent times much has been written about the mountains from two points of view, that of their scenery and beauty as landscape and also from the point of view of the scientific rock-climber. There are some famous climbs in Snowdonia, such as the Great Gully on Craig-yr-Ysfa, Tryfan, and Clogwyn Du'r Arddu, but the inexperienced and the inexpert should be warned against taking risks. There is real danger unless one has acquired the necessary knowledge and skill.

There are many places from which the mountains should be looked at, and one of the best vantage points is the Glaslyn lowland or marsh near Portmadoc. There the river winds slowly through the gorse-covered marshland to the sea, and beyond the flats rises the great semicircle of mountains, every mountain to be seen from foot-hill to summit, with Snowdon as the monarch of all. Skirting the foot-hills and crossing the marshland the road passes through the defile of the Aberglaslyn Pass, where there is room for only the road and the river, to Beddgelert and the heart of Snowdonia. Few today believe the story of Gelert, "the faithful hound" who defended his master's child from the wolf and was killed by his master in the belief that he had attacked the child, and "Gelert's grave" in the field near the village is quite modern. But the fact that there is no foundation for the legend does not lessen the charm of the village and the valley, which opens out into another valley, Nant Gwynant, with its lake set in green meadows.

TOWNS WITH LONG HISTORIES

Most of the towns in this part of the country are old. Bangor has a cathedral dating from the thirteenth century and its history as a religious foundation goes back to the sixth century. Caernarvon was a Roman station centuries before it became one of the boroughs of Edward I. Beaumaris has its Edwardian castle and was in the seventeenth century a port with vital Irish connexions. Harlech, famous for its castle and golf links, and Criccieth have their roots in the far past, and Dolgelley and Machynlleth have long histories. Criccieth, by the way, is near the village of Llanystumdwy, where Earl Lloyd George of Dwyfor, the famous statesman, was brought up in the home of his uncle, the village shoemaker. His grave is in a wooded slope above the little mountain river from which he took his title.

Barmouth was a fashionable seaside resort in the eighteenth century. Pwllheli, the key to the Lleyn peninsula and twenty miles of country without a railway, was a busy port long before the first English tourist tried to pronounce its name. Portmadoc, brought into being by the building of the great embankment in the early part of the last century, had many years of prosperity as a shipping centre, and there were many other busy little ports along this coast. Although the sailing ships have disappeared over the horizon of time and the quays are today deserted, there is still a tang of the sea and of seafaring to be felt wherever you may wander from Conway to Barmouth, especially along the lengthy indented coastline of the Lleyn peninsula, stretching out towards the west and the lonely island of Bardsey. There, on the heathery headland, three miles beyond the village of Aberdaron, where the tumult of the winds and the waves never ceases and the smell of the salt

CAERNARVON CASTLE

The castle of Caernarvon today dominates the town, as it did in the thirteenth century when it was built. In the left foreground can be seen also a section of the medieval walls of the town which are still almost intact. Caernarvon looks out over the Menai Strait, and was one of the chain of fortresses constructed in the reigns of Edward I and Edward II with the purpose of establishing a settled government in Wales. As the photograph shows, the power of the castle lies in the immense strength of its walls and turrets and does not depend, as did earlier castles, on a separately fortified inner ward.

spray mingles with the scent of the gorse, you come to the Ultima Thule of North Wales. There are a few farms on Bardsey and nowadays the islanders can reach the mainland by motor-boat. Even now the passage depends upon the weather and the Sound may be impassable for a week or more.

Everywhere in the season there are visitors, not only in the seaside towns and villages but in the farmhouses and cottages as well. The tourist traffic is an important industry, and just as it has coined the name of North Wales coast for the country from Prestatyn to Caernarvon, so it has called the country from Aberdovey to Pwllheli—including the Lleyn resorts such as Abersoch and Nevin—the Cambrian coast.

There are many deep, and sometimes narrow, valleys amongst the mountains, their meadows and streams green and silver in contrast with the surrounding austerity of bare slope and beetling cliff. In these valleys and on the slopes that run down to them you come into contact with one of the main industries of this part of the country, the slate quarries of Nantlle, Bethesda, and Llanberis, in Caernarvonshire, the slate mines of Festiniog and the quarries of Corris and Abergynolwyn in Merionethshire. Some of these quarries are amongst the largest in the world and the industry has made an abiding mark on the character of the people and on the landscape.

In Llanberis, rising above the waters of Llyn Peris to a height of 1,000 ft. and more, the vast open galleries of the Dinorwic Quarry show many varieties of colouring in the exposed rock and are, in their way, beautiful. Fronting the quarry across the narrow lake is the ivy-grown tower of Dol-badarn Castle, where, in 1282, Prince Dafydd ap Gruffydd made the last desperate stand for Welsh independence after the death of his brother Llywelyn, the last independent Prince of Wales. The castle rock is a good place from which to watch and to listen to the blasting operations in the quarry, and there is something very impressive in the boom and crash of the explosions while Snowdon and all the surrounding hills re-echo the sound. In Bethesda the Penrhyn Quarry dominates the road along which we go to the Nant Ffrancon pass. The Afon Ogwen washes the foot of some of the slate rubble heaps and here again there is a striking conjunction of industrialism and natural beauty. On one side is the great quarry, full of many sounds during the day, but strangely silent when the day's work is done, except for the far-off whisper of water trickling from the upper slopes of the hill and the sudden and startling noise of loose slates slipping down the slope of a rubble heap. Ogwen, with its hazel-shaded pools, runs between the quarry and the road, and on the opposite side of the valley, high and austere and far, rises the grey summit of Carnedd Ddafydd, one of the major heights of Eryri. In spring the lower slopes are white with hawthorn blossom.

The traveller who comes to Blaenau Festiniog, over Bwlch Gorddinan, popularly known as "the Crimea," by way of the Lledr Valley and the long climb of the road over the pass, with its magnificent panorama of the Snowdonian mountains, suddenly finds himself in a country of Cyclopean outlines, an incredible dream-landscape of gigantic hills of slate rubble, of rocks that appear to be on the point of toppling over, of long rows of houses that seem to grow out of the surrounding slate. Strangers have been known to call the landscape grim, and even sinister, and some have lamented that so much of the countryside has been defaced by slate rubble and quarry workings. But to those who know the kindly people who live in the shadow of the towering rocks there is nothing alarming in the prospect.

Many quarrymen are farmers as well. The hill slopes are brightened by their neat little holdings and the sturdy and beautifully kept cottages that go with them. In Merioneth and Caernarvonshire there are many of these

BLAENAU FESTINIOG

Slate-quarrying is one of the most ancient and most important of Welsh industries, since the greater part of the slate used in the British Isles is quarried in North Wales. In addition, slate is also found in North Devon, the Lake District, Scotland, and Ireland. Blaenau Festiniog, seen here, is traditionally one of the centres of the industry. The town, together with the village of Festiniog three miles away, lies in the midst of some of the finest scenery in Wales.

quarrymen-smallholders, people who work all day in the quarries—and a quarryman's work is a highly skilled occupation—and devote the rest of their time to cultivating the land and to participation in the life of the community. One would think that such men had little spare time, but they contrive to find time to read a great deal and they are often well up in current events. Some of them walk miles after the day's work to attend classes or lectures, drama rehearsals or choir practices.

Several of these districts have produced famous brass bands. In a word, in the slate and setts quarries—there are some of the latter in both counties— is to be found an industrial society, thoroughly Welsh in all its aspects, which has given Wales some of its best poets and novelists in the present century. Beyond Festiniog is the moorland village of Trawsfynydd.

Between Trawsfynydd and Bala there is some of the loneliest hill country in the whole of Wales. In autumn, when the berries of the mountain-ash are scarlet, the trees that line the railway track in some places in that solitude are worth going a long way to see.

ANGLESEY—LAND OF LARGE FARMS AND SMALL VILLAGES

Anglesey, despite the fact that it has no great mountains or rushing rivers, has a charm of its own. Llangefni, the county town, is little more than a village, but it is said that on market-day you can meet pretty nearly every farmer in Anglesey somewhere along its motor-car lined streets. It is certain that you can see a very fair cross-section of Anglesey life in Llangefni on that day. Holyhead is a place with a different tradition; it is still an important port, one of the gateways of Ireland and familiar ground to thousands of people who know no more of "druid-haunted Mona" than they have seen from the windows of the Irish Mail.

Beaumaris and its castle have been mentioned before; although the castle is Edwardian and one of the most perfect examples of its kind, the atmosphere of Beaumaris is that of a little town of the Regency period. Amlwch, by the northern sea, is a grey and busy little town with a harbour once crowded with shipping, when the copper mines of Mynydd Parys, above the town, were in full activity.

In the main, Anglesey is a land of large, silent farms and small villages. A good deal of the country might be called featureless, but for the fact that from nearly every point the long line of the Caernarvonshire mountains is to be seen, and in places like Cemmaes and Llanlliana there is magnificent cliff scenery; in some parts bathers dive from rocky pinnacles into water seething around hidden rocks. Ravens croak on Dinas Gynfor on cliffs at whose foot the water is always deep. There are other places where stretches of sandy beach attract many summer visitors, but all these places do not account for the fascination which Anglesey possesses and has always possessed, not only for her own children but for many others as well. Her greatest poet, Goronwy Owen, breaking his heart in exile in a bleak English countryside in the eighteenth century, when distances were formidable and travelling difficult, called her *Arglwyddes a meistres môr*—lady and mistress of the sea—and

SNOWDON FROM NANT GWYNANT

Nant Gwynant is a high-set valley that runs north and south along the east side of Snowdon and commands magnificent views of the craggy peaks that compose the summits of the range. The mountain torrent seen on the right of the photograph has cut a way for itself through the rock from the region of the high glacial lake called Llyn Llydaw. The photograph shows one possible ascent of Snowdon along the ridge in the background that leads up from the pass of Llanberis. Snowdon, 3,560 ft., is the highest peak in England and Wales.

COUNTRYSIDE OF THE MAWDDACH ESTUARY

Much of the countryside between Dolgelley and the Barmouth estuary is shown in this view. In the immediate foreground are the slopes of Moel Offrwm adjoining the famous "precipice walk." The town of Barmouth lies to the right behind the jutting headland in the distance.

spoke of the waves that were to her as a hundred defending towers. Some of her seaside places are busy, but it is her quiet, her ancient little churches, her stately old country houses, her haunts of ancient peace, that make Anglesey beloved of her sons and daughters, adopted or native.

Everywhere in the central highlands there are spectacular places, such as the sweep of sea and mountains to be seen from the high road as you approach Harlech from the Barmouth direction. There the road runs high above the water so that the sea is almost immediately below you, a great wrinkled expanse of blue and purple and green. Beyond are the mountains, from Snowdon to the remote grey bulk of Mynydd Anelog in Lleyn, and in the middle distance are the towers of Harlech Castle. Stretching along the coast from Harlech almost to Barmouth there is a long line of sand-dune country.

THE MAWDDACH ESTUARY

As we pass southward we come to the Mawddach Estuary, with its purple hills, golden sands and sunlit waters and, still farther south, to the wide flats of the Dysynni estuary and Towyn, with the abrupt cliff of Craig Aderyn conspicuous in the landscape. There are startling passes at Bwlch-y-Groes and Bwlch Oerddrws as you enter the old kingdom of Powys, and there is pastoral loveliness at Talyllyn, on the Merionethshire and Montgomeryshire borders. But after that the main character of the country is that of rolling green hills, with some large villages and small towns in the valleys. Machynlleth is the gateway to this part of the country. It has memories of Owen Glyndwr, who proclaimed and for a time maintained Welsh independence in the reign of Henry IV and who figures in Shakespeare's play of that name. Glyndwr's Parliament House still stands in the Machynlleth main street. The names of other towns and villages in this part of the country—Carno, Llanbrynmair, Meifod, Llanfair Caereinion, Llanfyllin, to name only a few—are familiar to Welsh people all the world over.

Here, too, there are moorlands and mountains. To the north, in the shadow of the Berwyn range is the artificial lake, Vyrnwy, from which Liverpool draws its water supply, a place known to anglers. Toward the southern border we come to the Plinlimmon country. The summit of that mountain— more moorland than mountain, despite its considerable height—is in Cardiganshire, but some of its bulk is in Montgomeryshire and here, till you come to Llangurig and the confines of Radnorshire, there is a stretch of highland country of hills and valleys, moorland and small lakes, much of it lonely and little known, approaching more nearly to the Hiraethog moorland in character than to the central highland.

The Welsh people speak of *mwynder Maldwyn*, the gentleness or pleasantness of Montgomeryshire, and the adjective is applied to more than the scenery. Here we have said farewell, not to the great mountains only, but also to the broad, open vowels of the Welsh spoken in Caernarvonshire and Anglesey. Here the accent is lighter and the voices are softer. Presently the musical sounds of the Powysland Welsh grow fainter and die away. English takes the place of Welsh. We have made the circuit of North Wales.

South Wales

SOUTH WALES is a complex of mountains and wide valleys, coalfields, manufacturing towns, and broad agricultural acres, that defies any attempt to define it exactly.

Diverse as is its scenery, the character of the people who have made it what it is must be still more diverse. Do they not include fisher-folk from Pembroke, yeoman farmers from Carmarthenshire, shepherds from the Brecon Beacons, steel-workers from Swansea, miners from Mountain Ash? It is impossible to include all these within a single group of the population, however much one is prepared to forget minor differences or harmonize inconsistent elements. Each one is poles apart from the other but each one is just as important to the economy of South Wales as the other. It is not only their work which is different. It is equally their outlook on their work and their outlook on life itself.

What do we mean by South Wales? It is certainly a district which has no exact boundaries. On the east the boundaries are precise enough—the borders of Radnorshire, Breconshire, and Glamorganshire. On the south and the west there is not much doubt either. The sea sets an adequate boundary. But where do you look for the boundary between North Wales and South Wales? There is very little either in physical characteristics or in the work or life of the

ON THE HILLS OF GLAMORGAN

North of the fertile Vale of Glamorgan and away from the narrow industrial valleys there are thousands of acres of hill and dale country untouched by modern development. Here the country is mostly rough pasture grazed over by flocks of sheep as large as those that range over the country of the Brecon Beacons. So great are the distances covered by the shepherds that many of them ride on horseback, accompanied by their dogs, tending their sheep.

TON-Y-PANDY IN THE RHONDDA VALLEY

The Rhondda Valley is the most highly industrial of all the South Wales valleys.
The town of Ton-y-Pandy is like a dozen others that straggle up the floor of
the valley, each having its own industry. In the centre is the Naval Colliery
with its ugly winding gear and pit-head buildings. Around it are set the serried
rows of miners' cottages reaching to the very edge of the dark hills, which
are a spur of the Black Mountains.

inhabitants to make a division anything but an arbitrary one drawn to the
whim of the writer or the geographer.

One easy answer is the boundary of the county of Montgomery, but this
is a purely artificial division. Look at a map and you will see that it winds
inconsequently from the mouth of the Dovey round the northern slopes of
Plinlimmon, cuts across the natural division of the Wye Valley and then
vaguely follows the watershed between the Wye and the Severn. Yet probably
that is as real a line of demarcation as any you will find. The only alternative
would be to draw an imaginary line from the coast near Borth over the

summit of Plinlimmon and along the ridge which stretches eastward from it, ultimately becoming the boundary between Montgomery and Radnor.

In either case the upper Wye Valley falls mostly within our area. That is as it should be, for if there is anything typical of this strange and lovely land, it is the valley of the Wye from its source to the little town of Hay, where it crosses into the Marcher county of Hereford.

In its upper reaches the Wye is a turbulent stream whose landscapes are alternately fierce and kind. Wild grandeur there is in plenty, where the stream rushes down from the heights of Plinlimmon, carving out an ever-broadening valley through the almost treeless moors, until it settles down into a broad valley stream beautifully wooded, and ranking with justice among the half-dozen most enchanting valleys of Great Britain.

Northward of the Wye is Radnor Forest, southward the massif of the Brecon Beacons, nearly 3,000 ft. above sea-level; in between is heavily wooded country and upland pasture, the very core of the agricultural life of South Wales. The towns in the valley, what few there are, such as Rhayader and Builth, are market-towns simply. (Builth is also a spa, like its neighbour Llandrindod.) Unlike so many English market-towns, they exist almost solely for their markets. They are each of them the shopping centre for people living in an area of many hundred square miles and they are the business centres where farmers come to sell their wares and meet their fellows. It is not an uncommon sight to see flocks of sheep being driven along the narrow, twisting roads to market with two sheep dogs for ever watching them from behind, and a gruff-voiced shepherd tending his flock with loving care.

THE BRECON BEACONS

This picture gives a fine impression of the wild, barren expanse of the highest ground in South Wales. In the distance is a small reservoir, effectively relieving the monotony of the scene. For mile after mile the landscape is treeless, with not a farmhouse or cottage in sight. It is a scene strangely reminiscent of the high moors of Northumberland and gives point to the name Black Mountains, which includes the Brecon Beacons and the high land radiating from them.

THE SUGAR LOAF, LLANWRTYD WELLS

The main road that climbs over the pass beside the Sugar Loaf can be seen winding its way from the foreground into the middle distance. This view is typical of the tumbled hill and vale country of central Wales, where there is much high ground, grass-covered but otherwise without vegetation, but the valleys are more spacious and more fertile than in the mountainous districts proper. Llanwrtyd Wells lies in Breconshire within the watershed of the River Wye, near the eastern borders of Cardigan and Carmarthen.

Sheep are indeed the chief preoccupation of the people, both here and farther south in the wild country of the Brecon Beacons. On a clear day if you stand on a spur of high ground and sweep the horizon through a pair of strong field-glasses, you will see near and distant flocks of sheep grazing on the highest ground and the lower slopes alike; but you will find that, whereas on the mountain-sides flocks are few and far between, on the lower ground they are numerous and large. There is scarcely enough grass to meet the meagre needs of sheep above the 2,000 ft. level but lower down the high rainfall combines with more fertile soil to make the pastures rich and palatable.

A less hardy and less determined race than the Welsh might have made no use at all of the mountain pastures, where the grass is rank and, if there are no bogs to impede the flocks, there are liable to be outcrops of bare rock. The Welsh use every acre of land, good or bad, and at whatever trouble, and even risk to their stock, drive the sheep up on to the high ground in the early summer to crop over the rough grass.

The leaders of the flocks have bells hung round their necks; the cheerful tinkling often comes unexpectedly upon the ear and can be heard miles away from the flock, and pinpoints its position, even when it is hidden under the shelter of the hill. When low cloud and mist blanket the whole scene in a dreamy vague outline of blurred shapes, the sheep bell takes on a new significance. In fact, the sheep rarely go wrong. They know by instinct how to avoid the sudden precipices. They find a foothold where no human could keep his balance and, what is more remarkable, in the densest mists they keep together bunched round their leaders, and led on by the tinkling of the sheep bells.

Brecon is a little town on the headwaters of the Usk. It marks a division between the comparatively quiet country of the Wye watershed and the grimmer landscapes of the mountain country which lies to the south. The Brecon Beacons are sometimes called the Black Mountains. The latter is a far more appropriate name. Black they are in every light, a black mass rising on the skyline from the verdant pastures of the lowlands and the wooded slopes of the river valley—black and lonely, but not unbeautiful.

Take any one of the tracks which leave the Brecon-Merthyr road on the east. It will take you by a more or less precipitous course toward the highest ground of the Beacons; if you happen to strike a sunny day you will be rewarded with magnificent views in every direction. Once you are above the 1,500-ft. contour you will see nothing growing; nothing, that is, except the sparse covering of grass which lies over all the Beacon country. At the summit you will find an outcrop of rock, but it is nothing compared with the screes and rock faces of the North Wales mountains.

Many visitors liken this countryside to Dartmoor. It certainly has the black and barren air of Devonshire's hill country, but it lacks something to make the comparison complete. It lacks the intimate views down the long narrow valleys which transform Dartmoor's austere beauty into a garden, on however large a scale or however severe a style.

There is nothing of the garden about the country of the Brecon Beacons. The only signs of life, as on the slopes of Plinlimmon, are the flocks of sheep with their shepherds; the only vestige of a habitation is thousands of feet below in the distant valley, and that only here and there—a tiny group of cottages or a single small farmhouse. Poor country, you will think it at first glance, and from the farmer's point of view you will be right. Wales has fine agricultural wealth but not in the country to the south of the Wye and Usk.

THE WEALTH OF WALES

Yet on the fringe of the Beacons there is wealth beyond dreams of avarice, wealth which has been tapped but not exhausted, wealth which has enriched not only the Welsh economy but the whole economy of Britain. This is the wealth of coal; some of the richest coal measures are found along the valleys which radiate from the mountains of South Wales. They have transformed the scene and changed everything in Brecon and Glamorgan, from the line of the Beacons southward to the Bristol Channel. In this sector there is the secondary development which follows the working of coal seams.

The steel industries here are linked with the coal industry and near the coast the shipbuilding industry, too. Successive trade depressions have hit South Wales, as they have hit few other parts of Britain, and there have been times, especially between the two wars, when about half the working population of towns such as Merthyr Tydvil were without employment.

How shall we describe this country, this changeling which a hundred years ago was like any other part of the rolling hill country of Wales and today

AFTERNOON SCENE, PORT TALBOT

The afternoon shift is leaving the steel works at Port Talbot. The town lies on the coast of Glamorgan facing Swansea Bay and looking across to the Gower peninsula, but there is little of the traditional brightness and gaiety of seaside towns about this industrial place with its 40,000 inhabitants. The buildings, new as well as old, are blackened by smoke from the blast-furnaces and factory chimneys. Even the country inland is industrialized, for the valley that runs northward from Port Talbot into the mountains is the Afon Valley, one of the chief centres of the iron- and copper-smelting industry in Britain.

THE ELAN VALLEY

One of the most striking man-made features of Britain's countryside is this reservoir in the Elan Valley, which joins the Wye Valley near Rhayader. The dam in the foreground was raised to hold back the waters of the Elan River, thus forming the large artificial lake behind. In all, three lakes were formed in this way and the water from them is conveyed by pipeline to the city of Birmingham, a distance of over seventy miles. The initial work was carried out between 1893 and 1904; further extensions not yet completed may raise the yield of water to more than seventy-five million gallons a day.

is like no other part of Britain? It remains a country of hills and valleys. That is the only clue to its former character. Long, long valleys run north and south from the high ground of the Black Mountains down to the broad Vale of Glamorgan.

Along each of these valleys there are strings of villages and towns, as grey as the hillsides above them, ugly because they have never been planned, mean because the population which they house is entirely a mining community which always needed houses to live in before the houses were built. The hillsides themselves are disfigured with the winding gear and slag heaps of the coal measures and lower down the valleys are marred by the stacks and factory buildings of vast industries.

When there is full employment it is a scene of vigour, but this vigour, perhaps because it is strange to its surroundings, has failed to modify the depressing qualities of the scene. By contrast, in this, the most thickly populated part of Wales, the cultural influences for ever associated with Wales have not been allowed to become dormant. Song is the modern as well as the traditional expression of Welsh character. Your Welsh miner sings as he trudges up the hill to work and sings as he trudges wearily downhill to his home.

There is a song in the very lilt of his voice and a poetic quality in his life in the dingiest surroundings, sometimes gay, sometimes sad, but always full of emotion.

In the far south of Glamorgan beyond the happy intervention of the fertile vale, Cardiff and Swansea are the twin centres of a land which is more conventionally industrial than the mining valleys, with docks and foundries and light and heavy industries, sustaining a teeming population, more stable in its prosperity and less influenced by the transient changes in economic conditions.

Here the population is not exclusively Welsh, though the traditions are Welsh to a degree. Folk have migrated to Cardiff across the Bristol Channel from Somerset and Devon. The rise of modern industry has attracted others from divers parts of England, so that there is something of the cosmopolitan character of England's metropolis in this, the centre of Welsh work and life.

Cardiff itself is the capital city of Wales—a most noble city with a civic centre in Cathays Park which can compete in good taste and magnificence with the civic centres of London or Edinburgh. Here government and culture have taken up residence side by side. The administrative buildings of the city, the law courts of Wales, the university and the art gallery are only a stone's throw from the medieval castle of Cardiff. This was one of the principal

THE KEEP OF CARDIFF CASTLE

The mound of Cardiff Castle and the shell keep, which surmounts it, are of Norman origin, having been built at the very end of the eleventh century. The castle, which was at one time the residence of the Marquis of Bute, was presented in 1947 to the people of Cardiff. The area behind the castle is known as Cathays Park; in it, in the classical tradition of architecture, are some of the city's municipal buildings.

strongholds when the Norman kings sought, with little success, to subdue the Welsh, led by their warlike chieftains, united as ever by a burning desire to keep the land of Wales free for the Welsh. So there is a defiance as well as pride in this centre of modern Wales.

Not only is Cardiff today a centre of international trade and industry of international importance; if you go back through the records of the centuries you will find that this south-east corner of Wales has always been the western limit of cultural penetration from England. That is partly because the southern plain of Glamorgan has always been a rich prize in the covetous eyes of potential conquerors from across the Severn. It is also because there is no natural bulwark on the English side once the Severn has been crossed and the hills of the Forest of Dean surmounted. So the outposts of Roman Britain were around Cardiff, though there is no evidence that the cultural influence of the Roman province ever spread far into Wales. Probably Caerleon on Usk in Monmouthshire is one of the farthest west of the larger Roman settlements. But at least Roman remains have been found in the south of Glamorgan, and there were military forays farther into Wales. Yet the Romans were never accepted as they were in England, as guests rather than conquerors.

The Saxons, too, penetrated as far as the borders of Glamorgan but never

KIDWELLY CASTLE

Now a roofless but still imposing ruin, Kidwelly is one of the castles built at the end of the thirteenth century to hold South Wales in check. It was built on the site of an earlier castle. The mound, which is shown clearly in this photograph, is an artificial one dating from the earlier fortifications. Together with the castle of Carmarthen, Kidwelly defended the fertile countryside that extends westward from the Vale of Glamorgan along the shores of Carmarthen Bay. It was never besieged until the great Civil War, when it fell after only a short attack and was then dismantled.

THE COUNTY TOWN OF CARMARTHEN

Typical of the country towns of South Wales, Carmarthen lies compactly in the valley of the Towy. For all that, it is the county town of Carmarthenshire and the largest place in an area of five hundred square miles. In the centre the fine tower of the church of St. Peter stands out clearly, surrounded by a number of old houses and a few modern office buildings. In the foreground are the meadows of the Towy, the traditional haunt of Merlin in Welsh mythology. Behind the town the rolling uplands of Carmarthenshire are divided by hedges into a chessboard pattern of ploughed land and pasture.

reached farther. So it was with the Normans, who were so well established in the west of England, and dominated the whole of Gloucestershire and much of Monmouthshire. They reached Cardiff but could go no farther; even there the tenure of Norman rule was slender.

The struggle between Welsh and English in medieval days has left its mark on the scenery of South Wales as it has on the character of the people. You will find a string of castles, mostly Edwardian in date, stretching from the borders of Wales westward to Pembroke and northward as far as Harlech and Caernarvon. It is these castles with which the English troops sought to hold the Welsh people in fee. Almost every one of them sustained a siege. Fighting went on around them for centuries, though it was not until the days of the civil wars, when the long struggle between England and Wales was finally ended, that, as in England, they were slighted and fell into the ruinous condition in which we find them today. A few of these castles have been rebuilt, but most of them are now only fragmentary monuments to the skill and industry of medieval castle builders, and silent witnesses to the temperament

THE HARBOUR OF TENBY

Tenby is a small and prosperous seaside resort on the coast of Pembrokeshire. It combines many of the beauties of the small fishing villages of Devon and Cornwall, which the Pembrokeshire scene resembles closely, with a growing but restrained residential quarter. Here is the old harbour with the fishermen's boats drawn up on the beach, and, behind, a row of Victorian dwellings, many of which welcome holiday-makers in the summer months. Tenby is one of the very few towns in Wales which may have been founded by Viking invaders in the eighth and ninth centuries.

of the Welsh people, which would not admit defeat even in the face of overwhelming might.

Pembroke Castle is one of the finest. At the other end of Wales Caerphilly is a magnificent and still impressive ruin. Between them are a dozen, such as those of Carmarthen and Kidwelly, which may be smaller but lack nothing of the interest of the others. They are links between all the counties of South Wales, symbols in the lively imagination of the Welsh people of English tyranny and Welsh independence.

Against this historic background of war the rural scene of the two more westerly counties, Carmarthen and Pembroke, is strangely peaceful. Carmarthenshire is a lovely county; the last ridges and peaks of the Black Mountains extend across its boundaries on the east. From them the land falls away toward the valleys of the many rivers which flow into Carmarthen Bay.

By contrast with the mountains, you would call Carmarthen a county of the plains. It is not flat in the way that the eastern counties of England are flat; rather it is gently undulating—a series of rolling hills and broad valleys with very little of the land uncultivated, and a charming coastline diversified by low cliffs and many indentations. One of these inlets actually divides the county from the Gower peninsula, which is part of Glamorgan. This is the Burry Inlet, a long, almost landlocked sheet of water, the yachtsman's dream and the painter's delight.

Some writers have compared Carmarthen with Dorset, just as Pembroke has been likened to Cornwall. There is certainly something of truth in both these comparisons. Carmarthen looks rich and, though it lacks the wealth of Dorset's Vale of Blackmoor, it has more than the average wealth of the Dorset heights. Woodlands are few and far between, but there is ample hedgerow timber and many little coppices and spinneys.

As so often in Britain, the people reflect the character of the landscape in which they live. Nowhere will you find a more quietly prosperous country community than the farmers of Carmarthen. The traditions are assuredly Welsh, but they lack the bitterness of eastern Wales or even of the Marcher counties. The people go about their business of ploughing the land, sowing and reaping, and tending their herds of cattle with the same sense of security

WELSH FISHERMEN AT CENARTH, CARDIGANSHIRE

Fishing is one of the traditional industries of South Wales. Round the coast of Pembrokeshire and Cardiganshire there are numerous fishing villages rather similar to those of Devon and Cornwall. There is fishing, too, for freshwater fish in the many rivers and streams that flow from the high ground of the interior into Cardigan Bay. Here beneath the Bridge of Cenarth three fishermen are following their traditional calling in the traditional craft of Wales, the coracle. These coracles are so light that the fishermen carry them easily on their backs between their own homes and the river.

as the farmers of central and southern England. Not every year is a good farming year, but the land is kind, and the weather (providing the right crops are grown) not such a menace to prosperity as it is in the mountain regions.

Carmarthen folk have gone about the same business of farming for centuries with much the same sense of security, for the wars between England and Wales passed over these western counties lightly; the cockpit of fighting was always towards the eastern border. By comparison with the meagre cottages, the tiny farmsteads of the central mountain district, the farmhouses of the Carmarthen valleys are comfortable and prosperous, often gay with colour wash, in contrast with the dull grey slaty look of the homes of the mountain people.

Carmarthen itself is a wonderfully well-kept and wealthy-looking town, the vast bulk of its houses ample and prosperous, its civic centre well built and spacious. It is a quiet town generally, but you would form a very different impression of it on market-days. It is not the only market centre of Carmarthenshire, but it is by far the largest and most important. Farmers and their families crowd into it from the farthest corners of the county. Its shops and streets and market-place are all thronged. Even today you will hear the Welsh language spoken, though the new generation of Welsh country people is being brought up entirely to the English tongue, and the only Welsh-speaking peoples of the next generation will be bilingual. It was very different even a hundred years ago, when Welsh was the principal language of the many and English the sign of an exceptional education.

Only one corner of this attractive county is marked by industrial scars. That is where the coal measures of the Vale of Glamorgan spill over into the county near Llanelly. But that is an insignificant fraction of the whole, though it gives visitors who approach from Swansea a misleading impression.

RURAL PEMBROKESHIRE

Pembrokeshire is even more rural. Until the beginning of the Second World War two-thirds of its total area was under permanent pasture. A great deal of it is still given over to cattle and sheep, though the area under root crops and oats has increased. Like their neighbours in Carmarthenshire, the farming people are prosperous and quietly confident. They have, too, a wonderful tradition of hospitality which a century of changing customs has not effaced. The stranger is indeed welcome within their homes, whether that stranger is a traveller from one village to another distant one, or a holiday traveller on foot from the towns of eastern Wales or even England. That is partly, of course, because the number of visitors to the hinterland of Pembrokeshire is small.

The coast is famous, though not visited as much as one would expect. The country of the interior is extraordinarily little known, and not much more frequented by holiday-makers than it was thirty or forty years ago. It has been described as dull country. Perhaps it is, in the same way as the interior of Cornwall might be called featureless. Well-wooded country is scanty and there is not the same richness of hedgerow timber as in Carmarthenshire. Mostly

FARMLANDS OF PEMBROKESHIRE

In many ways the countryside of Pembrokeshire resembles that of Cornwall,
but without the austerity of the Cornish moors. This view shows the three chief
elements which make up the typical Pembrokeshire scene. In the foreground
is good pastureland, in the centre cornfields, grouped round well-built two-
storeyed farmhouses, and in the background a rugged outcrop of rock on
which not even grass can grow because of the thinness of the soil.

the county is a tableland, though there are numerous small river valleys which
have cut a way through the high ground and give intervals of rich arable land
in contrast with the green grass fields of the higher ground. Altogether it is
not unlike Cornwall, and there is none of the prejudice here against things
English as there is in most of Wales. Again the reason is not far to seek. It is
found in the fact that the bitter struggles between the two countries only
slightly affected Pembrokeshire, and that mostly round the castle itself.

The coast is even more indented than that of Carmarthenshire and there
are many peaceful fishing villages as well as one sizeable holiday resort,
Tenby. This delightful town has beautiful sands and it is as unlike the large

holiday resorts of England as could be imagined. It is almost self-consciously retiring and attracts visitors by its very quality of peace and quiet, in spite of its growing population. A holiday at Tenby is a holiday by the sea and nothing else. There is little of the organized entertainment that marks, and for many country-lovers spoils, the attraction of most large seaside towns. There is a proposal to make the whole of the Pembrokeshire coast a national park. The high cliffs, the many bold headlands and landlocked bays well merit the distinction. Can there be anyone who has walked along the cliff paths by St. Govan's Head who has not returned from the expedition refreshed and invigorated by the clear sparkling air and by the beauty of the long seascapes and of the magnificent cliff scenery?

The cliffs are geologically old and of an uneven hardness. In many cases the breakers of the Atlantic have eaten away the cliff face and have undermined it, leaving weirdly shaped pinnacles and stacks standing out from the mass of the cliff proper. They have scooped out deep caves, to the innermost recesses of which the sea never reaches. These were smugglers' haunts in days long ago, and have saved the lives of many shipwrecked mariners whose

SNOWFIELDS OF SOUTH WALES

The climate of South Wales is temperate, the winters not usually more severe than those of eastern England, though the rainfall is higher. For years on end communications operate through the wildest weather of winter, but occasionally a great snowstorm causes complete dislocation. Then the railway lines that climb over many high passes and up long valleys, into which the snow drifts, are quickly blocked. Here a train is immobilized by snow on the track that climbs through the hills from Abergavenny to Merthyr Tydfil. The lie of the land is such that the snow is blown off the mountains and collects in the gully formed by the railway cutting. On the left of the picture a line of telegraph posts marks the course of the road, which is also totally blocked.

ISLANDS OF THE PEMBROKESHIRE COAST

There is no more rugged or more beautiful coastline in Britain than that of Pembrokeshire, a fact which is endorsed by the proposal to schedule the entire Pembrokeshire coastal region as a national park of the future. There are a number of islands off the coast which are natural sanctuaries for birds and sea fowl. This photograph was taken from Caldy Island and shows the irregular outline of the small St. Margaret's Island, with the coast of the mainland in the background.

boats have been dashed against the cliffs by the raging south-westerly gales which strike this coast with force unbroken, after their long travel across the wide waters of the Atlantic. Around these cliff paths there is the same sense of immensity, the same sense of power that comes to the visitor to Land's End and an infinitely greater sense of loneliness.

Numerous small and nearly barren islands diversify the seascapes, from Caldy Island in Carmarthen Bay to Ramsey Island off St. David's Head. These are the natural homes of millions of gulls and sea-fowl, where they nest and breed in unbroken quiet the year round, and multiply in the seclusion of their rocky strongholds. One or two of the islands are recognized officially as bird sanctuaries, but all of them are bird sanctuaries in the sense that there is not the human population to disturb the feathered citizens.

The coast is not the only attractive part of Pembrokeshire. There is interest of every kind to be found in the few small towns and the many quiet, forgotten villages. Pembroke and St. David's are the two places which should be sought out above all others. The latter is a cathedral city, the former the county town and a great showplace because of its castle. Yet neither could be described as a large town or a centre of industry. Indeed the cathedral city of St. David's is little more than a village. Many are the modern wayfarers who in the dusk have driven into St. David's along the high road and out again without realizing that they had entered it. In broad daylight the magnificent architecture of the cathedral is guide enough, but in the dim light of evening there is nothing to suggest that it is not just another village or insignificant small town. It is only a little walk from St. David's to the sea at either of two bays protected from the untamed might of the ocean by rocky headlands.

Pembroke is little different in that it has the same quality as St. David's of being out of the world of modern business, and the castle is by far its most significant building. But nearby is the bustle and activity of the dockyard and arsenal called Pembroke Dock, the biggest naval establishment in Wales, and one of vital importance to the whole country's defence.

There is one other port in Pembrokeshire—Fishguard, on the northern coast, with its regular service of steamers plying to and from Ireland. In spite of the importance of this traffic between the mainland and Ireland, it is a small and quiet place, set in an uncommonly beautiful bay, with the harbour a long way off from the town and standing alone, and the rocks and cliffs of Strumble Head dividing it from the western coast.

So you might go along the coast of Cardigan Bay, finding new delights

NEW QUAY, CARDIGAN

Twenty miles from the county town of Cardigan, New Quay resembles most of the coastal resorts of England and Wales in that it is a strange mixture of the new and the old, the modern holiday resort and the age-old fishing village. It differs, however, from most modern coast towns in that the impression it leaves is far more that of a fishing village than of a holiday resort. Here numerous small fishing boats are drawn up beside the hard, or quay, while the relatively new Victorian-like terrace dwellings which make up the holiday resort stand back from the sea-front.

ST. DAVID'S, PEMBROKESHIRE

The cathedral of St. David's, here seen behind the substantial and magnificent ruins of the bishop's palace, is the largest medieval church in Wales. The beautiful Norman windows of the cathedral can be seen in the centre. The cathedral was built between 1180 and 1250, though many of the details of the exterior date from the early fourteenth century, when the Decorated style of Gothic was in vogue. The most significant feature of the bishop's palace, which dates from about 1350, is the arcading, well seen in the picture above, as is also the unusual rose window (right) which was part of the great hall.

and new vistas as you come to each fresh inlet. That, too, is a coast little known but deserving of far more fame than it has achieved.

The university town of Aberystwyth marks effectively the division between North Wales and South Wales. This is a very different place from any so far explored, combining in itself the qualities of a university town, residential place, and seaside resort. It has a long promenade with a steep shingle beach, against which the Atlantic rollers break with a thunderous roar on the calmest of days, and in time of Atlantic storm hurl tons of shingle across the roadway, and cover the whole promenade in a whirl of spray. That is one of the most impressive sights you will see in this part of Wales—untamed nature at its wildest.

A few miles inland from Aberystwyth, at Devil's Bridge and in the wild country near, you will find another aspect of untamed nature; in this narrow valley of the Ystwyth are epitomized all the magnificence and all the breathtaking beauty of Welsh mountain-valley scenery.

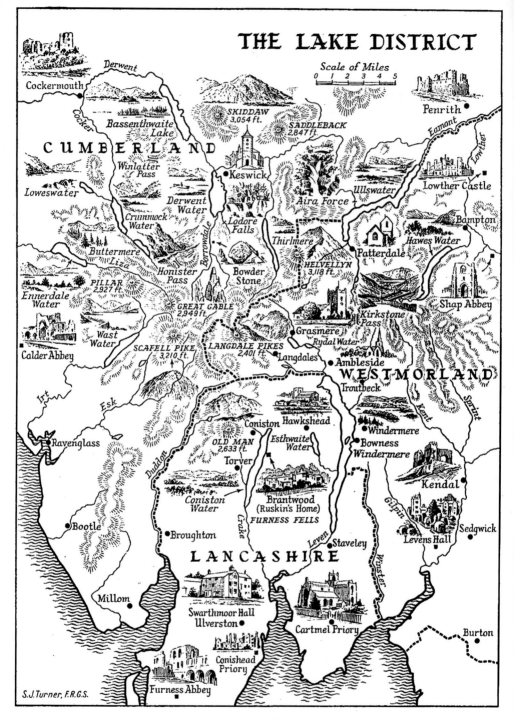

THE LAKE DISTRICT

Scale of Miles
0 1 2 3 4 5

Cockermouth

Derwent

Cocker

Bassenthwaite
Lake

SKIDDAW
3,054 ft.

SADDLEBACK
2,847 ft.

Penrith

Eamont

CUMBERLAND

Winlatter
Pass

Keswick

Lowther

Loweswater

Derwent
Water

Aira Force

Ullswater

Lowther Castle

Crummock
Water

Lodore
Falls

Thirlmere

Patterdale

Hawes Water

Bampton

Buttermere

Liza

Borrowdale

Honister
Pass

Bowder
Stone

HELVELLYN
3,118 ft.

Ennerdale
Water

PILLAR
2,927 ft.

GREAT GABLE
2,949 ft.

Kirkstone
Pass

Shap Abbey

Calder Abbey

Wast
Water

SCAFELL PIKE
3,210 ft.

LANGDALE PIKES
2,401 ft.

Grasmere

Rydal Water

Langdales

Ambleside

WESTMORLAND

Irt

Esk

Troutbeck

Kent

Sprint

Ravenglass

Coniston

Hawkshead

Esthwaite
Water

Windermere

Bowness
Windermere

OLD MAN
2,633 ft.

Torver

Kendal

Duddon

Coniston
Water

Brantwood
(Ruskin's Home)

FURNESS FELLS

Gilpin

Levens Hall

Sedgwick

Bootle

Broughton

Crake

Leven

Staveley

LANCASHIRE

Winster

Millom

Swarthmoor Hall
Ulverston

Cartmel Priory

Burton

Conishead
Priory

S. J. Turner, F.R.G.S.

Furness Abbey

126

The Lake District

THE Lake District, now apparently well set on the road to becoming the first of England's national parks, is so indelibly established as the foremost of the natural playgrounds of the British Isles that it seems hard to realize there was a time, not so very long removed, when its beauties of lake and mountain were little known outside the immediate vicinity.

It is, of course, almost impossible to separate the name of Wordsworth from any appreciation of the Lakeland scene and, indeed, so closely is the link affixed in the minds of many that today a form of "Wordsworth worship" is almost a cult among tourists visiting the Lake Country.

They make their pilgrimages to the little churchyard at Grasmere to see the plain grey headstone near the murmuring Rothay, to the poet's old home at Dove Cottage and the more pretentious house at Rydal Mount, and even to the ancient grammar school—no longer used for scholastic purposes—at Hawkshead, where the poet once carved his name on a desk, as any other schoolboy would have done. While such pilgrimages may do no harm, they do at any rate support an illusion better removed, an illusion that it was Wordsworth and his little band of contemporary, if less famous, poets who first called the outer world's attention to the beauties of the Lakeland scene.

Such an assumption is at least half a century too late, for it was not the poets but the painters who first "discovered" Lakeland. When Thomas West wrote his *Guide to the Lakes*, published in 1778, and forerunner of the innumerable volumes since turned out to put the visitor to Lakeland on the right track, he laid down a number of "stations," or viewpoints, to be included in any itinerary so that the tourist might see "the delicate touches of Claude verified on Coniston Lake, the noble scenes of Poussin exhibited on Windermere-water, or the stupendous romantic ideas of Salvator Rosa realized on the Lake of Derwent."

It was at the time when love of Lakeland was growing that Thomas Gray visited the district in 1769 and, as a commentary on the outlook of the period, he recorded that as his coach passed Skiddaw—a harmless mass of a mountain —he drew the blinds of his carriage lest his eyes feasted upon so frightening a sight! Beyond Derwent Water, Gray went up Borrowdale—as do thousands of present-day visitors—to the "awful amphitheatre" at Grange, where he stopped when he heard of Seathwaite and "a little path winding over the fells and for some weeks in the year passable to the dalesmen," a little path mountain-walkers today know as the Sty Head.

Such, then, was a popular poet's outlook on scenery less than two hundred years ago, an outlook that caused a barrier high as the fells between the mind of the tourist and the "innocent" dalesman, himself as rugged and often as unapproachable as the mountains themselves!

Familiarity, however, overcomes fear, and the tourists who followed Gray, while retaining a sense of the "horrible and terrific," were eventually induced to leave the dales and make their way up the mountain slopes. Before long, stout-hearted dalesmen were doing service as mountain guides.

So very far, indeed, had appreciation of Lakeland travelled by the time Wordsworth and his contemporaries began to add their praises.

For centuries the forebears of the dalesmen who made their homes in the very shadow of the "monstrous impending crags" have used the fell tracks and passes; for centuries they have built their homes in the dales and near the rocks. A country community is, of course, hewn from the rocks and soils of its immediate surroundings, and the very spirit of the hills—the spirit that had taken so long to make an impression in the mind of the visitor, save of the fearsome kind—was already part and parcel of the Lakeland dweller by the time the first tourists came along.

They had long since broken down the reserve of the woodlands that the early romanticists had peopled with various minions and spectres, for the woods provided them with fuel and building material. They had penetrated not only the secret tracks, but the depths of the mountains themselves in the search for metals and stone. Above all, they had found that the slopes of the fells, uncompromising as they were, provided sustenance for their sheep, the strange Herdwicks of almost legendary ancestry, and other mountain breeds.

A STORY OF UNBROKEN DEVELOPMENT

The story of the Lakelander is, indeed, one of unbroken development, for history has done as little to mould the Lakeland dweller as it has to fashion the landscape. Rather has the landscape fashioned the inhabitant and caused its reflection in the face of the buildings raised upon it, and, above all, in the habits and characteristics of the dalesman—farmer and villager alike.

Where then must we look for an interpretation of not only the Lakeland scene but its effect on those who dwell permanently within it? Guide-books there are in plenty dealing with the area, for since West started the fashion writers innumerable have gone to the Lake District, and, having been, have produced carefully planned routes and itineraries so that no one should miss the best of the scenery.

But West and his immediate successors hardly penetrated the thin surface soil of the mountains and never the skin of the Lakeland dalesman. Rather were they concerned with their own impressions, romantic enough certainly; but the real spirit of Lakeland, hard to the very core, was covered with an ultra-thick coating of what a more recent critic called "sloppy mush."

Modern novelists have done better, for their Lakeland has been peopled with living flesh against whose lives the hills and dales have been a dominating background. What Walpole has done for the Cumbrian dales, Constance Holme has done for the Westmorland valleys, and in more recent times

VII. AT THE HEAD OF BUTTERMERE, LOOKING TOWARD HIGH CRAG

VIII. VALE OF NEWLANDS, CUMBERLAND, FROM LITTLE BRAITHWAITE

IX. LOOKING FROM WYTHROP HILL TOWARD THE NORTHERN END OF LAKE BASSENTHWAITE, CUMBERLAND

Graham Sutton, Nicholson, and others have nobly carried on the tradition.

So much for the written word. It is necessary to bring the mind of the novelist to the routes of the guide-book in order to delve a little further than mere outline of fell and dale dictates.

Let us, therefore, first view the Lake District as a whole from some elevation that gives us an idea of the lay-out of the land. There is no need to be either climber or mountaineer to do that. Orrest Head, no more than half an hour's stroll from Windermere station, will do admirably. Measured in terms of the surveyor's theodolite its height is insignificant, a mere 784 ft., but few hills in the country command a wider prospect. Stand there, on a clear day, and you have an almost complete cirque of mountains, except to the south where the wide arc, yellow or flashing silver according to the state of the tide, of Morecambe Bay forms a natural boundary to Lakeland.

THE STAGE-COACH ROUTE ACROSS THE SANDS

In Wordsworth's day the route to Lakeland crossed the bay, the stage-coach following an almost forgotten route across the tidal channels and sands as it came from Lancaster and the south. Accidents there were, of course, and the parish registers of the villages south of the sands contain details of those who perished in the floods and stormy waters. Even today the Duchy of Lancaster maintains guides for the crossing; and sentiment, as well as a love of mild adventure, compels many people to cross under their leadership every year, for, even as Wordsworth said, the Lake scenery is never so fine as when seen after the passage of "its majestic barrier."

Northward, however, the prospect is one of mountains. Range after range stands out before us, all the main peaks clearly delineated. An indicator helps to position these and to mention them now would be to compile a mere catalogue of names. But that indicator does not show all the lie of the land. Among these mountains are the valleys and in those valleys are the people whose very lives are ordered by their close link with the heights.

Let us turn from the view and consult a map.

The railway from the south terminates at Windermere, at the foot of Orrest Head. A line runs up the coasts of Lancashire and Cumberland, with a branch to Coniston and a miniature railway up Eskdale. From Penrith, to the north-east and on the main route to Carlisle and the north, there is a branch line to Keswick and Cockermouth. The Ullswater Valley is connected to Penrith by road services which, in summer, link with steamers on the lake.

The railway, then, has penetrated but little into the Lakeland valleys. Apart from the visitors it brings and a speedy entry or departure from the fringe, its influence can be disregarded.

Even the main roads leave vast areas of country untouched. There is a good road from Windermere to Keswick, by way of Grasmere and Dunmail Raise, and one not quite so good from Windermere to Penrith, by way of the Kirkstone Pass and Ullswater. Roads, too, serve most of the valleys but rarely go beyond their heads; they also criss-cross some of the lower ridges. The real mountain sanctuaries, however, are left alone, save for walkers'

THE LANGDALE PIKES FROM KETTLE CRAG

The Langdale Pikes rise toward the southern end of the Lake District and are within the boundaries of the county of Westmorland. They rise steeply from Millbeck to a height of 2,400 ft. and from their summit the view extends westward to Scafell and eastward to Grasmere. This characteristic view from Kettle Crag, which itself consists of rough pasture divided off by low stone walls, shows the sheer rugged faces that provide some of the best rock-climbing in England. In the valley beneath is a group of farmhouses and cottages. The four peaks seen here are, from left to right, Pike o' Stickle, Loft Crag, Harrison Stickle, and Pavey Ark.

and shepherds' tracks across the mountains. From the head of Langdale to the head of Wasdale is a half-day's walk via Esk Hause and Sty Head; to travel by roads between the two is a good half-day's journey by fast car right round the northern and eastern fringe of Lakeland.

From Orrest Head the mountains appear compact and massed together. The idea of distance shrinks visibly. The map, however, puts us right and restores our true sense of Lakeland distances. Each dale becomes a separate entity, housing its farms and hamlets and walled in by the noble fells.

That being understood, it is time to leave our little hill and go farther into Lakeland proper.

Windermere itself is modern, despite the fact that appearances make it seem much older than is really the case. Before 1847 there was a cluster of cottages known as Birthwaite, but in that year the railway first came in from the south and the houses followed the engineers. In her *Guide to Windermere*, published almost a century ago, Harriet Martineau attributed the predominating old style of architecture to a vicar who had a passion for the old ecclesiastical ways of building, a passion that spread to his parishioners.

A hundred years, however, have been sufficient to mellow the buildings and, at the same time, to increase the briskness that attaches itself to life at Windermere. Let it be said that the tourist is all-important. One sees men and women laden with heavy rucksacks quickly leaving the towns and making for the hills; one sees motor-coaches and motor-cars laden with passengers also eager to catch their early glimpses of a Lakeland water from a lakeside road. Around these folk, modern Windermere lives and thrives.

True there are dalesmen coming down to the markets, perhaps bound for Kendal and the south. Their pace is slower. The outcome of generations of hill dwellers, their outlook on life seems more permanent; they know that the hills are there for eternity and life will go ahead in their shadows. They can be recognized not only by their more leisured gait, but also by their faces,

ON THE BANKS OF THIRLMERE

A new era of forestry has started in the Lake District and many new plantations of fir trees have been planted under the auspices of various official bodies. How well these hardy trees will grow is shown by the thick plantation on the island in the middle of the lake. Meanwhile the felling of older timber continues and there is a flourishing local industry in turning the felled trees into pit-props and other manufactured articles. When they are cut to the required length they are stacked, as shown on the left, ready for transport to the coalmining areas.

IN YEWDALE, CONISTON

Some of the most interesting features of the Lake District are in the Furness
district of Lancashire, which is wedged between southern Cumberland and
Westmorland. This area includes the greater part of Windermere as well as
Coniston Water, which is very near this attractive farm in Yewdale.

stained to deepest oak by the vagaries of Lakeland summers and winters.

From Windermere to Ambleside is a road that flirts first with lakeside gardens and then with the lake itself. Windermere is spreading, and spreading with a display of opulence that compels men to take great chunks out of the Lakeland landscape and fashion them to their own desire. But the opulence begins to fade after Low Wood and from there to Ambleside man has meant less to Windermere's shores than has Nature.

It might have been otherwise. Schemes were on foot to extend the railway as far as Ambleside—but even a century ago those concerned with countryside preservation were not mere voices in the wilderness. Wordsworth wrote a couple of sonnets and penned strong letters on the subject. His diatribes roused such a storm of protest that the scheme was abandoned.

THE OLD GREY BUILDINGS OF AMBLESIDE

At Ambleside we really begin to feel the hills. From the lakeside road they have been visible only as an inspiring backcloth to a setting of wood and water, but now their shadows spread across the narrowing vale and accentuate the greyness of the town.

There is, of course, as much variety in greys as in the more colourful paintings in oils. There is the greyness of a Lancashire industrial town, which is as completely alien to the Ambleside scene as is the warm grey of Cotswold stone.

Ambleside looks old and it is old, as the ages of towns go. The Romans had a station near the head of the lake and the Ambleside housewives pillaged it to use the stones, not for building but for scouring those spotlessly clean door-stones which were and still are their joy and pride. But in terms of individual houses Ambleside contains little that is really old. Its buildings have been erected time and time again on the same sites, and always the slate so readily obtainable from the near-by hills has been employed.

Ambleside, then, has been hewn from the Lakeland hills and in such a natural setting the dalesman assumes his rightful place. Now it is the hurrying tourist that seems incongruous to the scene. The native, walking along the road or gossiping with his neighbours, seems to have been there as long as the town itself, and so he has and, like the houses, has been renewed from time to time as one generation has been laid to rest in a little green mound beside the church and another fashioned in the same image has come along.

In Ambleside we are placed in a quandary. We can follow the main road farther into the heart of that district sometimes called Wordsworthshire; we can leave the main dale and go to the head of Langdale, where within a few miles we can stand in the very shadow of Lakeland's highest peaks, or we can turn southward and cross the lesser tumbled hills to Hawkshead and a countryside that centuries seem powerless to change.

If Wordsworth appeals our way is beside the Rothay, for preference on foot within sound of the prancing waters to little Rydal Water, a jewel among the hills, and by the lake of Grasmere to the village of the same name.

Grasmere, one must admit, has become a show-place and there are times

SCORE CRAG FARM, NEAR GRASMERE

This view shows the two distinctive features of Lakeland scenery, the placid green wooded valleys, with their charming farmhouses, long stone walls and lush fields, and the bare open treeless expanses of the moorlands and mountain tops. In the centre is Helm Crag which, though it rises only to 1,300 ft., commands an uninterrupted view over nearly a hundred square miles of country. From a fanciful resemblance when viewed at a distance the rocks on the summit have been called "the Lion and the Lamb."

when the quiet music of its river seems lost in the sonorous medley of the twentieth century. Then it seems as though the power of Wordsworth has been too much and the deep still waters of the poet's soul have burst their banks and become a flood-tide. Motor-coaches roar as one party after another comes from a visit to the churchyard or Wordsworth's old home at Dove Cottage and sets off to continue the mad rush of visiting as many lakes as possible in one day.

Perhaps it is not, after all, the still deep spirit of Wordsworth that overflows. Few people know that spirit today. The flood water is that of some tributary stream, skimming the deeper pool but never mixing and flowing out again in greater haste to leave the real pool still unruffled and undisturbed.

"Wordsworth himself, Dorothy, 'l'il Hartley' Coleridge, the dwarfish De Quincey, the gigantic Wilson are to be met with at every turn. People, ignorant people, will say sometimes that the Lakes are ruined by modern progress, by-roads, motor-cars, garages, and the rest. I can only say that eight months of the ten it will be Coleridge and Wilson and Hartley that you

will be meeting up Stonethwaite or by Newlands Church or on Striding Edge (new perch for Coleridge that!) or by the brook at Gordon Wordsworth's cottage at Ambleside. They rule the place now as they ruled it then." Those are the late Sir Hugh Walpole's words, written over a decade ago. There, then, is the deep still pool, as permanent and peremptory as of yore.

What of these dalesmen, progeny of poets and substance that made poets? Summer brings its visitors, but autumn brings peace. The work on the farms and in the quarries and on the hundred and one other jobs carried out in a village community goes on.

Darkness shuts out the monarchs of Steel Fell and Seat Sandal and that little community lives on. There are dances in the village hall; the members of the Women's Institute meet and discuss fruit-bottling and handicrafts and similar rural topics; the men select their football teams to do battle in the Westmorland League, and men and women together rehearse the season's play to be given by the local drama group.

All the time the summer visitor is back in his towns and cities, thinking wistfully of the Lakeland dales and lakes, all unconscious of the fact that life in a rural community goes on uninterrupted for the twelvemonth and that when he returns the next year he will find it following the same course as

NEAR KIRKBY LONSDALE, WESTMORLAND

The valley of the Lune, which for a part of its course divides Westmorland from Yorkshire, is in its upper reaches the effective division between the high ground of the Cumbrian mountains and the Pennine Chain. This view of the river near Kirkby Lonsdale is known as Ruskin's View and was described by him as the fairest and most satisfying scene in all England. The view-point is now protected for ever, for it was presented to the nation by a previous owner for the enjoyment of the people. In the background are the wooded slopes that rise toward the moorland pastures and the summit of Whernside, at 2,310 ft., one of the highest points in the Pennine Chain.

WINDERMERE

Windermere is the largest of the English lakes. Its name is held by some to mean winding lake, an epithet to which this photograph, taken from the high ground above Ambleside, gives point. Over ten miles long, Windermere is more than a mile at its widest. In the foreground is the River Rothay, which flows by Ambleside. On the left is the pier from which steamers ply along the lake to Bowness and Lake Side. Along the left bank can be seen some of the large country houses that occur at intervals round the lake.

before—the Lewises still tending their sheep, the Braithwaites still making the daily journeys over the fell to the quarries in the next dale, the Dodgsons still serving cakes and scones in the tea-gardens beside the river.

So does the pattern of Lakeland life fit in to the pattern of the landscape. It is time to cease dallying on the edge and go farther into the hill country.

From Windermere we saw the mountains as a satisfactory backcloth to a stage of wood and water; at Grasmere we came more completely under their spell. There are, however, other lakes where the mountains mould the scene and the outlook of the people to even greater effect.

Such a lake is Ullswater—like Windermere, resembling a river in general form but with the great fells, the Helvellyn range on one side and the High Street range on the other, coming down in a succession of folds right to the very shores. There is, however, a rim of greenery, wooded bluff and crag, that softens the scene and gives just the right touch to make Ullswater one of the worthiest subjects of the artist's brush.

Around the head the mountain wall is complete. Only the climbing road over the Kirkstone Pass communicates with the outer world, a road that runs along the edge of Brothers Water, set in permanent shadow, and then climbs stiffly over the watershed to the Troutbeck Valley and eventually to Windermere. For the rest there are only shepherds' tracks among the fells, tracks that lead past lonely farms and cottages where the postman often calls after a mad buffeting by the winter storms and, when the snow lies deep and the foot passes from dale to dale are blocked, fails to call for days on end. Here are some of the largest sheep-farms in the land, but more of sheep anon.

At the foot of the lake, Pooley Bridge, the starting place for the lake steamers, is five miles from the railway, although the railway tickets issued include the sail up the lake. Never does it throb with life as does Windermere. In normal times six thousand excursionists a day pass through Windermere. Pooley Bridge sees but a tithe of these. Near the lake's head are Patterdale and Glenridding, and there, like Ambleside, the passing of the years has seen much

ELTERWATER, WESTMORLAND

The dry-stone walling which bounds the winding tree-shadowed road, the stone-built outhouses, and the gay whitewashed cottages and farmhouses, are all typical of the countryside that lies between Ambleside and Coniston. This village is on the stream that flows down from the Langdale Pikes into Elterwater, and is about two miles across the mountains from Grasmere. The hills in the background are the outliers of the mountain mass that is centred on the Langdale Pikes. Here a scrubby vegetation rises to the summit but on the left there is the edge of bare open moorland.

rebuilding and renovating. Catering for the visitor looms large in the minds of the inhabitants. Nearly every house provides accommodation, which is at a premium in high summer.

Off Ullswater's eastern shores, behind the little pier at Howtown, lies Martindale, perhaps in many ways a kingdom of its own. There dwell the oldest inhabitants of the district, the wild red deer, survivors of the ancient herds that once roamed from the Scottish Border to the shores of Morecambe Bay, who have a sanctuary on the steep slopes of The Nab, a guardian buttress dividing two deep corries, or mountainside valleys. Summer and winter see the herd dispersed over much of eastern Lakeland, but mating time brings the wanderers back to the fell they consider home.

For centuries, the Hasells of Dalemain have held sway in this little mountain fastness, but even more powerful are the deer. Tenants hold their farms on condition that they shall accompany their lord whenever he chooses to hunt his deer—a condition never imposed because the Martindale deer are not hunted today.

In Martindale nested the last eagles in Lakeland. The wild cat, too, lingered here long after it had disappeared from the rest of the area, as did the kite and other birds. Such has always been the detachment of Martindale. After Ullswater, Derwent Water seems less enclosed. Keswick, once the

LOOKING ACROSS DERWENT WATER

This view of Derwent Water shows the rich vegetation and thick woods surrounding the lake. The mountain slopes of Skiddaw are more harshly defined and appear almost precipitous instead of a distant mass. This is the Keswick end of the lake and the view is that from Castle Head, a long-extinct volcano. Derwent Water is nearly three miles long, and over a mile wide at its centre. The River Derwent flows through Borrowdale to Derwent Water.

WATENDLATH BRIDGE

The wild scenery of the Watendlath Valley is the setting of Hugh Walpole's novel *Judith Paris,* the second book in the "Rogue Herries" series. It is typical of the beauty that never develops into prettiness, yet, except on the high peaks, is never so severe as that of the Scottish and Welsh mountains. In this view of the valley, where the river flows over tumbled rocks, the characteristic vegetation of the Lake District valleys is well shown, with fine deciduous woodlands in the distance, and on the right one of the plantations of conifers which seem likely to be the predominant vegetation in the future.

centre of a prosperous mining industry and still commanding fame as the place where lead-pencils are made, is the chief tourist town of Lakeland, but is a good mile from the lake. Behind the town is Skiddaw, urbane and high but finely sculptured so that every buttress pulls its weight; beyond the head of the lake, Borrowdale leads towards the highest mountains, Gray's land of "Chaos and Old Night." But Derwent Water is beautiful in its own right. Take away the mountains and the lake would be worth visiting for the "nabs and neuks" of its shore alone.

Buttermere is less easy to reach. To get there we must cross Honister Pass from Derwent Water, or go through Newlands Valley from Keswick, or even by way of the road from Cockermouth, an ancient place with a market dating from 1221 and the agricultural centre of a wide area. That last way would lead through the Vale of Lorton to Crummock Water and so to the little village near the foot of Buttermere, which consists of scattered farms and hotels.

To this valley the Vikings came in the late ninth century, mainly from the Isle of Man from where Harold Harfager evicted them after they had disputed his authority. They have left their impress in the typical inhabitant of the dale, who bears the blue eyes and fair hair of the Norsemen of old. Even in local art and music Scandinavian influence can be traced.

There is a track from the head of Buttermere that climbs over Scarf Gap on its way to the headwaters of the Liza, where the Forestry Commissioners have planted trees. Down the valley is Ennerdale Water, deep and lonely. Between the foot of Scarf Gap and the lake is the hamlet of Gillerthwaite, built around a farm renowned for its fine fell sheep. One cannot keep sheep out of the Lakeland scene. The slate quarries at Coniston, in Langdale, and on Honister employ their workers; the growing forests require more hands to continue the long-term work of timber production, and the village communities require their shopkeepers, postmen, and others, but the sheep are all-important in the scheme of Lakeland life.

Time was when there were hand-looms and spinning-wheels in many of the cottages, but these have long since passed into obscurity. From time to time one hears of attempted resurrections in the hope of interesting the tourist, but as work for the people they have lost their meaning.

WASDALE—WILDEST OF THE DALES

Another mountain pass, Black Sail, crosses the flanks of the great fells to Wasdale, wildest of Lakeland dales with a lake set black and deep with fan-shaped shoots of scree, or stone-covered slopes, plunging down from the side of Screes Mountain. The bunch of houses and the hotel at Wasdale Head have long been the Mecca of the cragsmen who disport themselves on the rocks and ridges of Great Gable, the Scafells, and the rest. Indeed, many a Wasdale farm relies as much on the climber for profit as on the fleeces of the sheep that populate the fells.

South of Wasdale are the lakeless dales of Eskdale and the Duddon, remote enough in their higher parts with sheep-farming as the sole occupation, and then at Coniston we find a good-sized lake again. The mountain mass of Coniston Old Man dominates the scene at the head of this lake; its slate quarries support the people who live in houses themselves made of slate in Coniston village and Torver, down the dale.

From Coniston we can cross the wooded hills back to Windermere, passing through the township of Hawkshead, loveliest of Lakeland towns.

Time has dealt kindly with Hawkshead. Clinging to a steep hillside, it contains as many odd corners and higgledy-piggledy collections of cottages as either Whitby or the Cornish St. Ives. Shut out the distant mountains and, indeed, you might be in some fishing port rather than an inland town.

Architectural changes seem to have been meaningless. Ambleside, Coniston, Glenridding—these have been rebuilt time and time again to meet changing needs. Hawkshead has remained steadfast and enduring. In more leisured years the spinning-wheels hummed incessantly in the upper storeys supported on pillars and protruding over the streets and even approached by flights of outside stairs. The spinning-wheels are silent; the cottages and stairs

WASDALE HEAD AND GREAT GABLE

On the west side of the Cumbrian range Wasdale cuts a narrow ravine into the
heart of the mountains. Here Wast Water lies between screes and fells. At the
head of the valley this pleasant group of tree-girt farm buildings is the key to
some of the finest climbing in England and Wales. Rising steeply from the head
of the valley is Great Gable, just under 3,000 ft.

remain. The hands that might have worked the wheels now perform more menial tasks about the home, but their skill has not departed. Handicrafts thrive under the aegis of the Women's Institutes and many a Hawkshead home displays its certificates showing that the work produced has caught the favour of the county judges.

From Hawkshead there are roads past Esthwaite Water to Windermere. We have completed the circle of the Lakeland dales.

We have looked in at the dales and the villages; we have seen the sheep on the fells. It is time we turned our attention more closely to these sheep.

There are, of course, sheep farms in other parts of the country, but Lakeland sheep-farming is of more than ordinary interest. Economically, it is difficult to see how Lakeland life could persist without the sheep; aesthetically, the animals are interesting because of the special breed to be found there and nowhere else in the world. The Lake District is the home of the Herdwick, that lithe, grey, agile animal, that, farming friends maintain, yields the sweetest mutton in the land.

The Herdwick is a true Lakelander. Take it away from its native fells and sheep-runs and it refuses to live. Even the mountains of North Wales failed to sustain Herdwicks sent there as an experiment, and when, following

SPRING BLOSSOMS AT RYDAL

Much of Wordsworth's work was inspired by the delightful cameos of beauty Lakeland offers in its many valleys and gentle wooded hillsides. This view at Dora's Field, near Rydal in Westmorland, is typical of Lakeland scenery.

NEAR LANGDALE HEAD

In spite of their ability to range over rocky country at all altitudes, sheep
sometimes stray and injure themselves on dangerous crags, from which the
shepherds must rescue them. This farmhouse, Blea Tarn Farm, typical of many
in the Lake District, is one of the first-aid stations to which the injured animals
are brought. The sheep on the extreme left has a hind leg bandaged; it will be
kept in the home pastures until the injury is completely healed. Like most of the
farmhouses of Lakeland this one is brightly colour-washed.

the First World War, sheep from the Lakes were taken to the Ardennes
country of Belgium every one perished in a short space of time.

Yet in spite of its allegiance to the Lakeland mountains, the Herdwick
is not a real native, and, indeed, its origin has been the subject of a deal of
controversy. Popular opinion has it that the first of the Herdwicks were introduced by the Vikings, and some have it that the sheep are of Spanish descent
and that some forty of them swam ashore from one of the galleons that
evaded Drake only to meet with disaster through the onslaughts of an Irish
Sea storm. No one seems to have sorted out the truth of the matter.

While these Herdwicks are the most typical of the Lakeland sheep, there
are other varieties to be met with on the great runs. All are hardy animals—
black-faced Swaledales from Yorkshire, Cheviots from the Border Country,

THE BLACKSMITH'S FORGE

In many parts of the country the blacksmith's forge is a feature of village life which has disappeared or in some cases has been converted into a filling-station or repair shop for motor-cars. In mountainous districts, however, and more especially in the Lake District, where the horse is still an essential factor in farming, the blacksmith's forge continues to perform a useful function with little less business than before the era of mechanization. The blacksmith is almost as important as he was two hundred years ago when he ranked with the baker as one of the two essential craftsmen in any village.

Rough Fells, and various crossbreeds. They are often buried in great drifts of snow, but these hardy creatures can live for days under the snow. The heat from their bodies melts the snow round them and makes an air space. The sheep feed on the grass and even the soil and, should their imprisonment be prolonged, will eat their own wool. Sometimes they have been buried for weeks and then, when released, have walked away to their farms.

One thinks automatically of these sheep when thinking of life in the Lake District, for the dalesman's calendar is formed round them and the character of whole dales has been moulded round the need for tending the sheep. Lambing time in spring, clipping time in early summer, shepherds' meets in autumn, and hunting in winter, for the Lakeland fox grows fast and cunning on the great hills and the foxhound packs are as necessary adjuncts of the farmers' lives as for the pleasure of the chase—these things mean much in a district still in geographical isolation from the rest of northern England.

Indeed, Lakeland sheep are by long association of tenure more part and parcel of the landscape than the farmer himself. They form part of the capital value of the farm; an incoming tenant takes over the sheep along with the buildings and land and pays rent for them. While in occupancy he receives the profit from their fleeces and flesh and, of course, increases his flock by breeding, but should he quit the farm he must leave behind a flock that corresponds both in numbers and in composition to that on the schedule of his lease.

Once the sheep have been clipped and other jobs of the farm have been attended to, however, there comes a time for sport and play before the crops in the dales have to be harvested and the autumn work begins, and then the various Lakeland villages hold their annual sports meetings and gatherings, meetings that excite an enthusiasm out of all proportion to the importance of the events in the athletic world. Most of the contests are for money prizes but these are never large sums and although it means the competitors are professional athletes, the word "professionalism," when applied to the native sports of the Lake Country, has a very limited meaning and competitors are mainly local men.

Just as the famous Highland gatherings at Braemar, Oban, and other Scottish centres have earned renown as the scenes of great feats by throwers of the hammer and tossers of the caber, so have the north country sports of wrestling and fell-racing become typical of these Lakeland gatherings. Flat races and leaping competitions are held, but interest in these is slight compared

HOUND-TRAILING
In this picture hounds are seen leaving the field at the start of the trail, which is a course previously laid by dragging aniseed-soaked rags on the ground. The trailer can be seen in the background.

with that shown in the more strenuous contests. The dalesman's daily life is hard and vigorous; he looks to these same qualities to dominate his sports.

The wrestling is in the local "Cumberland-Westmorland" style and this is entirely different from either the "catch-as-catch-can" or "Cornish hug" methods. The contestants face each other in the ring and a "hold" is secured by placing the arms round the body of an opponent, the left arm under the arms and the right over the shoulders. As soon as both competitors have got a good grip, the signal to commence is given and the first one to touch the ground with any portion of his body save the feet is the loser.

Wrestling is always an important feature of the famous Grasmere sports —most picturesque of these gatherings—usually held on the third Thursday in August, but there is no doubt that this form of wrestling was in vogue in the Lake District many centuries before the first sports were held at Grasmere in 1865. Some authorities attribute a Norse origin, and there are definite

SPRING GLORY IN WESTMORLAND

Mountain country covers most of Westmorland, for where the Cumbrian mountains fall away to the east the Pennine Chain rises on the other side of the Eden. Even so, apart from the mountain valleys, there are many odd corners in the county, such as in the valley of the Eden itself and in the south toward the borders of Lancashire, where a vigorous agriculture is carried on. The wealth of damson blossoms seen here near Lyth promises a rich harvest of fruit, while sheep and their lambs are pasturing on the rich herbage of the valley. There is a reminder of the mountain country in the steep hills of the background and the stone walls, but the promise of the lowlands in the hedges that take the place of stone walling when once the mountainous country is left behind.

THE BEAUTY OF BORROWDALE

Borrowdale is one of the loveliest of the narrow fertile valleys that intersect the mountains of the Lake District. This view is looking south up the valley, which is watered by the River Derwent, here seen near its junction with Derwent Water. From left to right can be seen Scafell Pike, the highest summit in England; Lingmell and Great Gable in the centre; and Brandreth.

records of "wrustling," as the dalesmen call it, at Grasmere soon after the eleventh century.

Equally spectacular are the fell races held as part of the sports meetings, and that at Grasmere has been claimed as the stiffest event of its kind in the land. From the sports field near the village, the runners make the climb of the thousand-feet-high Butter Crags, go along a rocky ridge to a farther peak, and then come back down the long slopes of heather, bracken, and scree to the sports field. Practically the whole of the course is visible from the field.

There are other fell races at Keswick, where the route lies up and down Latrigg, the "cub" of Skiddaw, at Ambleside (where a route is made on the slopes of Loughrigg Fell), and Patterdale (with a climb in the direction of St. Sunday Crag, on the Helvellyn range), so that there are plenty of opportunities for visitors to witness these fascinating and strenuous contests.

The passing of the years has, indeed, resulted in something of the very texture of the hills being thrust deep into the inner hearts of those whose ancestors have long dwelt in their shadow. Take away the dalesman, with his sheep and his sports, his homes and his villages, and you turn Lakeland into a lifeless museum of scenery without a soul.

147

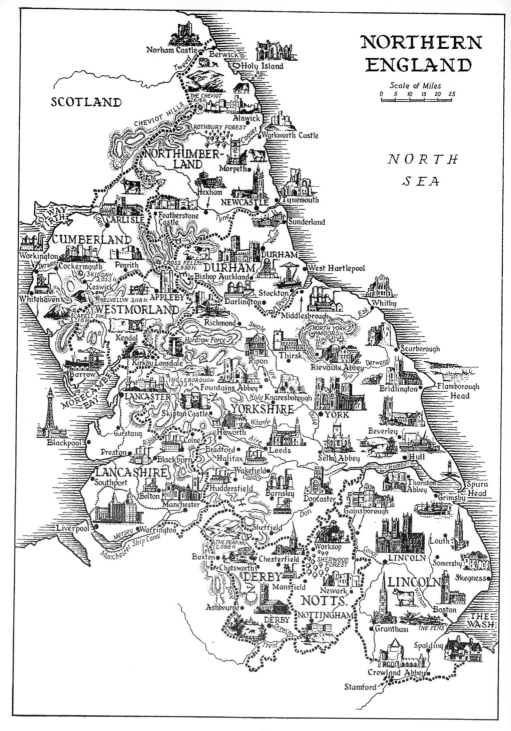

NORTHERN ENGLAND

Scale of Miles
0 5 10 15 20 25

SCOTLAND

NORTH SEA

Norham Castle
Berwick
Holy Island
Tweed
THE CHEVIOT 2,676 ft.
CHEVIOT HILLS
ROTHBURY FOREST
Alnwick
Warkworth Castle
NORTHUMBER-LAND
Coquet
Morpeth
Hexham
NEWCASTLE
Tynemouth
SOLWAY FIRTH
CARLISLE
Featherstone Castle
Tyne
Sunderland
Eden
CUMBERLAND
Workington
Derwent
Cockermouth
Penrith
CROSS FELL 2,930 ft.
DURHAM
Bishop Auckland
West Hartlepool
Skiddaw 3,053 ft.
Keswick
Whitehaven
HELVELLYN 3,118 ft.
APPLEBY
Stockton
Darlington
Whitby
SCAFELL PIKE 3,210 ft.
WESTMORLAND
Tees
Middlesbrough
Esk
Richmond
Swale
NORTH YORK MOORS
Kendal
Hardraw Force
Rievaulx Abbey
Scarborough
Kirkby Lonsdale
Ripon
Thirsk
Derwent
MORECAMBE BAY
Barrow
INGLEBOROUGH 2,373 ft.
Fountains Abbey
Bridlington
Flamborough Head
LANCASTER
Nidd Knaresborough
YORKSHIRE
YORK
Skipton Castle
Wharfe
Garstang
Haworth
Ure
Beverley
Blackpool
Preston
Colne
Ribble
Bradford
Aire
Leeds
Selby Abbey
Hull
Blackburn
Halifax
Humber
LANCASHIRE
Wakefield
Calder
Thornton Abbey
Southport
Huddersfield
Barnsley
Doncaster
Spurn Head
Bolton
Manchester
Don
Gainsborough
Grimsby
Liverpool
Mersey
Warrington
Manchester Ship Canal
Sheffield
Louth
Worksop
THE PEAK 2,088 ft.
Buxton
Chesterfield
SHERWOOD FOREST
LINCOLN
Somersby
Chatsworth
Dove
DERBY
Mansfield
Newark
Skegness
Ashbourne
NOTTS.
NOTTINGHAM
LINCOLN
Boston
DERBY
Derwent
Grantham
THE FENS
Witham
THE WASH
Trent
Spalding
Crowland Abbey
Stamford

148

Pennine Country

COACH-ROADS today pass through those upland areas where the moorland pastures lie, where once the cyclist, the pedestrian, the farmer with his horse and trap making a way along an indifferent highway, a lane, or a rough cart-track, were lonely and diminutive in a wide emptiness. The city dweller on tour is becoming familiar with the areas, their great expanses, their emptiness, their silence, and as he passes through villages which are little more than hamlets, or catches sight of a native tramping over the moorland, it is incredible to him that such emptiness should be the home of man, that its wildness should sustain a people. If it is the scenery he remembers, and nothing of the man who dwells and works among it, it is because the very circumstances of his travel give the holiday-maker little chance of getting in touch with the upland farm folk. A pity, that, for here live folk of as rugged an individualism as any to be found in Britain.

It is a people which in its speech, its manner, is the embodiment of these high places. They are areas where hard winters are common, where the growing season is short, enduring a high measure of cloudy weather so that hours of sunshine are fewer than elsewhere, where the soil is poor, and many of the homes are wellnigh inaccessible, perched as they are just under the summits of the hills. They are people of strong characteristics. That man trudging along ahead of the coach is a figure to catch the eye. He tramps it heavily, as one accustomed to broken ground, but at a pace that covers miles steadily and unwearyingly, and he is peculiar because of the way he carries his ash stick—clipped against his side by his forearm and held with an ease and assurance that is inborn. He will make no reply to a greeting flung at him, save perhaps a brief word, for these upland folk are a dour people. They are, it may be said, intelligent, resourceful, self-reliant, but they live a remote life, their speech is slow, brief, with a suggestion of reluctance. Against the advances of the quicker speaking, quicker thinking man of the town he presents a brusque monosyllabic manner of reply. It is self-consciousness, but there is no suggestion of inferiority about it. His manner is a defence against ways of speech that are unfamiliar to him. The millstone grit that throws up a rugged and broken rampart against the skyline is in his nature; it gives him stubbornness and a hardness. The white limestone, that outcrops and gives to the green fellsides a charm, outcrops in the man, too; it reveals itself in his hospitality, his generosity, when once you know him intimately. Thus you will find the northern hill farmer; in like manner the red sandstone of South Wales is embedded in the nature of the moorland farmer there.

NORTH OF THE PENNINES

The Pennine Chain at its northern end joins the Cumbrian Mountains on the one hand and the Cheviot Hills on the borders of England and Scotland on the other. This view of the Cheviot country looking south into Northumberland gives a fine impression of the bare outlines of the moors. This is a countryside that has never been inhabited on a large scale or cultivated at all. It is the country of the great wall which the Romans built from the Tyne to Solway Firth. Its farms are few and far between and are confined to the valleys. Their stock-in-trade, as in the whole of the High Pennines, is their flocks of sheep, their tillage mostly confined to the kitchen garden and a field or two ploughed to grow fodder for their livestock.

One must live among these qualities for some years before their richness becomes apparent. The native has a way of treating a stranger residing in his midst with courtesy, yet holding him off at arm's length. He has a term for such residents. Off-comers, he calls them; in some Yorkshire dales the term is "comers-in," pronounced all as one word "kummersin," and among his own kin he will comment on these strangers with a shrewdness that can be devastating. For, in spite of common opinion that runs to the contrary, that laughs at his apparent slowness, his mental processes that work leisurely, he is a shrewd man, alike in observation and in business.

To understand the hill farmer he must be put against his background. In their total, the moorland pasture areas run to some five million acres, or about one-sixth of the total agricultural area of England and Wales. There are four main regions, all high land running up to 1,400 ft. and over, and they differ in their physical characteristics. In Northumbria, under the Cheviots, there is grand rolling moorland where one may stand and see earth and sky meet in the distance encircling one. Here are some of the finest and most expansive moors in the country, and on the lower slopes of the heights, as may be seen along the road from Barnard Castle to Alston, the expansiveness is often accentuated by sparsely dotted whitewashed farmhouses and cottages.

The features of the Lake District surely need no description, but it may be said that here the quick steep sides of the hills make the transition from hill to lowland farming a sharp one. The northern ranges of the Pennines, both on the Lancashire and the Yorkshire side, are notable for their dales, and, on the eastern or Yorkshire side, the miles and miles of stone walls criss-crossing the fellsides are a feature of these dales. Many of these walls, straight, curving, twining across the green fields like wind-blown ribbon, must be hundreds of years old. They endure, perhaps, because they are dry walls—walls, that is, built without lime for bonding. The building of them is a craft, and so that it may not share the fate of other local crafts and vanish, competitions in dry-wall building are held and fostered. The dales of Durham and of Derbyshire, bleak, wall-girt spaces, share many of these characteristics. The ranges of Snowdonia and the Black Mountains of the Welsh border are also extensive hill-farming areas. Those mountains of South Wales, the great striding ridges

THE WASHBURN VALLEY

The large lake in the background is the Swinsty reservoir, which supplies Leeds with much of its water. It lies in the midst of the Washburn Valley, the scenery of which is characteristic of much of the moorland foothills. Here there are the same stone walls and long views that are typical of all the Yorkshire moors, but the scene is enlivened by generous scattered timber and a few larger woods. Here, too, is good pasture-land over which range the flocks of sheep that help to supply the Yorkshire woollen mills with their raw material. In the trough of the valley there are a few fields which have been ploughed and have responded with an abundant harvest.

of the Black Mountains, have a character of their own. Here is perhaps the most beautiful of all these moorland pastures; softer, smoother, than the northern moorland regions. The long ridged bulk is tree-clad, the valleys are sweet and clean. It is a red-sandstone region, with but one or two limestone caps. to the summits of the ranges. Here, in Brecon, with these mountains, with the Brecon Beacons, is some of the most attractive inland country that Wales can show. Yet just south of it, thrusting up their dirt and squalor, their smoke, the slag heaps that ever creep out and out swallowing up the land—here are the Welsh valleys, the blackened and ravaged valleys, the home of the coalpits, the iron works, the tin works, the blast furnaces. Not even the industrial towns that crowd along the eastern and western foot-hills of the Pennines show so striking and so disheartening a scene as is to be found here.

A typical farm consists of unimproved moorland, intake, which is enclosure won from the moorland and is also known as in-bye, or allotment; and some lower-lying arable or meadow land. As a sheep farm it is a small unit, and in terms of invested capital, turnover, and size of flock it is a small business. The labour is that of the farmer and a hired youth, or members of the farmer's family, and this cost, and that of rent and hire for winter grazing, are the chief costs of working the farm. Because of the fluctuations in the price of sheep, of wool, and of cattle, and in the yearly yield of lambs, it is a specula-

THE HIGH PENNINES
This panorama of well-known scenery is best seen from the road that connects Buckden in Upper Wharfedale with Hawes in Upper Wensleydale. In this photograph a part of this road can be seen winding from the bottom right-hand corner down into the slightly wooded valley until it disappears in the middle distance. The high plateau is known as Fleet Moss and exceeds 1,850 ft. above sea-level. The only access to the farms that nestle in the distant trees is by steep roads, which in winter are often blocked by snow.

UPPER WHARFEDALE

The most famous part of Wharfedale is between Bolton Abbey and Ilkley.
Above Bolton Abbey the valley narrows until here at Yockenthwaite it is little
more than a broad cleft between the ridges that radiate from the central mass
of the Greater Whernside. The grey stone walls which match the walls and
slates of the farmhouses and outbuildings are characteristic of the district.
A few fine trees and stunted bushes near the stream straggle up the hillside.
There is a monotony in the colouring of the scene even in sunny weather,
but there is beauty in the contours and bold lines of the landscape.

tive and precarious way of livelihood. To increase his income, and also to
steady it, the farmer breeds and rears cattle, fattens store cattle on his lower-
lying land, goes in for butter-making, and sells milk and poultry. Where this
extended farming is not possible, where the holding is really small, as in
many instances in Wales, the man will also work in quarries or on the roads.
For some years now, too, catering for holiday-makers has been an important
source of income, but where this has meant the letting of a cottage for the
summer it has added to the local housing difficulties.

The "statesman," a term once well known in Cumberland and Westmorland and in the northern dales, has gone. He was the man with a farm of
his own, an "estatesman," the yeoman proud and independent. But the farm
was too small to sustain such a family as was common in Victorian days;

too small to be divided among the numerous sons, and there were few farms to let, or sell, to which the younger generation could go. There began a town-ward drift; the young men to the dockyards of the north-east coast, to the textiles mills of Lancashire and Yorkshire, to the mining and iron and steel industries of South Wales; the daughters went into domestic service or to the looms. It was a process that continued and still continues. But these migrants, and their descendants, are still of the hill-farming community. However attenuated the relationship has become, they are welcomed as one of the family when they visit the homes from which they spring. Neither off-comers nor comers-in, they are of the blood, and so are given entry to that close and clannish inner life of the community that no outsider can enter.

This is the background against which is produced the taciturn, self-reliant, stubborn, slow-speaking hill farmer. He is apiece with the enduring hills, and as stubbornly unresponsive to outside influences. He is a difficult man to approach; best approached, perhaps, when he has come down from the mountains to the market-town. There, among folk he knows, people of his own type, he moves and speaks with a freedom in sharp contrast to his manner when encountered at home. He is down on business.

THE SHEEPDOG AT WORK

For his shepherding work, still more for that great day when all the sheep have to be swept up off the moor and brought down for the annual dip, an August event in most of the areas, a farmer depends upon his dogs. To see a big flock cascading down the hills, with the farmer in their rear, the dogs weaving in and out and along the flanks to keep the fleeces on the move, is a striking sight. But still more striking it is to see the man directing his dogs over what appears to be a silent and uninhabited, heather-covered area. Out of that cover emerges here and there a blob of white. The numbers increase, huddle together, and presently the whole flock is on the move, the farmer's whistle, fingers in mouth, being the only method of command for the dogs. To watch their response, to see them dart off this way, then that, to stop abruptly and crouch, is to marvel at the intelligence of the dogs. But seldom is it the good fortune of the casual visitor to these highlands to witness such a performance, but he will see it, and marvel, at the sheepdog trials which are usually held at each local agricultural show. He may see it, carried to a higher degree of cleverness and intelligence, at the national sheepdog trials. Here Welsh farmer contests with Welsh farmer, Scot with Scot, English with English, and the winners go forward to the international trials. These are an enthralling sport; here the best shepherds and farmers meet in contest; here are the best sheepdogs the country can produce.

The contests take place in a large enclosed field. Down one side of it are spaced two, sometimes three, upright posts, something like goalposts without the crossbar. Towards the end of the field is a crossroad built up of hurdles; near the other corner is a pen, also of hurdles. There is one more post, near the judges, and here the competing farmer takes his stand, his arm passed through the loop of a rope. At the farther end of the enclosure are three sheep,

NIDDERDALE

The valley of the Nidd, which rises on the slopes of the Greater Whernside
and runs in a general easterly direction into the Vale of York, is one of the most
picturesque and varied of the Yorkshire dales. This photograph looks down into
the valley from the ridge that divides Nidderdale from Wharfedale. In the
middle distance the old town of Pateley Bridge can be seen, while beyond are
the moors that separate Nidderdale from Wensleydale.

MILLSTONE EDGE, DERBYSHIRE

The main road from Sheffield to Hathersage passes through some of the most
magnificent scenery of the southern end of the Pennine Chain bordering on
the Peak District of Derbyshire. For part of the way it runs between high
limestone cliffs and then emerges on high ground near the rocky outcrops
shown here. The weather has moulded the rocks into fantastic shapes owing
to the uneven hardness of their composition. In some places the lower parts
of rocks have been worn away while the upper part has resisted the forces of
erosion. In the background is a rock known as the Rocking Stone, the base
of which has been almost worn away so that it moves as on a pivot.

straight down from the hills, wild and nervous, held by as many perspiring
attendants. The farmer's aim is to drive the sheep through the uprights,
through the crossways, and pen them. Points are awarded for time, for neat-
ness of performance, for the handling of the dog.

With the farmer at the post, his dog at his feet, the judges give the signal
and the sheep are let loose. Immediately they bolt, then stop and nibble at the
grass, which after their moorland fare is a tempting food. A nod by the judges,
and the farmer turns to his dog, waves his arm and says "way by." In a
second the animal is tearing up the side of the enclosure. As the dog nears the
sheep a long low whistle shrills out, and the dog swings in, still on the run, to
rear of the sheep. They throw up their heads in alarm and race off. Now begins
the guiding of the startled animals, the manoeuvring of the dog by the man.
With fingers in his mouth he sends forth whistle after whistle; now short and
sharp, commands that bring the dog to an abrupt stop, prone on the grass,
then send him weaving on the right flank, the left flank, heading the bolting
animals toward the centre of the posts. If in their alarm they race away on the
outside of the posts they have to be swung about and steered all over again,
and with ears cocking the dog makes instant response to every command,
never barking, never biting, which is the trait of a good sheepdog.

It is when the sheep have emerged through the last of the posts that the real work begins. A straight run is one thing; to head the sheep through a short lane of hurdles is another. It is an obstacle that sends them speeding about in fright, breaking away in all directions—or they would thus break away but that the man is now free to join and help his dog. They hesitate, those frightened sheep, about the entry. A whistle, and the dog drops prone, and wriggles towards them. They break away but in a flash they are back again, for the dog is on every side of them, and the man with slowly waving arms, a silent man, is also there to head them back. They retreat, facing the dog, their sterns pointing to the entrance. Down goes the dog again, belly flat, and at a soft whistle, from pursed lips now, he wriggles nearer; a yard closer. One sheep swings about, facing the entry. The dog suddenly sits up, panting at the two others, tongue lolling. They swing about, bump against the one with its head in the entry, and push it farther in. It drives through the road, the others, being sheep, burst through after it—to meet dog and man on the farther side, waiting to swing them through the second of the crossroads. It is pretty work. If, as the sheep break away, the man loses his temper and shouts to the dog, issuing contradictory commands and so confusing the

THE HEART OF WENSLEYDALE

Bainbridge on the River Ure, here seen flowing swiftly under the humpbacked stone bridge, is typical of the Wensleydale villages as it is of the villages of all the Yorkshire dales. It affords an interesting comparison with Yockenthwaite in Wharfedale, shown on page 153. All the chief elements are the same —the colouring, the stone walls and stone buildings and the moors in the background—but here in the heart of Wensleydale the trees are more numerous and more stately and the land on the lower ground more fertile.

animal, much time can be lost. The experienced farmer or shepherd is quiet and cool; dog and man work as one in a partnership marvellous for its unity. After the crossroads are safely won the sheep are driven to the pen. Again they are stubborn, hesitant at entering an enclosure from which they see no exit. But man and dog are insistent; one sheep falters and pokes in his head. Again the dog wriggles closer, sits up and pants; the two others burst in, carrying the first before them. The dog drops prone along the mouth of the pen, ears cocked, waiting on his master for the next command, but it is all over.

The prettiest work, the prettiest handling, and the intelligence of the dogs is even more manifest, when two are worked together to pen six sheep, a selected three in one pen, the remainder in the other. The manner in which the man and one dog detach the named three, shedding them from the others, and penning, whilst the second dog keeps guard over the other three, is something to command nothing but the greatest admiration. Yet of these trials, packed with interest as they are, it may be said that they are no more than a refined edition of the actual work done on the moors. There is a difference between a long, level enclosure, where three sheep, or six, are always in sight, and the rough, broken moorland where there are dips and hollows and thick heather to hide a flock. Nor on the trials field is there to be seen what can happen on the moor—a proud and heavy ram, indignant that his lordship of the moor should be thus challenged, planting his feet sturdily and with lowered front defying the dog. The dog wins, of course; he knows his business; he knows how to handle the toughest of rams.

Hard as is his life, rough as is his nature—until you have broken through the crust and discovered the geniality and the generosity beneath it—the moorland farmer knows how to play. He relaxes at the local agricultural show, he jests with his fellows. At the annual feast of the village on which his workaday life centres, he is a man intent on enjoyment. The folk have ways of their

A MOORLAND ROAD
All the austerity of the high moors of the Pennines is reflected in this grey monotonous landscape. For mile after mile there is rank grass and no other vegetation in sight, the vista being limited only by the mistiness of the atmosphere. The rough road that twists round the isolated hummocks connects farm with farm and cottage with cottage. The only traffic passing over its rough surface is an occasional farm car or delivery van.

FOUNTAINS ABBEY
This is judged by many to be the most beautiful abbey ruin in Britain. It is set in a picturesque situation near Ripon where the outliers of the Pennine Moors merge into the Vale of York and the ruins are mostly in the late Norman and Early English styles of architecture. The photograph shows the contrast between the round arches of the earlier and pointed arches of the later period. Only the tower in the background, known as Abbot Huby's Tower, is a later addition and was built about 1500.

own of conducting these affairs. At an agricultural show, for example, as you enter by the field-gate which does duty as a turnstile, a burly red-faced farmer —or it might possibly be the local constable—will take you by the hand and pat it, with perhaps more vigour than seems necessary. A curious welcome, and the gate-man will smile as he sees the astonishment on your face. With a jerk of his head he will indicate your hand. There, at the base of the thumb and forefinger, is the impression of a rubber stamp. Your pass for the day.

The homes of these upland people, farmhouses and cottages alike, reflect the character of the people and of the countryside. They are, traditionally and rightly, built of local material—the rock on which these moorland pastures lie. There is no great pretence of architectural distinction, especially in the houses that are remote up the hillsides, unless one includes the thickness of their walls; but thick walls are needed to carry the weight of the stone-slab roofs. Those roofs, standing up to the weather for centuries, have in that time collected a covering of moss and lichen whose sheen of green and grey and old gold not only harmonizes with the landscape, but gives some distinction to the building. On the lower slopes, in the villages strung out along the road like beads on a string, many of the farmhouses were originally halls or manor-houses. They, too, are of stone, with ponderous walls, stone-slab roofs, with mullioned windows that are evidence of the skill, the artistry, the craftsmanship of those bygone days. Among them are found houses with a panel over the door or over the porch, bearing some initials and a date; "J. & E. C. 1689," one may read; local history will confirm that John Craven, on taking to wife one Elizabeth, built this house for their dwelling, and, as custom was in those days, carved the initials of himself and his bride and the date. A true yeoman's home, solid and enduring as the race from which he sprang, the race which he continued. In later years his descendant, as rugged and as stubborn as his forbear, blocked up many of the windows rather than pay the window tax which was essayed as a freakish effort to increase the country's revenue.

These old halls, these manors, are spacious, but the farmer today makes use of few of the rooms. There are treasures here, however. Long oaken tables, of undoubted age, in the great disused dining-room, musicians' galleries, oak furniture, deep kists or chests that hold old-time garments, chairs of pedigree. They are rich and rare, and musty from disuse, for the farm household lives in the kitchen. Things run almost to the other extreme in houses that were built as farmhouses. Here, too, are rooms seldom used, furnished with horsehair couches and chairs, the fireplace filled with coloured paper, the purpose being to stop down-draught. Home-made rugs line the floor. There are pot dogs and other pot ornaments on the mantelpiece, funeral cards of deceased relatives on the walls, and of pictures, not unseldom two engravings that appear to have had some popularity in the worst of the Victorian days— engravings of the Plains of Heaven, and Judgment Day. Of them it may be said that they reveal the artist as a man of lively imagination, and in matters theological a pronounced Fundamentalist. Still, they were popular, and appealed to a remote-living, lonely upland folk.

The unused rooms are there because the life of the farmhouse centres in the kitchen. A homely spot it is, and comfortable. Oaken beams cross the ceiling, and in the gap between a beam and the floor-boards above the farmer keeps his shaving tackle. A gun hangs from a beam, and from another swings the oil lamp. In the corner, where the farmer monopolizes a stout armchair, a grandfather clock ticks somnolently. Under the window that looks out on to the farmyard is a long couch covered with dressed sheepskins, and a capacious fireplace is fed with logs as well as with coal. Peat was once the staple fuel in the days when coal was costly in transport and not easily available; peat is still used in the more remote farmhouses. The farm wives have a quick way of inducing a blaze in the smouldering logs. A handful of swealings, the thin dry twigs of the coniferous trees, is thrown on the fire; in a moment they blaze and hiss furiously, filling the kitchen with the aroma of pine.

POSTY—MESSENGER, CONFIDANT, AND FRIEND

There is one man of special standing in these districts; the postman. Posty, for short, may rank as a Government official, distributing letters, parcels and the like all along his round, calling at farmhouses, cottages, taking short cuts across fields as a matter of right; collecting letters and parcels on his return round for outward post. He is a figure to take the eye. Begirt with bag and slung about with parcels, wearing his sou'wester and oilskins on rough days, flourishing his stick as he tramps along—he occupies the road. But to the farm folk he is more than all this. He is their link with all the district. As he travels his round, with a word for everyone, he picks up the gossip of the district and retails it at every house of call; he keeps the district in touch with all its little doings, the messenger in whom all confide.

WINTER IN THE PENNINES

When, as they often do, winter snows block the upland roads of the Pennine country, wheeled traffic becomes impossible, but the postman still goes his rounds on foot, as here, to serve the scattered farmhouses of Upper Wensleydale. Sometimes the snow lies three or four feet deep with drifts much deeper. Even today, when snow-ploughs are used to clear the main roads and many of the by-ways, the farmhouses often make a practice of laying in enough provisions to last a month or longer.

Here and there in these regions another man lingers on the scene who is sure of a welcome. The clock dresser is today no more than an aged and scarce survival of a craftsman once a well-known figure, as much part and parcel of the local life as Posty. He is of the days when grandfather clocks were to be seen in every household, a piece of furniture regarded with pride. From his little shop in a small down-valley town he went forth at intervals up to the farms and cottages in the hills, keeping the old clocks in repair and in the way of recording the correct time. But so many of these old clocks have gone, snapped up by visitors, holiday-makers, people with cars who take a cottage for the summer, and, finding these things in the farmhouses, offer a tempting price; a younger generation, too, prefers smaller, handier clocks that take up little space on the mantelpiece or hang against the wall instead of occupying a good deal of floor space. There are no new long-case clocks; the craft has died out through the competition of cheaper machine-made things. So the old-fashioned clocks, wonderful timepieces though they are and despite the beauty of their casings, are scarce and dear; indeed a younger generation would find one difficult to acquire.

So the old clock dresser, the last of his race, makes but intermittent appearance these days. He comes unannounced. A welcome place is made for him at the table, and after the meal he and the farmer sit about the fire, pipes going, in homely but shrewd talk on things past and things present; on men and affairs. Then, tapping out the ashes of his pipe, the old man will say that he "might as well have a look at her," and out of his bag come screwdrivers, pliers, other small tools, a bottle of oil, one of varnish, and some cleaning rags. The clock works are taken out and laid on the table, cleaned of dust, oiled, carefully put back. Then with loving care, with all the concentration of a man skilled in, and proud of, his craft, he gives the clock case a thorough polish. This done, he sets the pendulum swinging, with the assurance that now "She'll go for ivver."

There are superstitions in the moorland pasture regions, legends, but today they are becoming dim memories. Yet they linger. What else is to be expected in these lonely spaces; lonely—the Black Mountains alone can offer some eighty square miles of real solitude. Tales of the Marches, of the phantom riders, are not wholly forgotten. Under the Cheviots, too, there surely linger the ghosts of those who fought in the Battle of Chevy Chase, the subject of one of the most stirring ballads. Here Douglas and Percy met, here Witherington, as the ballad tells, fought on his stumps after his legs had been hewn off. All this is the very substance of legend and superstition, to be told to the children over the fire at night, the very time, the very kind of

BEDALE, YORKSHIRE

A small market-town seven miles from Northallerton, Bedale lies on the banks of the River Swale at a point where the outliers of the Pennine Chain fall away into the broad Vale of York. It is the market-town for the countryside between Lower Wensleydale and the Great North Road. In many ways it is characteristic of a dozen other small market-towns in Yorkshire, with its stone-built houses, its modest Georgian fronts and its picturesque church. Its air of activity is largely confined to market-day, when brisk business is done in all manner of household articles as well as in farm produce.

RICHMOND CASTLE

Richmond is an historic market-town between the Pennine foothills and the Vale of York, more likely the home of the traditional "Lass of Richmond Hill" than its southern namesake. It is built on both banks of the Swale; an ancient ford over it was guarded by a castle, to which the town owes its name from Norman times onwards. The massive medieval walls and the square Norman keep are clearly shown here, as also is its impregnable position on a cliff overhanging the river. The name of Richmond in Surrey is derived from it in an interesting way, for it was Henry VII (Henry of Richmond) who gave the name also to his Surrey palace on the banks of the Thames.

tale, to send shiverings all down their spines. And there is the demon dog which haunts the broken limestone and grit lands of the northern Pennines. Laughingly, yet with pride as of ancestry, Wharfedale folk will tell of the school run by the Devil in the dale; a school that meets but one day a year, as the little Wharfedale devils are so clever that the one day suffices. In mid-Wharfedale the natives will tell of a village boy, born at Appletreewick, who went to London to seek his fortune—and found it. He became Sir William Craven, Lord Mayor of London, a man noteworthy in the district for the benefits he conferred on his native place. His son was a gentleman adventurer who took service with the Elector of Bohemia, brought home that famous lady, the Electress, sister of Charles I, when she became widow, and, according to tradition, married her and became the first Lord Craven. For his assent to the marriage, so runs the story, Charles I accepted a gift of £40,000 from Lord Craven.

On the lonely heights, too, it may yet be possible to find a farm where a light is left burning in the window at night. Its original intention was to keep away evil spirits during the darkness, but the upland farmer will be reluctant

SLOPES OF THE
This photograph from the slopes of Mam Tor is taken looking across the grassy
slopes of the Edale Valley and shows the Peak itself in the background. The
Peak forms the southern end of the upland plateau of the Pennine Chain and
fills the northern part of the county of Derby. On its slopes there rise a number
of rivers, whose valleys, where they flow southward toward the Midland
Plain, give some of the most magnificent scenery of all the Pennine country,

today to admit this. He may go so far as to suggest that the light is sometimes useful to the wayfarer who for want of its guidance might become lost
on the moor. He might tell, also, if his confidence is won, that no longer ago
than his immediate ancestors, those forebears would carry the leaves of the
rowan tree, the mountain-ash, in their boots—again to fend off the attention of
mischievous evil spirits. Guardedly, the upland farmer may say that there
might be something in it. Of some article of oak, standing in the window,
plenty may still be found, even though a young housewife may not know that
here, too, is a charm against evil spirits. It is a superstition that dates as far
back at least as the days of the Druids, who had a special reverence for the
mistletoe, a parasitic growth of the oak. It is out of that veneration, with its
mysteries, that the superstition has grown and persists today. Yes, persists,
for though we may laugh at it, a little oak article is even today to be found in

EDALE VALLEY

not excluding the Yorkshire dales. There is the valley of the Wye (not to be confused with the river of the same name in Wales and the Welsh Marches), which flows by Buxton and Haddon Hall to Matlock and includes in its course Ashwood Dale and Miller's Dale. There is the valley of the Derwent, which flows down to the east of the Peak and, finest of all, the vale of the Dove. The Forest of the High Peak, which this photograph shows, is treeless.

the windows of thousands of town houses. What of that little knob at the end of the blind cord? A bit of wood turned on a machine; but examine it. It is an acorn, conventionalized to be sure, but none the less an acorn—an oaken charm against the evil ones.

But superstitions, maybe old folk-tales, are dying in these changing times. They lived and flourished when the moorland people lived remote and contact with their fellows, other than neighbours and those they met in the market, was well-nigh impossible. All is changing under the influence of the coach-road and the motor-bus. Where the farm folk gathered about the fire at night, the younger generation today, with higher wages and shorter hours, take advantage of the bus services to get into town on Saturday nights when milking and other farm tasks are over. They meet people, make friends with a much wider community than could their elders. The cinemas attract,

165

OVERLOOKING DOVEDALE

For a few miles before it bursts out of the hills into Derwentdale the Dove has carved for itself a deep narrow valley in the limestone hills. Thus exposed to the effects of weathering through the ages, the soft limestone rocks have been carved into sharp pinnacles and many other curious shapes. Here on the summit of the cliffs overlooking the valley is Thor's Cave, which has been cut out of the rock, probably by a stream that once flowed through it from underground springs. Such underground rivers are numerous in the limestone country and are responsible for the formation of the well-known "potholes"; many of these caverns have still to be explored.

and this wider company, the life depicted on the screen, false as it may be, introduces them to a world hitherto unknown, and it broadens their outlook.

These young people are back home before midnight, with minds refreshed. The week's work becomes easier because of this week-end background. But they still breed true to their stock; they are rugged individualists, as rugged as are their parents, but now with a wider outlook on the world. Perhaps it is as well, for they are a declining people. Hard winters, bad summers, poor prices, have for some time been forcing the abandonment of the smaller farms, and the farm unit is consequently growing bigger as the small farms are absorbed into their neighbours.

East Anglia

AN ISLAND within an island, East Anglia was cut off from the rest of Britain for hundreds of years in the course of its development, and this insular history is reflected in the character of its people at the present day. The historical background of the East Anglian husbandman determines perhaps more than any other factor his attitude to modern life and, above all, to innovation.

Norfolk and Suffolk (the land of the North Folk and of the South Folk respectively) comprised one of the principal independent kingdoms in the days of Saxon supremacy before the Norman Conquest. They were colonized by the Angles, a race of men who came principally from Denmark and the Low Countries and who sailed up the eastern estuaries in their longboats, razing with fire and sword the Roman towns which had flourished for four hundred years and sweeping away the civilization which had been built up.

So the purer Celtic strain which is inherent in the people of the West Country is less apparent in East Anglia; for hundreds of years the Angles intermarried and built up a racial strain which has been permanent. Their nearest neighbours were the East Saxons, who dwelt in Essex. There was war at first between the two tribes, but inevitably they merged together to form a single unit and a valuable Saxon element was introduced into the Anglian heritage. Thenceforward the area which is covered by the present counties of Norfolk, Suffolk, and Essex was visited by many invading peoples.

If you look at a map you will see how unique was the position of East Anglia in medieval history. The sea bounds two sides of Norfolk and sweeps round the coast of Suffolk and Essex into the Thames Estuary, which forms a natural barrier on the south. In the Middle Ages, a wide belt of impenetrable marshland fringed the Thames. To the west were the Fens, pointing a long finger from the neck of the Wash into the very heart of England. In those days the Fens were not what they are now. They were an undrained area of salt marsh, with only two or three islands, such as that of Ely, rising above the general level and a single causeway connecting Ely with the "mainland."

It was inevitable that the East Anglians of tradition should have all the conservatism and the brave independence of island folk. Moreover, with invasions usually coming across the North Sea from the Continent, the East Anglians had to stand and fight, instead of, as in other parts of the country, retreating toward the west. The Fens were not only a grand defence from attack, but they were sometimes an equally effective obstacle to retreat.

Time has not really changed the picture. The Fens have been drained and become one of the richest agricultural areas in the whole of Britain, but, except to the fensman, they are inhospitable and have never invited migration from other parts of Britain. It is as though they were still a barrier to encroachment and you will find surprisingly few engaged in tilling the ready soil of the East Anglian farms who have not been born and bred in the district and are not descended from a long line of East Anglian husbandmen. But, alas, they are no longer a barrier to "retreat"! East Anglia, like every other rural part of Britain, has lost all too many of her sons to the industrial towns of other parts of England, and you will find thousands of East Anglians working in London, Birmingham, and Manchester.

RURAL CONSERVATISM

There is a certain innate conservatism in all the rural peoples of Britain, and for that matter in all the rural peoples of the whole world, but it is accented in East Anglia, especially in Norfolk and Suffolk. Essex, though rural enough, begins to look a little towards London, which in turn has begun to spread into its rural domain. "What was good enough for my father is good enough for me," is still the slogan of the Norfolk or Suffolk yeoman farmer.

It has taken two wars and the agricultural crisis which each brought to introduce machinery on a big scale into a countryside which, above all others in Britain, lends itself to intensive mechanical treatment. Even two wars have not done much to affect the outlook, the traditions or the view-points of the older men and women on the land, though the young men who have served overseas and returned to their native country have inevitably brought with them an attitude of more ready progress and their quota of new ideas. But even on them tradition has its effect and has tended to mould those views into a local rather than a national democratic ideal.

To some extent East Anglians have always been "agin the government." This attitude dates from the time when the central government found it well-nigh impossible to rule over a district which was effectively separated from it by physical barriers—perhaps from the still earlier time when the pride of the people would not admit the authority of a central government in London.

So the ideas brought home by the warrior sons of the soil in the First and Second World Wars tended to invigorate a tradition which was already dominant rather than to introduce something entirely fresh or contrary to the traditional outlook. Only time can show how much longer this independence of view-point, as of expression and dialect, can continue in the face of growing uniformity, which broadcasting has done much to foster.

But it is safe to predict that the independence of spirit which underlies the East Anglians' unorthodoxy is something so deeply rooted in heredity and environment that no influence, however strong and insistent, will ever entirely eradicate it. Quite apart from the traditional factors and the physical characteristics of the country, there is another important difference which has contributed to the individuality of East Anglia. That is the fact that industry has almost entirely passed it by.

In all the three counties, if we exclude that part of Essex which lies within twenty-five miles of the metropolis, there is not a single town in which

EAST ANGLIA

Scale of Miles

THE WASH

Blakeney Cromer
Burnham Thorpe
Sandringham Blickling North Walsham
Houghton Foulsham
West Walton King's Lynn Castle Acre Elsing Wroxham The Broads
Downham Market Swaffham NORFOLK NORWICH Acle Bure Great Yarmouth
Denver Watton Hingham Ore
March Oxborough Wymondham
Whittlesey Methwold Stow Bedon Hales
Little Ouse New Buckenham Waveney Lowestoft
Ramsey The Fens Thetford East Harling Harleston Bungay
HUNTINGDON Ely Diss Blythburgh
St. Ives Soham Brandon Eye Southwold
HUNTINGDON CAMBRIDGE Little Saxham Bury St. Edmunds Framlingham
Bourn Swaffham Prior Ickworth Stowmarket Aldeburgh
BEDFORD CAMBRIDGE SUFFOLK Orford
Elstow Henlow Melbourn Linton Lavenham IPSWICH
BEDFORD Ickleton Long Melford Woodbridge
Baldock Saffron Walden Sudbury Little Wenham Felixstowe
Woburn Hitchin Buntingford Thaxted Finchingfield Harwich
Luton Knebworth HERTFORD Braintree
Bishop's Stortford ESSEX Colchester
HERTFORD Coggeshall St. Osyth Clacton-on-Sea
St. Albans Layer Marney
Hemel Hempstead Cheshunt Greenstead CHELMSFORD Maldon
Woodham Ferrers
Watford Waltham Abbey Burnham-on-Crouch
Laindon Hadleigh
East Ham Southend
Tilbury Thames

manufacturing industries hold a dominant place. Ipswich and Norwich are the nearest to modern industrial towns, but each of them in its own way has contrived to absorb a certain amount of industry and to give employment to populations of hundreds of thousands without ceasing to be a country town. So the impression that the visitor to Norwich will carry away with him is of a cathedral city or of a great market centre, and certainly not of a manufacturing town, even though its manufactures are numerous and locally important.

So, too, the traveller to Ipswich will most probably remember it as an old river port still carrying on its maritime trade and a great distributing market centre, but it is only if you climb up on to the hills above the Orwell and look down on the close-packed centre of the town that you will notice the number of factory chimneys which bespeak a flourishing and impressive list of industries. But here, as at King's Lynn, Great Yarmouth, Lowestoft, and Chelmsford, with their engineering works, sugar-beet factories, chemical works, and so on, which all give employment to many thousands of the people, industries are always subsidiary to the pulsing life of country towns.

By no means all of East Anglia is rich farming country. Much of what has long been felt to be most attractive has defied the farmer's effort to make it productive. Particularly is this true of the windswept slopes of Breckland. But most of the central districts of all three counties, from north Norfolk down through Suffolk into northern Essex, contain some of the finest arable

NORFOLK MANOR-FARM
All over the corn-lands of Norfolk and Suffolk farming is prosperous and the old farmhouses and manor-farms are well kept and well stocked. Here at Colney, only a few miles from Norwich, is a typical group of Norfolk farm buildings, with the round tower of Colney Church, the church of the original manor, behind it. The round towers of Norfolk churches are a feature of the scenery, especially in the area between the Yare and the Waveney.

BRANDON BRIDGE, SUFFOLK

The bridge over the Little Ouse is a link between Brandon in Suffolk and the Norfolk countryside on the other bank. Until recent years, Brandon itself has been the only surviving centre of the rural craft of flint-knapping, the making of flints for guns and other purposes from the flint nodules found in the chalk strata. On Breckland, a stretch of open warren-country in the neighbourhood, there have been flint-mines since prehistoric days, including Grimes Graves, which has traces of workings four thousand years old.

land in the whole of Britain. And this arable land is particularly suitable for wheat, so that East Anglia has become the true granary of Great Britain.

The soil is not Nature's only benefaction. Indeed, here and there it is rather thin and light. The climate is just as important a factor. Wheat, to give a good yield, must have a dry climate and a soil that is porous. Winter wheat, particularly, is destroyed in heavy soils when they become frostbound in January and February. Now, East Anglia as a whole is the driest part of Britain, particularly towards Essex. Shoeburyness, in point of fact, has less rainfall than any other recording station in the British Isles, with an average annual fall of only eighteen inches. Northward and eastward from this point rainfall increases, and if you look at a weather map of East Anglia you will find that lines joining points with equal annual rainfall are arcs of concentric circles with their centres at Shoeburyness, rising to a maximum in the Norwich district, which has very nearly half as much rainfall again as Shoeburyness. But a good deal of this excess falls in heavy summer showers and thunderstorms, when the rain quickly drains away and little damage is done to the corn crops except in those unhappy years when a series of heavy thunderstorms lays flat the fields of oats during the first half of July. But wheat is sturdier and suffers less frequently from this catastrophe.

The years in which the East Anglian farmer does not reap a fair reward for his labours are few compared with the vicissitudes of other parts of England. Most farmers follow the four-year rotation of crops, so that part of their land is always under wheat.

It is not only wheat, oats, barley, and clover which make the ploughed fields of East Anglia so important in British rural economy. Since the turn of the century another crop has attained equal importance, that is the sugar-beet crop, which though not entirely confined to East Anglia is largely centred there, particularly in Suffolk and towards the borders of Cambridgeshire.

The sugar-beet factories have followed the crops, and the making of sugar has become the characteristic local industry of all three counties. Between them they produce almost enough sugar to supply every single member of the population with half a pound a week throughout the year. How great a difference this comparatively recent development has made to Britain's self-sufficiency in food was proved during the Second World War, when the sugar-beet factories produced enough sugar to satisfy the entire domestic ration and so freed a vast tonnage of shipping for other more vital tasks.

AN ESSEX MILL-HOUSE

Essex, as befits one of the counties which form the granary of England, is rich in ancient mill-houses, many of them timber-built. Originally the mills were worked by water power, but in almost every case where the mills are still in action modern forms of power have replaced water. Many of the mills no longer grind corn, like this fine one at Littlebury near the borders of Cambridgeshire. But here, as in many other places, the handsome Georgian house, which was the miller's home, has been kept in repair and is still good for many years' service as a dwelling-house.

LAVENHAM CHURCH
The church at Lavenham is one of the most impressive of East Anglian churches, the tower exceeding 140 ft. in height. The building was erected from money given by the rich cloth-merchants of Lavenham between 1475 and 1525, on the site of an earlier church of which the chancel survives. It is in the same tradition as the church of Thaxted (page 197). The long rows of windows with their plain straight tracery gave the name of Perpendicular Gothic to this period of architecture.

Nor has the rural mill disappeared from the East Anglian scene. The days of the windmills, at least those used for grinding corn, are over, though among the last windmills to operate on a commercial basis were two in Essex. The modern mill has taken its place and is a feature, if not of every village, of every small town. The miller and the manager of the sugar-beet factory represent big business in many a township of Suffolk and Norfolk.

Traditionally, Essex is a wool country, almost as famous in the annals of British sheep as the Cotswold country. Almost every farmhouse and cottage was a unit in the medieval woollen industry. Great wealth followed the medieval boom in wool, and the wealthy merchants and producers banded together to provide funds to build the great Perpendicular Gothic churches, which reached their greatest perfection in the fifteenth century. It seems to the wayfarer that almost every other church through the length and breadth of the three counties belongs to this period and some of them are most elaborate and beautiful in their interior decoration as well as in their outer fabric. Three outstanding examples are those at Thaxted and Saffron Walden in Essex, and Lavenham in Suffolk, but these are only three among a great number of others almost equally superb.

In Norfolk, by contrast, it is not so much the great parish churches of the towns as the small village churches which reflect the prosperity of those times, and one must remember that in Norfolk there are many famous names among the villages which contributed something to medieval prosperity. Worstead, where the famous cloth was first made, is only a small village, but its church, a fine example of the period, is a landmark for miles around.

The art of those times was not confined to architecture, but expressed

THE FERTILE MARSH

Impenetrable swamp a few hundred years ago, the land bordering the flat coast of Essex round the estuaries of the Blackwater and Stour, has, by the building of sea-walls and the cutting of drainage canals, been brought under the plough and now yields a magnificent harvest of corn crops. This scene of corn in stook near Southminster gives an idea of the enormous fields which characterize the region, and of the unrelieved flatness of the landscape, which for miles on end is not even diversified by a single tree.

itself as much in the kindred craft of woodcarving, which appears at its best in the carved figures of the lofty hammer-beam roofs, which are the crowning glory of many of these fifteenth-century churches. Though there are many which may equal it, there are none to surpass that of Mildenhall.

As the centuries have passed wool has declined in importance in East Anglia, just as it has in every other part of Britain. Its decline is more noticeable in these parts because of their modern wealth as a land of ploughed fields. Today sheep are no more numerous than in any other county and far less so than in many. Sheep-walks have become fields of waving corn. Where there are grass fields they are usually cropped by cattle and by the dairy herds which range along the river valleys and complete the tale of a country rich by nature and further enriched by the stubborn efforts of the farming people.

The gently undulating contours of the corn country are not picturesque in the sense in which the mountains or the moors of Britain inspire the author or artist. There is rather the quiet beauty of growing things, which appeals to the true countryman who sees beauty in fertility and does not crave for the spectacular. Two districts of Suffolk combine the two, the valleys of the Stour and Orwell. There are many things in common between these two; each has inspired a great English landscape-painter, each has claimed the loveliest river of rural England, each is a rich country, well kept, well tilled. But there the resemblance ends, for where the Stour Valley has an intimate beauty, which depends on the combination of gently rolling hills and broad meadows, and the colourful variety of the copses and the ploughed fields, the Orwell yields essentially more dramatic views, in which the broad river, with its manifold craft, takes an important part.

The Stour Valley dividing Suffolk from Essex, is Constable country. Near its stream the great artist lived and worked, and he has immortalized many of its most famous beauty-spots, from East Bergholt and Flatford Mill to Sudbury and Bures. The characteristic row of poplar trees on the skyline, the tall tower of some village church, the flowing willows by the river's brink, the rapid alternation between the dark greens of the meadows and the browns and greens of the cornfields—those are the beauties of Constable's Stour.

No motor road can do full justice to the river's charm, but for the traveller on foot there are numberless field-paths and tracks which follow the higher ground on either bank. From Bures long paths lead downstream on the north bank, sometimes near the river's brink, sometimes on the crest of the hills, now dropping steeply to one of the many dry valleys which break up the contours of the hills, now ascending to some wooded slope, from which the silver

CONSTABLE'S COUNTRY

The valley of the Stour, which divides Essex from Suffolk for many miles of its course, is the countryside which the artist Constable has immortalized in his canvases, from Flatford Mill near its mouth to Sudbury in its middle reaches. Nowhere are these landscapes more lovely than here near Bures, where the wooded slopes of the low hills make a perfect background for the winding course of the river and the sheep-pastures of the nearer slopes.

bends of the stream are seen occasionally through breaks in the trees. For the connoisseur of the quiet beauties of the English landscape there are few finer walks in all the country.

The Orwell is Gainsborough's river, for Gainsborough lived long in Ipswich, which lies where the little River Gipping broadens into the estuary which is known as Orwell. Like Cobbett, who says of Ipswich: "You can go in no direction to a quarter of a mile without finding views that a painter might crave," Gainsborough appreciated to the full the attractions of his native soil and never needed to go far afield for inspiration for his landscapes.

This countryside, too, is one which is best seen on foot, though there is one road which leads out of Ipswich beside the estuary to give the traveller some idea of the loveliness which lies so close to the busy town. But for the footpath walker there is a long path that starts almost on the southern outskirts of Ipswich and traverses spreading parklands which fall to the very brink of the river and lead ultimately to Pinmill, a tiny place, though now a

KERSEY, SUFFOLK

Kersey shared with Lavenham (page 173) and many other places in East Anglia the prosperity which came from the late medieval woollen boom. The neighbouring countryside was ideally suited for the rearing of sheep. The farmhouses won additional wealth from weaving and the cloth merchants lived in the small towns, every one of which had a flourishing wool market. So, though the church of Kersey, here seen in the background, is smaller than that of Lavenham, it is large in proportion to the size of the village and in the same style of architecture. The pleasant houses were typical of the homes of the merchants in the sixteenth and seventeenth centuries.

KENNINGHALL, NORFOLK

A typical centre of the rural countryside of Norfolk, Kenninghall has had a continuous history, like so many other East Anglian villages, going back to early Saxon days. Like so many others, too, in this purely farming countryside, it has retained an identity of its own, partly because it is many miles from the nearest large town. Its name shows that it was once a Saxon tribal centre of far greater importance than many of the East Anglian towns which have outstripped it in modern fame.

well-known yachting centre, nestling beneath low grassy cliffs and hemmed in by woods which end only at the water's brink.

Just east of Ipswich there is another of the highlights of Suffolk scenery, as different as could be imagined from the river scenery of the Stour and the Orwell. This is the stretch of heathland, never yet brought under the plough and never likely to be, which embraces a wide triangle of countryside between the road to Felixstowe and the road to Woodbridge. The heathland is known by many names. The Ordnance map shows one common following another, one heath after the next, but essentially it is all one, starting at the very point where the Ipswich trolley-buses have their terminus, and extending almost as far as Woodbridge, unbroken, unspoilt, until the traveller comes to the aerodrome at Martlesham. There are clumps of pine trees and a few scattered beeches, but for the most part it is heather and gorse-covered common, a feast of colour in the spring and again in the autumn when the heather flowers.

This is only one of several wide expanses of sandy heathland which diversify the East Anglian scene. The largest and the most famous is Breckland, which lies between the corn country in the west of Norfolk and Suffolk, and the level expanses of the Fens. Centred on Thetford and Brandon, extending northward to Swaffham, southward nearly to Newmarket, it is a little-known, seldom-visited "forest," where you can travel on foot or awheel for mile after mile without coming to a single farmhouse or cottage.

This is one of the great centres of archaeological research, where traces of prehistoric man have never been erased. Many attempts have been made to bring it into productive fertility, but every one has failed. The latest was little more than a century ago, when a well-meant scheme of development caused much of the sandy wastes to be turned into vast fields called brecks. A number of small farmhouses were built in hope and faith, which time quickly showed were ill placed. Now the vast majority of the brecks have reverted to their native heath, though in recent years a fresh effort has been made to draw wealth from as nearly barren countryside as any in Britain by the planting of large areas of Scots firs and other conifers. These not only take root in the shallow soil, but tend to bind it together so that in centuries to come it may well be that useful crops will be coaxed from it.

RABBITS IN THE BRECKLAND

Even now a change has come over the scene. All early writers record how in dry weather the light sands were constantly shifting. More than one hamlet has been engulfed by them in historic times. But today, though a high wind will produce flurries of sand-laden dust, there is nothing of the shifting sand-hill about the country; yet for hundreds of square miles there are still only the sparse bracken and heather and the bright splash of the gorse bushes.

Breckland was the last home of the bustard, now unhappily extinct. Today the rabbit represents the principal wild life of the region. In the sandy warrens they have become so numerous that many square miles are completely undermined and trapping them has become a minor industry of its own, necessary if only to prevent them from descending into the level of the Fens or into the rich fields of high Suffolk, where they might be as disastrous as they are in the fertile districts of Australia.

Brandon, which lies in the very centre of Breckland, is the home of a local industry as old as it is important, namely flint-knapping. From Brandon gun flints are exported to every part of the world, and there is perhaps a continuous history of flint-knapping since Stone Age man four or five thousand years ago quarried his flints at Grimes Graves and fashioned them into tools and implements which were the stock-in-trade of the prehistoric craftsman and hunter.

Between Swaffham and the coast there are several other outbreaks of heathland on the high ground, which is a part of the East Anglian Heights, ending at Hunstanton cliff. Most picturesque are the heights and commons round the King's Sandringham estate which, like many other great estates of this countryside, was fashioned out of the barest, most heart-breaking country, and through the years by unremitting toil has been brought into a measure of cultivation. The map of north-west Norfolk shows many vast estates such as Sandringham and Holkham Hall, near Wells. All of them were

RIDERS OF THE FOREST

Travellers in Epping Forest pass over tracks that were used by the Ancient Britons, when Ambersbury Banks was fortified by Boadicea, in her unsuccessful rising against Roman rule. In the Middle Ages Epping Forest was part of the Forest of Waltham. Today it is an open space under the London County Council.

ON THE NORFOLK BROADS

The white sails of boats bring colour and life to the level lands of the Norfolk Broads and the Rivers Yare and Waveney. So level is the landscape in this part of Norfolk that the sails of the boats moving along the streams can be seen across the flat countryside from many miles away.

once sandy heathlands, many of them today have been afforested, though at intervals there are, as ever, untilled stretches of native heathland to diversify the landscape, which is always attractive and occasionally supremely beautiful.

Another of East Anglia's famous districts is Broadland. Now Broadland is like no other place in the world, and though nowadays visited by many thousands of holiday-makers every summer, is still one of Britain's loneliest districts.

The Broads are really a freak of Nature. Many centuries ago the estuaries of several rivers, the Wensum, the Bure, the Yare, and the Waveney, met in a wide delta which comprehended much of the country between Happisburgh and Lowestoft. In the days of the Roman occupation certainly, and perhaps much later, this was a totally uninhabited waste of salt-marsh and shallow tidal waterways. Through the centuries the delta slowly silted up as the rivers brought down from their higher reaches an accumulation of soil and debris which they deposited in the sluggish channels near the sea, and so the Broads gradually took shape, though it remained for the hand of man to complete the transformation by draining a good deal of the land.

When this drainage was completed many thousands of acres of good pasture-land resulted, so that Broadland today is an agricultural country which, if it cannot rival the fertility of the Fens, at least bears its part in the Norfolk economy. The method of draining adopted was to cut dykes through the marsh-land, as in the case of the Fens, and to set up windmills to provide the power to make the surface water flow down the dykes and keep it moving. So the windmill has become a characteristic feature of the Broads landscape. Together with the even contours of the land and the absence of trees it helps to give a sense of a limitless skyline and a breadth of vision. To find its parallel one would have to go to the dyke-land of Holland.

For the visitors who sail up the Broads in a yacht or motor-boat there is a never-ceasing change of scenery, an endless succession of water vistas which relieve any possible sense of monotony, as the rivers now broaden into a wide tree-fringed lake, now narrow into a secluded waterway. Every few miles there is a village with an inn by the riverside thronged by a gay crowd of holiday-makers in the season, but deserted and lonely for eight months of the year.

The Broads are a great haunt of wildfowl, with many rare species of duck, and to the south, Fritton Lake, tree-fringed and lovely, has become a bird sanctuary in fact as well as in name.

The Broads vary in size from an acre or two to a square mile or more, and number several hundred. Among them, Oulton Broad, Hickling Broad, and Ormesby Broad stand out in the memory, though these three are no more

ONE OF THE KING'S COUNTRY RESIDENCES

Sandringham Hall is one of the country homes of the Royal Family. Though the estate is an ancient one, the house itself is comparatively modern, built in 1862 for Edward, Prince of Wales, later Edward VII, with Albert Humbert as architect. The country surrounding Sandringham is some of the most picturesque in Norfolk. Sandringham estate itself covers 15,000 acres and includes extensive pine forests traversed by long drives.

NORFOLK REED
HARVEST
The many stretches of
water which make up the
Norfolk Broads, together
with the sluggish streams
which connect one with
the other, are the gathering grounds of Britain's
most important reed har-
vest. At the end of the
summer the reeds are
cut, roughly dried and
then tied into bundles to
be transported, often, as
above, by water, for
further processing. The
wealth of the reed harvest
is reflected in the great
number of cottages and
barns in Norfolk which
continue to be thatched
with these reeds.

beautiful than dozens of others. In a few places, such as Potter Heigham, the landscape is ruined by an outcrop of modern bungalows and buildings, and most of the people are devoted to the business of catering for the amateur yachtsmen. But for the most part the villages remain small and unspoilt, though few of them have the antiquity or the intrinsic interest of most of Norfolk's villages. The people who dwell in them are even hardier than most of Norfolk's sons of the soil.

The tall reeds, the characteristic flora of the Broads, are not wasted. Towards the autumn scores of villagers, the womenfolk as well as the men, can be seen collecting them. Then they are dried and make an ideal material for thatching. The chances are that the many charming thatched villas which the wayfarer will find up and down the Norfolk landscape are thatched from this source.

Some of the pleasantest scenery in East Anglia lies near the coast, and some of the most characteristic and historic old towns as well. It is a very long coastline, which starts at Hunstanton, facing the Wash, and ends at Southend-on-Sea, facing the Thames Estuary.

In the north there is a charming line of old-world villages, now separated from the sea by a few miles of salt-marshes, which are themselves unique in Britain. In the hills which look down on to the sea there are stone quarries and, as a consequence, most of the village cottages and churches are stone-built. The result is a chain of old-world villages with winding streets and tiny harbours, very little changed since the sixteenth and seventeenth centuries, when they had their heyday.

From west to east there is Brancaster, which is traditionally the centre of the mussel-fishing industry, a little town of fisher-folk and seafarers. Next comes Wells, just as old-fashioned, just as unspoilt, but with a more sizable harbour, to which come the coastwise sailing or motor barges from as far afield as the Port of London, but more especially from the Lincolnshire coast.

The road which leads from Wells to Sheringham inevitably reminds the wayfarer of a scenic railway on a grand scale, as panorama succeeds panorama and the crest of every hill brings a fresh glimpse ahead over scenery of infinite variety, stretching from the cliffs inland to wooded hills. These, though they seldom exceed three hundred feet above sea-level, dominate the more level countryside around and, with their jagged uneven contours, simulate hills far higher.

Between Wells and Sheringham a large stretch of salt-marsh has been set aside for a bird sanctuary, where it is hoped that the many rare birds that

BLAKENEY QUAY, NORFOLK

Along the whole of the north coast of Norfolk the sea has receded, compensating for its constant advance along the east coast. Now a wide area of salt marshes separates the erstwhile ports from the open sea, though the marshes are broken at intervals by narrow creeks coming up to the old quay-sides, now for practical purposes reserved for pleasure yachting. Blakeney is one of these medieval ports now left high and dry. In the Middle Ages, though it had less fame than its neighbours, Wells and Cley, the port had flourishing commerce with those of Lincolnshire and East Anglia. Today the marshes beyond the town form a bird sanctuary vested in the National Trust.

dwell there, as well as hundreds of kinds of marsh flower, will be preserved.

Something of the medieval prosperity of the port of Blakeney is reflected in the lovely hammer-beam roof of the fifteenth-century church, but though it is still a fishing village, the trade of the port has almost ceased to exist. But if the seafaring prosperity of old has deserted these once-famous Norfolk ports, the people of Sheringham and Cromer have reaped a new harvest of prosperity since the advent of good roads and railways, which are the very things which doomed them as ports. In brief, they have become holiday resorts, quiet and relatively small, it is true, with few of the "improvements" which have changed the face of many south-coast watering places; but they attract year after year a faithful and ever-growing band of visitors for whom the east coast, with its tranquillity and bracing air, holds something which more famous resorts have lost.

Cromer and Sheringham are the gateways to some of the most exciting scenery of Norfolk, which rises across heather-covered commons to a lovely ridge overlooking the sea. The hill is crowned by an ancient entrenchment which is popularly known as a Roman Camp, though probably it was built several centuries earlier than the first of the Romans set foot in Britain.

THE NORFOLK COAST

Beyond Cromer the coast turns southward and low cliffs continue through Trimingham and Mundesley to Happisburgh, whose high-set church is a landmark along miles of lonely coastline. Finally, as the area of the Broads is approached the cliffs are replaced by shifting sand-dunes which are for ever encroaching inland, and have left more than one hamlet stranded on the beach.

There is another dramatic change in scenery to the south of the Broads. Here are East Anglia's two modern ports, Great Yarmouth and Lowestoft, twin centres of the herring-fishing industry, which has made Yarmouth herring and Yarmouth bloaters world-famous. The hardy sailors who man the fishing craft—trawlers and drifters—are the backbone of both towns' teeming population. Even though the old days when every fishing boat was individually owned are past the owner-captain is still a force to be reckoned with and is the East Coast equivalent of the Kentish yeoman farmer, master of a traditional craft, determined, rugged, with a responsibility not only to himself but to his crew.

Every year in the herring season there is a great influx of "fisher girls" from Scotland, who travel down the coast with the herring fleet and whose task it is to clean the herring, cure those which are being stored and box the rest for transport to London and the other great centres of distribution.

From Lowestoft to the estuaries of the Stour and Orwell it is nearly fifty miles, and it is still a matter of wonder that in all these fifty miles there is not a single large town, nor yet a single town which has spread far beyond its nineteenth-century boundaries. As far as Southwold there is scarcely even a village after the outskirts of Lowestoft are passed. The low cliffs here are constantly being eaten away by the sea, and though many elaborate schemes of coastal defence have been proposed, none has been carried through to a con-

THE SEA HARVESTERS PREPARE

This scene on the dockside of Great Yarmouth shows the drifters mustering for the East Anglian herring harvest, the great event of the year for Yarmouth and Lowestoft as well as for the fishing ports farther north. The herring season opens first in the far north of Scotland and is later at each more southerly group of ports, following the average course of the shoals.

clusion. Much of Pakefield itself has fallen downcliff, and ten miles farther down the coast Dunwich, which was once a busy port, has virtually ceased to exist, only a part of the church remaining on the cliff top, and that destined to topple on to the beach before many years have passed.

Aldeburgh, another medieval port, has suffered less dramatically than Dunwich, though the medieval moot hall, formerly the centre of the town, now stands on the promenade and all that part of the town which was to seaward of it has disappeared.

All the way down the coast the tale is of an uncertain struggle between man and Nature, and it is not until we come to Felixstowe that we find a place where the man-made defences have sufficed to stem the ravages of the sea and weather. Here a bright and flourishing seaside town has been built, to which come thousands of Ipswich workers every summer weekend.

A VALLEY OF SUFFOLK

Suffolk is watered by scores of small rivers dividing the county into a succession of low tablelands and narrow valleys. It is on the higher ground that the corn for which East Anglia is famous is chiefly grown, while the lush meadows of the valleys give pasture to herds of cattle and occasionally, as here in the valley of the Deben, to horses, which are still bred in many parts.

There is plenty to reward the traveller who is willing to make the effort to explore this lonely coast, and a real effort is needed, for the railway comes only to Aldeburgh, and other communications are few. There is no coast road, and the few roads which lead to the sea, except at three or four points, are narrow, winding lanes. There is heather-covered heathland fringing the cliffs for many miles, particularly from Dunwich towards Aldeburgh, and between the estuaries of the little rivers Deben and Alde. Some of the views are almost breath-taking in their beauty. From one point on the hill above the great Norman fortress of Orford the traveller on foot can pick out nearly twelve miles of the Alde River, which, after coming to within a quarter of a mile of the sea at Aldeburgh, changes its mind and flows southward for five miles or more separated from the sea by only a wide shingle bank.

Probably the loveliest point of all the coastline is Easton Broad, not a broad in the true sense of the word, but a lake, reed-fringed and almost completely surrounded by woods, with the sea on one side of it pounding against the steep shingle beach, and cliffs rising from either end of it.

By contrast, the coast of Essex is comparatively unexciting, though much of it is pleasant enough, and for many miles is as lonely as the coasts of Norfolk and Suffolk. And there is the port of Harwich, whence steamers cross the North Sea to the Hook of Holland, and the line of low cliffs which extends from Walton-on-the-Naze to Clacton.

But there is never the loneliness here that we find on the cliffs of Suffolk. Since the railways brought London within a two-hours' journey, building has proceeded apace and we are here within the region in which there are many season-ticket holders who travel daily to and from the metropolis.

Frinton-on-Sea has a very special history, which is no more than an exaggeration of the story of many of the Essex seaside towns. No insignificant place in the Middle Ages, it lost so much to the encroaching sea that by the turn of the nineteenth century the census revealed a population of only sixty-four. Within twenty years these sixty-four had increased to over three thousand and the bulk of these were the families of London business men who made this their seaside home. The new Frinton was not designed as a popular resort, but as a model estate of fine houses carefully laid out, with ample space for lawns and gardens—one of the very earliest experiments in modern town-planning. Nor has Frinton lost its personality, in spite of the vicissitudes that the Second World War brought to all the sea-coast townships. It remains to all appearances one of the most prosperous places in Britain and plans a continued though strictly controlled growth.

A JACOBEAN MANOR-HOUSE

The seventeenth century was a great period of building in East Anglia and especially in Norfolk. The stepped gables of this finely proportioned house at Bawburgh, near Norwich, prove its Jacobean origin. The house is much more recent than the two small buildings in stone which adjoin it, one of which may have been a resting place for pilgrims to the well of St. Walstan, the Norfolk saint, the other, shown here, a chapel attached to the shrine.

South of Clacton there is another aesthetically less satisfying, though possibly not less successful, experiment in seaside building, for here one of the phenomena of the twentieth century, the holiday camp, has made its appearance and has transformed what was previously a completely deserted expanse of marsh-land into a thriving holiday centre.

The rest of the coastline is in its pristine state of quietness and remoteness, its inhabitants as far remote in spirit and demeanour from the people of London, a bare fifty miles away, as could possibly be imagined. But there are no cliffs to diversify the scene. It is essentially the country of the eastern estuaries, a stretch of low marshy grass-land broken up by innumerable streams and separated from the low shelving beach by a grassy sea-wall. It is a countryside dedicated to the fauna and flora of the eastern marsh-lands, which seems to some visitors dull, but to others who can commune with unspoilt Nature, even if it is not associated with bold contours, a land of infinite promise and fulfilment.

Near the estuary of the Blackwater is Brightlingsea, one of the great centres of the immemorial oyster fisheries which gave Colchester so much prosperity in years gone by and which are still celebrated by an annual feast and ceremony. There is much yachting on the broad estuary, as in the

AN ESSEX VILLAGE GREEN

Essex is famous for the beauty of its villages, but this beauty is to be found more in the charming grouping of village buildings than in any outstanding excellence of architecture. Among the most attractive kinds of East Anglian villages are those grouped round a green, as here at Writtle, where the village pond with its weeping-willows and the broad green form a perfect setting for the seventeenth- and eighteenth-century houses which are set round it. The rural quiet of Writtle is almost unbelievable when it is remembered that Chelmsford, the county town, is less than two miles away.

GALLEYWOOD COMMON

A feature of the Essex scene is the number of breezy upland commons, especially on the high ground which separates the Crouch from the Chelmer. Galleywood Common, *above,* lies in this area, the tall spire of its church a landmark for miles around. In a county where the lowlands have always been liable to flooding, very many of the villages have been built on the hill-tops. So Galleywood Church looks across the valleys to other high-set land-marks—in one direction to Danbury, its church marked, like Galleywood's own, by a tall spire, in the other direction to Stock and Billericay.

estuary of the Crouch farther south, where Burnham is one of the favourite east-coast yachting centres.

Far more typical is the little village of Bradwell, with Bradwell Quay looking west to the Blackwater, and the tiny Saxon chapel of Bradwell-near-the-Sea looking out across the North Sea. The latter is on the site of the great Roman fort which was built here by the Count of the Saxon Shore in the fourth century A.D. as a protection against the inroads of the savage barbarians of the Continent.

So, finally, to Shoeburyness and the modern urban growth which is called variously Southend, or Thorpe Bay, or Westcliff, or what you will. Southend, entirely a modern town, was formerly only a hamlet at the south end of Prittlewell. It has many virtues, but it is not really an East Anglian town. It looks toward the eastern confines of London. It is to London what Coney Island is to New York, what Blackpool is to the cotton country of Lancashire, a healthy, bracing place of many amusements and many ways in which the visitor may spend his time and money, to return to his work refreshed in mind if not in body.

The fisher-folk on the sea-front are an anachronism; their main purpose in life is now catering for holiday-makers, most of their boats are now devoted to a trip round the pier for a shilling. There is, of course, the pier, a mile long, which won fame in the Second World War as H.M.S. *Leigh*, and maintained itself as a naval establishment, in spite of hundreds of attacks by German bombers. The people of Southend are proud of H.M.S. *Leigh*, for was it not one of the very few piers in Britain which were not cut in half as an anti-invasion measure?

What now of the historic towns which have seen so much of East Anglia's storied past and still retain many a romantic link with times gone by? Up and down the country there are hundreds of places sacred in the hearts of the typical East Anglian, and happily these for the most part lack the self-consciousness which has overtaken so many of the famous places of southern England, in an age which has commercialized historic fame as well as natural beauty.

Most illustrious of all is the shrine of Our Lady of Walsingham, which on and off has had a part for nearly a thousand years in the story of the East Anglian people. To it in the Middle Ages came thousands of bare-footed pilgrims along the Peddar Way. Peddar Way actually means pilgrims' way,

CASTLE ACRE PRIORY, NORFOLK

Of Norfolk's two most famous ruins, Walsingham and Castle Acre, the former is historically the more important, the latter aesthetically more satisfying. Acre was a Cluniac priory, one of several which owe their foundation to William de Warenne toward the end of the Norman period. This photograph shows the west front of the priory church, one of the loveliest examples of Norman architecture in the kingdom.

CASTLE HEDINGHAM, ESSEX One of the three great Norman strongholds of East Anglia, Castle Hedingham is comparable with the castles of Norwich and Colchester and was originally in the same tradition of building as the great Norman castles of London and Rochester. Immensely strong in defence, the walls many feet thick have withstood the ravages of time even though the castle is now only a shell, its battlements and fittings dismantled at the end of the Civil War by order of Oliver Cromwell.

and though the pilgrims who go to the shrine today come but rarely on foot, there still are pilgrims in their thousands and a brand-new twentieth-century shrine fashioned after the manner of the medieval one.

For all its religious fame, however, Little Walsingham has not grown. It is still a charming ancient village with many old houses along its single main street. Only the character of its shops has changed, reflecting in their wares of religious books and emblems the spirit which has given it fresh purpose and life. Here, too, are the picturesque ruins of an abbey, one of the many religious foundations which were an integral part of life in the Middle Ages. The dignity of the ruins is an ever-present reminder, both of the devoted life of a large section of the medieval community and of the art and artistry of medieval architecture. Among those which have bequeathed to the materialism of the modern age a more than usual legacy of beauty are Wymondham and Castle Acre in Norfolk, Bury St. Edmunds in Suffolk, and Colchester, Little Coggeshall, and Waltham in Essex.

Outstanding also are the ruins of Norman and later medieval castles, which represent the other extreme of medieval life, the military protection which the lord of the manor gave to the villagers whose homes nestled round the bulwark of the castle. In Essex alone there are two great Norman buildings, wonderfully preserved over the thousand years that have intervened since they were built. These are Castle Hedingham and Colchester Castle, the latter almost entirely built from the materials of the Roman town of Camulodunum. They were two of the great fortresses designed to the order of William the Conqueror to hold the Saxon people in check. Together with the fortresses of Castle Acre and Norwich, they were enough to ensure peace in all the country east of the Fens.

ESSEX PARGE WORK

Parge work, or pargeting, is the characteristic exterior decoration of old houses in Essex and Suffolk. This photograph shows pargeting on the old Sun Inn at Saffron Walden.

Reference has already been made to the late-Norman castle of Orford, near the estuary of the Ore in Suffolk, which was built at the time when the need for military forts was less, and was half manor-house and half castle. It remains one of the most perfectly preserved buildings of the eleventh and twelfth centuries.

All over East Anglia, too, there are numerous old houses which are links with the medieval life of the country. Many of the finest of them date from the fifteenth and sixteenth centuries, when the wool merchants were beginning to build rich houses in the towns. At Lavenham and Bury some of these old houses and some more modern ones, too, are decorated with plaster carving known as parge work, or pargeting, which is a traditional East Anglian craft, arising naturally from the fact that stone-built houses are rare. All through the ages man has sought to decorate the other less-characteristic forms of building materials. The finest example of parge work in East Anglia, and for that matter in the whole world, is the Sparrowe's House at Ipswich. Among other numerous examples, Saffron Walden and Coggeshall in Essex can boast some of the oldest and most attractive. But it is to be found in all sorts of out-of-the-way places, a simple and unassuming decoration of even tiny cottages, sometimes nearly effaced by time, but often preserved well enough for us to admire the skill of the medieval decorator.

The lack of stone in East Anglia has affected the life of the country at every age, and has led to some distinctive and very interesting types of architecture. The Romans imported thin red bricks, or tiles as they are called, and used these to mix with rubble to construct all the great buildings in Colchester, which is the most important of the Roman towns in East Anglia, and at numerous other smaller stations, ranging from Ongar in Essex to Caister.

From the time of the Romans until the late Middle Ages the production of bricks ceased and the import of building material virtually ceased, too,

THE LAKE AT HATFIELD FOREST

Hatfield Forest, now vested in the National Trust, is a densely wooded expanse of countryside between Bishop's Stortford and Great Dunmow, the lake is one of its most attractive vistas. Apart from the beauty of grassy clearings and dense thickets, Hatfield Forest has a special claim as one of the few places in eastern England where mistletoe grows wild, clustering densely on the boughs of numerous thorn trees. Here, too, are some of the most ancient oaks in Britain.

CHURCHES THE SAXONS BUILT

The church of St. Peter on the Wall, near Bradwell (*left*), rivals in interest the church at Greensted-juxta-Ongar (*right*). Like Greensted, it is of Saxon foundation. Like Greensted, it retains part of the Saxon fabric. The church of St. Peter is built of cobblestones (much repaired with brick) as befits a church near the seashore in a county which has no local building material. The "wall" which appears in the name is not, as many have thought, the sea wall, but the wall of a Roman fort. The church of Greensted, a church continuously since Saxon days, still retains the split trunks of oak trees which have formed the walls of the nave since the foundation of the church.

because the fine Roman roads were allowed to fall into disuse and navigation up the eastern estuaries was always a perilous undertaking. It was the lack of roads in medieval East Anglia that made the builders turn to whatever material lay to hand. The result is an extraordinary conglomeration of materials and styles, which is characteristic of East Anglian churches as much as of the private dwelling places.

First, the medieval masons made use of the material which the Romans left behind them, building, for instance, the castle and churches of Colchester from the ruins of the Roman city, so that even today the courses of Roman bricks are clearly visible, and there is a reddish tinge about the castle of Colchester.

All over the three counties these tell-tale thin bricks can be seen in the fabric of the churches. Wherever they are found it is safe to assume that there was a Roman town or village or grange somewhere in the vicinity.

In Essex there was abundance of timber, and so timber-built houses were the order of the day. There is even one church of late Saxon origin, Greensted-juxta-Ongar, whose nave is composed entirely of the split trunks of oak trees taken from the thickets of Epping Forest. Though a thousand years of use caused some of them to decay, the nave is still recognizable in its original form, another link with the distant past which is unique in England.

In the central districts, particularly of Suffolk, there was little timber to hand, so recourse was had to rubble, and lath and plaster, while the very early style of "wattle and daub" survived in the homes of the labouring class far into the Middle Ages.

In the eastern districts of East Anglia, again, there are signs of the growing import of building materials, particularly near the medieval ports. Later bricks began to be imported from the Continent. Flemish and Huguenot settlers brought their own particular styles, and so the large farms and manor-houses, and the churches, too, are a miracle of improvisation, while at Layer Marney, which is near to the Mersea Island estuary, is one of the loveliest and one of the earliest of the brick-built manor-houses of England, ranking in beauty and building merit with Hurstmonceux Castle in Sussex.

Time has done nothing to ravage the glory of Layer Marney Towers, or to make it obsolete as a dwelling place. But for the changes in the pattern of social life, which have tended to turn all the great British homes into schools or communal institutions of one kind or another, Layer Marney might well have continued as a manor-house for the next five hundred years. Indeed, the tendency for great estates to break up under the stress of death duties, and the

LAYER MARNEY TOWERS, ESSEX

Probably the earliest brick-built mansion in Essex, Layer Marney Towers was constructed between 1500 and 1525. Though in the tradition of the medieval castles, it was more a castellated manor-house than a castle, its defences meant for show rather than actual use. The gatehouse seen here is one of the finest examples of early Tudor architecture in Britain.

disappearance of the servant class, has been less rapid in East Anglia than in most parts of the country.

A few of the great estates have been turned into limited-liability companies, but the old tradition of the squire with his manor-house as the centre of village life is one which has been miraculously preserved. This is partly because the typical manor-house of East Anglia is smaller than in most other parts of the country; the medieval manor-house has quite naturally and, indeed, inevitably, merged into the large farmhouse; this remains the centre of village life, with the farmer's wife often the chairman of the Women's Institute and the farmer on the rural district council, exhibiting in their new environment the twentieth-century equivalent of the feudal rights of their ancestors.

Perhaps in the rural districts far removed from the influence of the big towns the feudal system will never entirely die, so strongly embedded is the idea of service to the squire and the reciprocal service of the squire to the community implied by it. Many half-timbered farmhouses of the sixteenth century are still surrounded by a moat, a reminder of the troubled times of the

INTERESTING ESSEX CHURCHES

The shortage of local building material in the Middle Ages caused architects to make shift with whatever supplies were available. In some village churches brick, cobblestones, rubble, and slabs of sandstone can be picked out, as well as more conventional building materials. At Blackmore (*left*) a three-storey tower has been added, the lower storey half-timbered, the upper storeys entirely timber-built. On the *right* is Chelmsford Cathedral, which is the old parish church of St. Mary the Virgin. The oldest parts date from the fifteenth century, which was a great period of church-building in East Anglia.

AN ANCIENT MOOT HALL

The ancient Moot Hall, or Guildhall, of Thaxted, with its handsome half-timbered facade, dates from 1480 and is one of the most perfectly preserved of Britain's medieval local-government buildings. The Moot Hall is almost contemporary with the famous church whose lofty spire can be seen in the background, one of the finest of the late Gothic churches which were built in East Anglia during the boom in the medieval wool trade. The photograph shows also one of the many ancient houses of Thaxted with overhanging upper storeys and gives some idea of this place as it was in the sixteenth and seventeenth centuries when its prosperity was at its greatest.

Middle Ages. They are as characteristic a feature of life in Essex and Suffolk as they are a part of the charm of the landscape.

There have been many changes in this landscape in the course of the last five hundred years, most of them arising inevitably from the social and industrial changes which we have already noted. The greatest change of all is the disappearance of the vast belt of forest-land known as the Forest of Waltham or the Forest of Essex. In medieval times this stretched from the valley of the Lea eastward as far as Chelmsford and northward as far as Saffron Walden and Great Dunmow. It is true that a few fragments have survived, especially Epping Forest, which is now an open space permanently dedicated to the enjoyment of the public; Hainault Forest, between Romford and Abridge, and the detached woods round Blackmore in the Chelmsford area. For the rest, it has utterly disappeared and only some fine hedgerow timber and the names of a few towns, such as Hadleigh, remain to carry on its tradition. (Leigh means a clearing in the forest, and every English town which has this termination must have lain in forest land.)

Another great change has been the disappearance of the endless pastures which were the home of the sheep and which were the basis of the medieval woollen industry, their place now taken for the most part by arable land, with its conventional rotation of crops, corn, roots, and clover. This, too, is a change that has taken place over almost all of the three counties.

Nevertheless rural life has gone on almost unchanged in spite of these great differences. It is a stronger thread running through history than any temporary or even permanent change in the way in which the rural people have earned their living. The same is true of the townspeople, for the towns of today in East Anglia are very largely the towns of yesterday, grown somewhat, and in a few cases sprawling over erstwhile untouched countryside, but essentially old and traditional centres of urban communities. We must exclude from these the satellite towns of London, such as Romford, though it still centres about an age-old market-place, which retains surprisingly a number of old buildings.

For the rest, there are Colchester and Chelmsford in Essex; Ipswich,

A NORMAN CASTLE OF ESSEX

Colchester Castle, now a museum, was one of the early Norman castles built, along with Castle Hedingham and Norwich, to check possible rebellion of the Saxon people in East Anglia. The photograph shows the moat where it was crossed by a drawbridge leading into the main entrance of the keep, still retaining its rounded Norman porch, though the windows are later additions. The courses of thin red Roman bricks which make up part of the fabric can be seen. The castle, like the rest of the Norman town of Colchester, was built largely from the ruins of the Roman city of Camulodunum.

THE SQUARE OF KING'S LYNN

King's Lynn is the only port of the north Norfolk coast which has retained some of its medieval prosperity. It is still a seaport, though its trade has diminished out of all proportion since the time when it was the fourth port in Britain. By King's Lynn's quays the River Ouse merges into the Wash, its course kept within limits by tall earthen banks.

Bury St. Edmunds, and Lowestoft in Suffolk; Norwich, Great Yarmouth, and King's Lynn in Norfolk, the latter a famous port of the Middle Ages, which still has the look of a medieval town, though the port no longer takes large vessels and its industries are modern. To these we must add Newmarket, the aristocrat of racing towns, whose chief substance is derived from the "sport of kings."

This short list almost exhausts the large towns of East Anglia. Apart from these, the people live in equally old but much smaller market-towns, whose number is legion and whose mellow quiet is enduring. If you drive into Fakenham in Norfolk, or into Sudbury in Suffolk, or into Saffron Walden in Essex, you will have the impression that you are entering a true country town, busy perhaps on market-days, but still a country town thronged by country people. You will feel, whichever one of these or fifty others you are visiting, that you have come to a place which depends for its existence on the countryside and which, in turn, gives life and character to the surrounding farms and villages. Whichever one you choose, you will have reached the heart of East Anglia, or, in other words, the heart of rural England.

SALISBURY CATHEDRAL

The greater part of Salisbury Cathedral was completed by 1260, and the crowning glory of the cathedral is due to the fact that it is built throughout in one style, unlike the majority of the cathedrals of Britain, which were enlarged and altered many times through the centuries.

The Southern Downlands

THE downlands are the most distinctive feature of the English landscape south of a line from the Wash to the Severn, and the distinction of the scenery is matched by their historical background and by the character of the rural people whose homes are set among them.

The downsmen are a rural people; for in the downland country proper there are no large towns, and certainly no centres of industry such as have changed the character of northern England's industrial region. London alone points long fingers toward the unspoiled countryside, northward toward the Chilterns and southward toward the North Downs. Here many thousands of London workers have made their homes, following the inevitable tendency which has characterized city folk in the nineteenth and twentieth centuries in search of homes secluded from the noise and bustle of the metropolis. So, to some small extent, the character of the people who live among the hills within thirty miles of London has changed, too.

The coming of the electric railways and frequent bus services has allowed them to look away from their native country towards the specious attractions of the first city of the Empire. This urban influence has extended beyond the first ridges of the North Downs and Chilterns, so that even towns like Sevenoaks and Oxted, both set beyond the escarpment of the Downs, have become suburban in the sense that very many of their inhabitants use them only as a dormitory and week-end resort, travelling each day to London to work, and looking to her for their relaxation and partly for their shopping.

Added to this is the regular invasion of the downland at week-ends by train, coach and bus from the centre of London, by car and cycle from every part of the metropolis. "London's country" has become something more than a name. It has become an area of still beautiful countryside, but of a landscape in which the signs of London's proximity are never long absent.

But this does no more than scratch the surface of life in the English downlands. For the rest there is a marvellous uniformity in the pattern of rural life, yet with a marked distinction in types, for instance, between the Kentish downsmen and the Sussex downsmen, which no influence on earth will ever eradicate. Throughout the whole of the area, in place of great industrial centres, there is a chain of little market-towns, nestling at the foot of the Downs or in the valleys which run between them. These are the true centres of rural life, unspoilt and largely unchanged.

There are strings of villages, too, along the valleys which intersect the Downs, and along the courses of the little rivers which rise near the upper

slopes and flow toward the Avon or the Thames. Many of these villages are no more than a manor-farm, a church, and a few cottages, self-contained and self-sufficient, conservative in the extreme, their horizon bounded by their own particular valley, their only link with the outside world the weekly bus which runs into the market-town. This is a picture which all the manifold influences of the twentieth century have failed to alter in material respects, a picture which will probably be as true in a hundred years' time as it is now.

The country which these rural people work is not agriculturally rich, so the people themselves have few reserves of wealth, but for compensation they have a great store of independence—the independence which is part

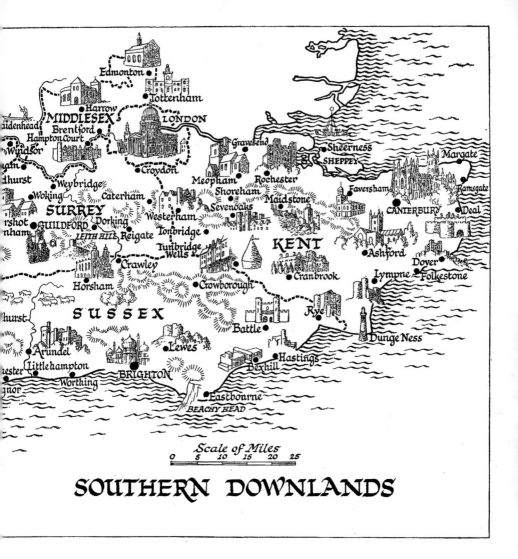

SOUTHERN DOWNLANDS

and parcel of the character of the yeoman farmers of England. They draw only a modest return from the soil, but their houses and cottages are spick and span and their manner of life is as certain and as predestined as it was in the days of the feudal system.

These market-towns are the true centres of rural life. Many of them are quiet, unspoilt places which have changed little in appearance during the last fifty years. In Kent there are several less than twenty-five miles from London, two typical examples being Sevenoaks and Westerham. These two make an interesting contrast, for whereas Sevenoaks has spread down the hill on which the old town was built toward the railway station, Westerham has scarcely increased in size at all though there has been some expansion.

203

CLIFFS OF SUSSEX
The chalk cliffs, where the South Downs are broken off at the sea, extend from Kemp Town, at the eastern end of Brighton to Beachy Head by Eastbourne. They are seen here from Rottingdean, protected now from the erosion that has steadily cut them back through the centuries.

In Surrey, Reigate remains the old market-town, whereas its near neighbour Redhill has grown out of all proportion because it is served by the main railway line to the south.

The farther away you go from London, the quieter are the downland towns. There is Wantage, sacred to the memory of King Alfred; Marlborough, one of the finest Georgian towns in England; Devizes, a place with many old buildings ranged round its broad square. Most characteristic of them all, Shaftesbury in Dorset is an ancient settlement on one of the spurs of the chalk downs, a place which has become the market centre of the fertile Vale of Blackmoor as well as of the more arid downlands of Cranborne Chase.

There is a similar string of market-towns under the north face of the Chiltern Hills as there is beneath the North Downs, though some of these, like Luton and High Wycombe, have been industrialized. But there is nothing industrial about Princes Risborough or Wendover, or indeed about Royston under the eastern extension of the Chilterns.

The geographical centre of the southern downlands is the great upland mass which includes Salisbury Plain and fills the greater part of the county of Hampshire and a large slice of Wiltshire as well. This is an old plateau into which many pretty little streams have eroded deep fissures, but hundreds of square miles of the upper slopes have never been ploughed from time immemorial and remain for all today as the richest storehouse of prehistoric man's activity in all Europe.

From this central mass of downland long ridges radiate like the spokes of a wheel. Eastward the North Downs extend through Surrey and Kent, to end in the sheer face of Shakespeare's Cliff at Dover, the "white cliffs of Albion" which greet the traveller on his return from the Continent. South-eastward another long line of Downs, the South Downs, traverses the whole length of Sussex to end in Beachy Head, which is thus a companion head-land of Shakespeare's Cliff.

North-eastward there is a still longer ridge, which starts as the Berk-shire Downs and goes down to the Thames at Goring only to rise again immediately on the other bank, and as the Chiltern Hills to give its distinctive character to Buckinghamshire and Hertfordshire. With a change of name but no change of form this downland ridge continues as the East Anglian Heights through Suffolk and Norfolk, to end in the cliffs of Hunstanton on the shores of the Wash. Yet once more the ridge is continued on the other bank to form the wolds of Lincolnshire and Yorkshire, which are essentially an integral part of the downland country of England, and end in the supreme grace of Flamborough Head, which is the most northerly point to which the chalk extends in Britain.

Westward from the central plateau of Wiltshire, the North and South

VIEW OVER THE WEALD OF KENT
The North Downs cross the boundary of Kent above Westerham. From there they extend in a long line to Shakespeare's Cliff near Dover, broken only by the valleys of the Darent, Medway, and Stour. Over all their length they command magnificent views across the well-wooded Weald, as here near Brook, where the landscape across ploughed fields and pasture-lands extends to the valley in which rise many tributaries of the Medway and Stour.

STONEHENGE: PREHISTORIC TEMPLE

More spectacular than Avebury and built about the same time, between 2000 and 1800 B.C., Stonehenge was probably a temple to the sun; one of its stones is in direct line with the rising sun on Midsummer's Day as seen by an observer standing in the centre of the circle. These magnificent trilithons (two upright stones supporting a horizontal slab) are part of the outer circle. They are formed of blocks belonging to a layer of sandstone that originally covered the whole of Salisbury Plain and of which there are still fragments known today as "grey wethers." The face of the vast stones was tooled and the horizontal slabs are fixed by rough toggle-joints.

Downs of Dorset reach the sea near Lyme Regis, which stands as the most westerly outpost of the chalk.

If it is remembered that the Kentish Downs which break off at Shakespeare's Cliff are continued on the other side of the Channel, where the flashing sides of Cap Gris-Nez are sometimes to be descried on clear summer days with the naked eye, it will be realized how far-flung is this part of Britain's scenic and historic heritage. Cap Gris-Nez has added significance, because a trackway followed the higher slopes of the hills which joined Cap Gris-Nez and Shakespeare's Cliff before the English Channel had been formed. It was along this trackway tens of thousands of years ago that the first inhabitants of Britain came from the Continent in search of fresh pastures and new wealth. From that time onward, before the days of railways or roads, before even the lowlands had been cleared of the impenetrable swamps which formerly covered them, the downland tracks were the only means of travel and the only arteries of commerce between Britain and the Continent, as well as between different parts of Britain. They continued to be used through successive civilizations until, less than two thousand years ago, Britain came under the influence of the Roman Empire. Because of this, and because the uplands over which they ran have never again been brought under intensive cultivation, the trackways remain to this day as the green ways of England, which we can follow on foot or on horseback for mile after mile in the footsteps of these earliest inhabitants of Britain.

It was about two thousand years B.C. that the civilization of these downland peoples came to its highest fulfilment, about the time when what the archaeologists call the Stone Age was ending and the Bronze Age beginning. This means that the men and women who built such magnificent monuments at Stonehenge and Avebury had no tools or weapons with which to work other than the rough tools which they fashioned from flint, the native stone of the chalk downs, which they found all over the chalk country, in places as far apart as Cissbury in Sussex and Grimes Graves in Norfolk.

Stonehenge and Avebury, which lie only a few miles from each other, are the two greatest prehistoric monuments in Britain and for that matter two of the most elaborate and the largest in the whole world. Most probably

THE STONES OF AVEBURY

The southern downlands were the chief centres of population in prehistoric times. These stones survive from a vast temple constructed between 2000 and 1800 B.C. at the end of the New Stone Age, about the same time as the near-by monument of Stonehenge was being constructed. Avebury consisted of outer and inner stone circles surrounded by a bank and trench, the whole covering an area of more than twenty-eight acres, the entire circle almost four hundred yards in diameter. The medieval village of Avebury, seen in the background, is built chiefly within the orbit of the prehistoric circle.

they were temples, and Stonehenge may well have been a temple of the sun god, although that is still a matter of conjecture. But at least it is certain that the peoples who lived there four thousand or more years ago were a powerful and industrious people, welded together by some kind of firm government and practising a fully fledged tribal religion. For the labour of collecting, tooling, and erecting the vast stones of Stonehenge, or raising the great ramparts of Avebury, could never have been achieved unless a whole tribe had combined to tackle the work with might and main. Even then it must have taken them years to complete, just as the building of medieval abbeys was sometimes spread over thirty or forty years.

FROM STONE AGE TO ROMAN OCCUPATION

The prehistoric inhabitants of the downlands buried their dead in stone chambers covered by earthen mounds. If you wander over Salisbury Plain today you cannot fail to come upon dozens and dozens of these "barrows," as they are called, partly levelled by time and weather, but still clearly visible. Here and there the earthen covering has been washed away and only the burial chamber remains, as for instance at Wayland's Smithy in Berkshire and Kit's Coty in Kent.

Then there are the hilltop fortified villages, strung out at intervals along the downland tracks, like Cissbury Camp in Sussex and Eggar Dun in Dorset. Most of the ramparts and ditches which make up these fortified villages were rebuilt in the third or fourth century before the beginning of the Christian era, and belong to a later civilization than that which was responsible for Stonehenge and the other stone monuments of the downlands. Most of them had their origin in the Stone Age and were adapted and enlarged by the tribes of ancient Britons, the Celts, who were still ranging over the downlands and using the trackways in the years immediately before Julius Caesar brought his legions across the Channel in the first expedition against Britain.

These wonderful links with the distant past are only the beginning of the attraction of the downlands for the wayfarer of today, but they are a heritage which no one can overlook and which somehow gives a tone to the countryside, a particular charm which is quite apart from its scenic delights.

To capture the full spirit of the downlands one of these prehistoric trackways must be followed from beginning to end, for so one will come upon many of these links with the past and be rewarded with an ever-changing scenic panorama. The Ridgeway over the Berkshire Downs and the Pilgrims' Way, which follows the ridge from Winchester to Farnham and Guildford, and then along the side of the Downs to the Stour near Canterbury, are the two most easily followed, and the two which give the greatest sense of unlimited space, the greatest variety of scenery and views of historic town and village.

Whilst of old the high plateaux were the centres of the people's homes, today the upper slopes of the Downs are bare of habitation except for an occasional isolated farmhouse and a very few high-set villages, like Ranmore

X. DORSET DOWNLANDS NEAR WINTERBOURNE ABBAS

XI. A VALLEY IN THE HAMPSHIRE DOWNS NEAR ANDOVER

XII. DAIRY HERD IN A KENTISH ORCHARD NEAR SITTINGBOURNE

XIII. HOPFIELDS AND OAST-HOUSES AT YALDING IN KENT

XIV. EAST GRINSTEAD, SUSSEX

XV. CORFE CASTLE, DORSET

XVI. CASTLE COMBE, WILTSHIRE

and Headley. All the towns and almost all the villages are in the valleys, and they illustrate how completely methods of working the land have changed over four thousand years. In the days of Stonehenge and the prehistoric hilltop villages, the lowlands were an impenetrable mass of bogland and oak forest. It was only when the Romans colonized Britain and brought with them skill in clearing forests and draining bogs that the fertile soil of the lowlands was brought into cultivation. It was actually the Saxons, little more than a thousand years ago, who founded most of the villages along the banks of the downland streams, and the towns and villages of today are the direct descendants of these Saxon settlements.

SOIL AND THE LANDSCAPE

So we shall find that the high ground is untilled, though in the First and Second World Wars, under the stimulus of a national emergency, the plough reached higher up the slopes than it had done for hundreds of years. For the most part, however, the high ground is pasture-land, the rich grass country which has nurtured many famous breeds of sheep and cattle, while it is on the lower slopes where the chalk lands merge into the clay of the valleys that the land is ploughed, and around the small farmsteads there are fields of corn, vegetables, and clover, while dairy herds find rich verdure in the water-meadows beside the streams.

This is no country of vast farms like East Anglia. There are very few farmers who possess a combine-harvester and it is only in the last thirty or forty years that the old-fashioned method of cutting the corn by scythe has given place to the tractor-drawn cutter and the horse has given place to the mechanical plough.

As you wander along the Pilgrims' Way, or the Icknield Way in the Chilterns, you can see the swift transition between the flinty soil of the uplands and the richer clay loam of the valley. Where the upper slopes are ploughed, the land on a sunny day gleams almost white—so thick is the chalk, so near the surface the hard bed-rock—but, lower down, the fields are a rich brown, and in some of the deeper valleys, almost black, with something of the wealth of the black lands of the Fens.

There is brilliant colour in the landscapes of some parts of the Downs. At every season of the year the browns and greys of the fields are picked out by the dark green of the clumps of pine trees, which are only a recent addition to the trees of the Downs and which have proved wonderfully well adapted to the chalk country. In spring and summer the generous woods which cloak many of the middle slopes of the North Downs and the Chilterns range through every variation of colour, from greens so light that they are almost yellow, to the russets and purples of the beeches in autumn.

Of all the trees which flourish in the downland, perhaps the beech is the most distinctive. There are noble isolated clumps on the North and South Downs like Chanctonbury Ring in Sussex and Knockholt Beeches in Kent, but it is in the Chiltern country that this noble English tree reaches its highest perfection, for here there are endless groves traversed by narrow

EARLY SPRING IN THE CHILTERNS

The beech woods are the crowning glory of the Chiltern Hills. From the
Thames gap in the Downs at Goring they cover the hillsides until the bare
expanse of the Dunstable Downs is reached. The woodlands extend back from
the main ridge into the Chiltern valleys and dominate the landscape. They are
especially beautiful in autumn when the mellow colouring, browns and golds
and yellows, of the beech trees is at its finest. The woods are beautiful also
in the early spring when, as here, the close-woven pattern of trunks and
branches is reflected by the bright sunshine on the greensward and there is
promise of summer in the palest green of the early shoots.

tracks which go on and on for mile after mile and reach to the very crest of
the Downs. Burnham Beeches itself, the most famous of south-country
beauty-spots, is in the foothills of the Chilterns, while the vast trees of
immemorial age which cover many acres of the country round Ashridge
Park are very near the crest of the Downs where they overlook the Midland
Plain. On Aldbury Common, near Ashridge Park, is the monument built to
commemorate the Duke of Bridgewater, known as "the father of British
inland navigation," since in 1762 he constructed the first canal in England
forty-two miles long linking Worsley with Manchester and Runcorn.

On the North Downs, too, on either side of the old Drove Road, the
long green track which links the valley of the Wey at Guildford with the
valley of the Mole at Dorking, there are wide expanses of woodland, in
which flourishes almost every type of tree found in the forests of England,
though the oak, the most characteristic tree of the lowlands, is generally
absent, and its absence causes a strange sense of emptiness.

Here and there in the downland country there are small areas where a
particular kind of tree or plant has become localized, as has the box tree on

the slopes of Box Hill, and the juniper on the ridges round Mickleham. Though the woodlands add diversity to the scene, they are foreign to the landscape of the central plateau. The most noble of the ridges here are bare —utterly bare save for the short-cropped stringy grass, which makes walking over them a pleasure, and the myriad little flowers, mostly flowering in late summer, which give added beauty to the scene.

Some of the finest parts of the South Downs, too, are bare ; so is Cranborne Chase in Dorset, and the high ridges that swing south-westward towards the sea around Cerne Abbas and Sydling St. Nicholas. Bare, too, are the upper slopes of Salisbury Plain, and the beetling brow of Old Winchester Hill, and the whole line of the Berkshire Downs, save for an occasional clump of trees planted a century or so ago to mark the site of some prehistoric earthwork or burial place, or in memory of some distinguished local person.

In the cultivated valley of downland country there is the characteristic bright splash of the poppy fields in summer. If you plough fresh ground in the autumn, plant what you will in it, the poppy will be the most conspicuous part of the crop as the longest day passes. The year after, there will be a better harvest of corn and fewer poppies, but the poppy will ever be the emblem of the chalk country, its bright head will forever bespangle the greens and golds of the harvest fields.

If we look at each of the counties which fall within this great range of chalk hills, we shall see how completely the Downs dominate the scene and

TWO INTERESTING CHURCHES

Mickleham, with its distinctive medieval church (*left*), is typical of the many charming villages of the North Downs. The shingled spire and the generous use of flints in the fabric of the church are interesting points. Tring is one of the market-towns of the Chilterns. The square tower of the church (*right*) is a fine example of the late Gothic style.

KENT ORCHARD-LAND

Where the North Downs fall to the valleys of the Thames and Stour is the centre of the Kent orchard-land. This scene near Chilham shows all the character of the downland foothills, with their spreading orchards, their well-wooded slopes and rolling contours. The thatched and half-timbered cottage in the foreground is like many of the smaller Kentish yeomen's houses and makes an interesting comparison with the manor-house shown on page 215.

how, too, they influence the life of the people. Let us look first at Kent, where the North Downs are the very backbone of the county. From one end of the county to the other, the ridge is continuous from the point where it crosses the boundary near Westerham to the point at which it ends in the cliffs of Dover.

The rivers which break through the Downs, and incidentally lend them an added variety of scene, are only three in number. First there is the Darent, which waters the deep cleft valley in which lie Eynsford, with its castle and old-world ford, Shoreham, clustered about its fine church, which stands on the very brink of the river, and Otford, at the point where the river finally breaks through the chalk barrier into the broader valley beyond.

Next comes the Medway, proudest and finest of Kent rivers, with two ancient and historic towns upon its banks—Maidstone in the plain below the Downs, and Rochester to the north only a few miles from where the Medway flows into the Thames beside the Isle of Sheppey

Here in this river valley is the very spirit of Kent. In its upper reaches it is a meandering, elusive stream, which waters hundreds of square miles of valley country between Tonbridge and Maidstone—a countryside to which the hopgardens, a traditional feature of Kent, still bring thousands on thousands of Londoners in late summer to gather in this most characteristic of Kentish harvests. From the river banks at every turn the wayfarer can see the oast-houses, whose conical towers rise above the hopgardens and mark the often half-timbered farmhouses which are the centres of this flourishing rural industry.

Farther downstream the river is broad and stately, but modern industry has laid a hand on the countryside. Under the brows of the green ridges of the Downs, for instance, are cement works, and at Chatham, one of the greatest dockyards in the world. Here, too, modern industry and historic monument look down on the river side by side. Rochester's historic castle keep was built by the Normans at this point, where the Roman and medieval road from the coast to London forded the Medway. With its help, along with the similar castles of London and Canterbury, William of Normandy held sway over all the country south of the Thames.

Near the mouth of the Darent, too, there is industry—cement works, chemical works and, above all, the paper mills which have made the name Cray Valley (the Cray is one of Darent's tributaries) world-famous.

THE MEDWAY BRIDGE AT AYLESFORD

The Medway divides the chalk Downs of west Kent from those of east Kent, flowing through a wide valley in the chalk in which there are numerous cement factories and also some charmingly pretty villages. Aylesford, only a few miles from Maidstone, is one of the loveliest of these. Its trim houses and small Gothic church make an effective background to the bridge, which is one of the oldest in eastern England, almost unchanged since the fourteenth century, when it was built to replace an important ford over the river.

It is the Medway, too, which divides Kent into two parts, for those who live to the east of the Medway have for centuries been known as the Men of Kent, to be distinguished from Kentish Men, who include all who dwell within the confines of the county. It is the Men of Kent who have been the yeoman farmers of south-east England since the time when they secured special privilege from William the Conqueror by which it was agreed that the Saxon custom by which a man's land was divided among his children should continue, instead of passing to the eldest son, as by Norman custom.

So arose the tradition of the prosperity of the Men of Kent, who were freemen owning their own plot of ground and who continued prosperous in their own right, instead of becoming tenant farmers after the breakdown of the feudal system in other parts of the country. Indeed, if the prosperous half-timbered Tudor and Elizabethan farmhouses are any guide, they must have been a very prosperous race of men. There is something solid and comfortable about these homesteads (ranging from the magnificently proportioned black-and-white manor-house of Boxon to the many small three-room timber-framed farmhouses in the country to the south of Maidstone), which gives a real distinction to this part of Kent. It is something also which makes the descendants of those medieval yeoman farmers proud of their heritage, proud of the soil that reared them, and of the fine homes in

VILLAGE OF THE KENT DOWNS
This quaint village street in the central Downs of Kent near Bredgar is typical of scores of others. A variety of materials has been used at different times for cottage building. The half-timbered style is side by side with more modern brick-built cottages. The cottage in the left foreground is weather-boarded in the style characteristic of the south-eastern counties.

A MANOR-HOUSE IN KENT

The half-timbered manor-houses of east Kent are a feature of the southern downlands. They recall the traditional prosperity of the Men of Kent, who won special privileges for themselves at the time of the Conquest and became a by-word for wealth and loyalty in the Middle Ages. The half-timbered manor near Bredgar, shown here, is one of the finest of these old houses. Dating from the sixteenth century, it has all the grace of half-timbered houses in general, and in addition a spaciousness and design equalled by few others. The oriel windows were the forerunners of the modern bay-windows, and the Elizabethan porch developed from the medieval gatehouse.

which their fathers and their grandfathers and their great-grandfathers before them lived, struggled and won their perpetual fight against the vagaries of Nature and the sometimes not over-bountiful nature of the soil.

The third of the rivers which cut through the Kentish Downs is the Stour. Two of the county's most important towns lie on its banks. Where the gap of the Downs opens out into the Weald there is Ashford, historic market-town, through which runs the modern highway from Maidstone to the coast at Folkestone and Dover. Beneath the northern foothills of the Downs is Canterbury, the most historic and romantic city in the whole country, a centre of population since the very earliest times, Roman city, Saxon borough, Norman castle and medieval centre of the religious and cultural life of south-east England. Its magnificent cathedral, its castle ruins, its old houses and its hundred and one links with the Flemings and the Huguenots and, above all, with the life of Thomas à Becket, make it a real mecca for the historian of today. It was to the tomb of St. Thomas that thousands of pilgrims came yearly throughout the Middle Ages bringing

THE PILGRIMAGE PASSES SEALE CHURCH

The prehistoric Pilgrims' Way follows the line of the North Downs from the area of Salisbury Plain as far as the valley of the Stour near Canterbury. There is a tradition that this ancient trackway was used largely by pilgrims to the shrine of St. Thomas at Canterbury. In the spirit of this tradition a party led by three Franciscan friars from Cerne Abbas, Dorset, makes its way on foot following, as far as possible, the course of the ancient road to Canterbury. Here the party is passing the church of Seale, a village lying under the Hog's Back between Farnham and Guildford.

trade and prosperity to this city of so many abbeys and priories that it became known as the British Rome.

Tradition relates that the pilgrims who came from Winchester and beyond first trod out the Pilgrims' Way which, as we have seen, runs along the length of the Downs. In sober fact, tradition, as so often, lies. Medieval pilgrims, wise in their ways, came along the high road by way of London and Rochester, and put up at the many inns which line that road, first made out by the Roman engineers to link the port of Dover with the metropolis of London. Some pilgrims may have come by the Pilgrims' Way, but they certainly did not give it its name, which arises from the romantic imagination of nineteenth-century antiquaries. Rather, as is now certain, it was a highway three thousand years and more before St. Thomas was martyred.

Around Canterbury the Downs rise on the west towards the wooded hills about Lenham, where from the high ground the wayfarer looks across thousands and thousands of acres of orchard-land towards the broad silver belt of the Thames. Just as the hops are sacred to the Weald of Kent, so the orchards are the soul of all the country between Gillingham and Canterbury. Rising from the level of the Thames marshes, they ascend toward the four-hundred-foot contour line—apples and plums and, above all, cherries. It was here, incidentally, around Teynham that the first cherries were cultivated, and Teynham has remained one of the chief centres of cherry culture through the centuries.

In this mass of downland, too, is one of the loveliest dry valleys in south-east England. The Elham Valley is a narrow belt of rich land in the very heart of the chalk, once watered by a considerable river, down which even now there flows every few years an intermittent stream, associated in local folk-lore with impending misfortunes for the nation.

The downlands are not all Kent. In area they fill scarcely a third of it, but they are the county's most important physical characteristic, and dominate its scene for miles away. So across all the Weald from Romney Marsh to the Medway, the long ridge of the Downs stands out rock-sharp against the northern skyline, beckoning the traveller as he moves northward across the lush meadowlands and through the rich hopgardens.

In the west of the county, near the Surrey boundary, there is another line of Downs, which, though they are distinct from the chalk-lands and belong rather to the sandstone of the Weald, still form a single unity with them. Here are the heather-covered pine-clad slopes of Crockham Hill,

VIEW ACROSS THE BERKSHIRE DOWNS

In the background is the main ridge of the Berkshire Downs, which links the Marlborough Downs with the Thames gap at Goring. In the foreground is one of the many shallow valleys that have been eroded in times past by rivers rising in the Downs, but are now dry. There are herds of cattle, as here, and of sheep, too, on the rich pastures of the upper slopes, and ploughed fields in the well-wooded trough of the valley. Wheat, oats, and barley all bring a good harvest to this district, which has doubled its acreage under the plough since the beginning of the Second World War.

Toys Hill, and Ide Hill, and the parklands of Knole and Ightham, a land in which there is a riot of wild flowers, and the rhododendron flourishes profusely to give a splash of brave colour in the spring.

Only the narrow clay-soil valley separates these hills from the line of the North Downs. This is the lovely valley in which lie Westerham, sacred to the memory of Wolfe, and Brasted. In a single day's modest walking the wayfarer can comprehend both ridges and enjoy the startling contrast and the wonderfully varied changes of scene, from the close-cropped grass of the Downs to the bracken and heather of the sandstone hills.

To the south of this again is another charming corner of Kent, where we reach once more the valley of the Medway in its higher reaches and find the Tudor villages of Hever, Chiddingstone (the latter with a whole row of beautifully preserved cottages dating from the time of Henry VII) and Penshurst, with its vast manor-house which still retains its medieval hall complete with minstrels' gallery.

Croydon at the extreme northern end of the chalk country has become a county borough in its own right, and is a vast dormitory for London's teeming millions. But in rural Surrey most of the big market-towns lie just under the Downs—Redhill and Reigate, astride the main highway to Brighton, Leatherhead and Dorking, where the Mole strikes a bold course through

SURREY FARMHOUSE

In Surrey and the Home Counties generally most of the old farmhouses have been restored and repaired, a few of them being the homes of prosperous London people who have made country life a hobby. This ancient farmhouse in the countryside that lies between the Hog's Back and the Hindhead Hills shows an interesting mixture of the half-timbered and stone-built styles, with the traditional hanging tiles of the southern counties.

THE GOLDEN VALLEY, SURREY

Unlike the greater part of the South Downs, much of the North Downs is well wooded, especially that portion of the ridge which lies between Guildford and Reigate. Some of the most beautiful vistas in the whole downland country occur in the Golden Valley, a deep cleft in the hills from Headley to the valley of the Mole, which lies on the far left in this photograph taken from the slopes of Box Hill. The dark mass of conifers and the lighter green of the deciduous trees make an effective pattern.

precipitous hills, Woking and Guildford where the parallel course of the Wey cuts through the western Downs.

Guildford, the county capital, is even more a downland town than its Kentish counterpart, Maidstone. It spans the River Wey and its steep streets mount abruptly to the very crest of the hills, westward to the summit of the Hog's Back, eastward to Pewly Hill and Newlands Corner. Though little more than thirty miles from London, it is still very much the county town, with its castle standing on a cliff, where it has guarded an important ford over the Wey since Norman times, its many old houses and churches, and its broad market-place. The bold outline of the new cathedral, now many years abuilding, stands out on the skyline to the west. Perhaps, of all the towns within sixty miles of London, Guildford most perfectly presents the character of a typical rural market-town.

Near here, too, are some of the finest view-points and most exciting trackways of the North Downs. The long line of the Hog's Back stretches as far as Farnham, a little town on another loop of the Wey near the romantic ruins of Waverley Abbey, which gave Sir Walter Scott the title of one of his most famous novels. From the summit of the Hog's Back, which is traversed by a motor road as well as by the line of the Pilgrims' Way, the wayfarer looks north to the misty shadows of the Thames Valley and southward over a deep gulf to the pine-clad heights of Hindhead and Kettlebury Hill. Thousands and thousands of acres of barren heather common intervene, where Elstead and Thursley are typical of the tiny villages which nestle in the folds of the commons.

The Hindhead Hills and the sandy country which surrounds them are not a part of the North Downs, but belong to the same parallel range of hills which in Kent are Crockham Hill and Ide Hill. Between the two is the tumbled country of heather and pine trees, rising to its highest point at Leith Hill, which is actually one of the highest points in the Home Counties, and with the help of its tower just touches the thousand-foot contour.

DIVERSITY OF THE SURREY SCENE

The lovely villages of Friday Street and Holmbury St. Mary rank with the most beautiful in England. Between them and the line of the North Downs is the narrow valley of the winding Tillingbourne, with Shere, Gomshall, and Abinger Hammer. This is the countryside of many surprises, of steep hills, of local arts and crafts, which defies easy transport and millions of visitors to destroy its charm or to impair its beauty.

Northward again is the grand view-point of Newlands Corner, famous for its long vista across the Tillingbourne Valley, though in fact it is a no finer viewpoint than a dozen along the old Drove Road which connects it with Ranmore Common, overlooking the valley of the Mole.

Box Hill, the Mickleham Downs, and Headley Heath are all three part of the Surrey downlands. So are the breezy expanse of Walton Heath and the precipitous front of Colley Hill, every one a name to conjure with among the highlights of English scenery.

Indeed, Surrey is far more a county of famous downlands than even Kent, but grandeur of scenery is not often allied with fertility of soil. For all its beauty, Surrey is one of the least productive counties. The husbandman faces a greater poverty of soil and reaps a poorer harvest than in any other part of the south-east. So much of the county is heather country and common-land, so little fertile clay, that farming is always precarious and in bad years disastrous, except in the river valleys and in the lowlands of the Weald.

Perhaps largely because of its very lack of fertility, Surrey is a county of large parks with many head of fallow deer, whilst the abundance of wild flowers and the many rare forms of animal life owe their survival to the wide areas which have not been brought under intensive cultivation. The hedges round Thursley are a butterfly-hunter's paradise. The lanes between the Hog's Back and Hindhead are full of rare ferns, far more reminiscent of the deep enclosed lanes of Devonshire than they are of a countryside which nowhere is more than fifty miles from the centre of London.

A feature of the country, too, which strikes every wayfarer in Surrey is the number of sunken lanes. In more fertile and therefore more developed counties most of the sunken lanes have vanished, having been turned into metalled roads, but in Surrey there are dozens which were first trodden out in the early Middle Ages and sank gradually under the weight of traffic.

PINE COUNTRY OF SURREY

Most of the trees that grow on the chalk are deciduous. The beech is the most
frequent of them all, but in the sandstone hills, which are separated from the
main line of the downs by a narrow valley, evergreen trees and shrubs are
a constant reminder of the change of soil and make the scenery entirely
characteristic. This view is of part of the village of Friday Street.

Beachy Head is where the South Downs begin. It rises sharply five hundred feet from the waters of the English Channel. From its crest to Seaford there are ten miles of some of the loveliest cliff scenery of all England, with the Seven Sisters, peerless among chalk cliffs, linking Birling Gap with Cuckmere Haven.

Then there is the narrow mouth of the Cuckmere itself, and the abrupt slopes of Seaford Head, followed by the wide valley of the Ouse and the cliffs which stretch from Newhaven to the Kemp Town end of Brighton, once as lovely as the Seven Sisters, but now despoiled by the urban spread of Brighton itself and the mushroom growth which is Peacehaven. Thereafter the coast is flat and the Downs recede, but they have receded only in comparatively recent ages. In prehistoric times the sea washed against the southern flanks of the Downs, right through Sussex and Hampshire. The coastal plain, where the new seaside resorts like Worthing and Littlehampton and Bognor now stand, is land recently formed by the silting up of many rivers and the gradual building up of a sea-bed from the debris washed from the Downs. Just as Nature is for ever eating away the land on the Norfolk and Suffolk coasts, so for compensation she is constantly laying down fresh land under the sea, and here under the western Downs of Sussex she has created a thriving countryside of market-gardens, pasture-land, and cornfields which is one of the most prosperous parts of the whole county.

LEGACY OF THE PAST

But Nature meant the South Downs to be uncultivated, and the struggle between man and Nature has been unstinting, with Nature generally winning the struggle. Even the extensive fresh ploughing of the Second World War left thousands of acres of the turf untouched, where only herds of sheep and droves of oxen find rough pasturage and the shepherd wending his way slowly across the open hills ever seeking fresh pasturage for his flock is a familiar sight, and the sheep bells make the sweetest music of the Downs. Inland the hills form tumbled ridges, rising to a final scarp which looks steeply across the Weald.

Like the North Downs, the Downs of Sussex are broken by several rivers whose valleys contain some of the most attractive scenery. The Cuckmere Valley is narrow and intimate. Before it widens into the Weald it holds to its gracious breast the little town of Alfriston, whose inns recall the days when smugglers frequented all the lonely inlets of the southern and eastern coasts. On the other bank nestles Litlington and Lullington Church, which many claim to be the smallest church in England.

Looking northward over the Weald between the Cuckmere Valley and Eastbourne is the Long Man of Wilmington, the vast figure with a staff cut out of the turf above the village which gives it its name. Like most of the other hill figures it was obscured during the Second World War.

No man can tell with certainty the story of the hill figures of the Downs. Some, like the White Horse of the Berkshire Downs, are of immemorial antiquity and were probably figures cut by prehistoric man as part of his

222

THE CUCKMERE VALLEY

This view from High and Over, near Alfriston, Sussex, shows the winding course of the Cuckmere River with Fore Down in the background. The Cuckmere is one of the many streams that rise in the Sussex Weald.

THE WHITE HORSE OF BRATTON

From prehistoric times to the present day, figures have been cut in the downs simply by removing the turf and exposing the bare chalk. One of the earliest is the White Horse, Wantage (see pages 234-5); one of the latest, the Peace Memorial Cross (1919) above Lenham in Kent. This horse on Bratton Down, near Westbury, Wiltshire, probably belongs to the eighteenth century, though tradition has it that it celebrates one of Alfred's victories.

religious observances. Others, like the Giant of Cerne Abbas, are also almost certainly prehistoric. A few, like the Westbury white horse and the figure of George III on the hills behind Weymouth, are certainly modern.

Between Seaford Head and the Hampshire boundary, three rivers break through the barrier of the Downs. Each is justly famed for its scenic beauty. Each has a small port at its mouth, each has a medieval castle guarding the point where the valley is narrowest.

First is the Ouse, with Newhaven at its mouth, whence the cross-Channel boats sail for Dieppe, and Lewes, the old county town, a few miles upstream, its castle on a cliff two hundred feet above the river. From early medieval days the Ouse has been navigable to Lewes, as witness the round towers of the churches of Southease and Piddinghoe, and Lewes itself, which were built in this shape strange to Sussex, though common enough in Norfolk, as guides to mariners navigating the treacherous bends of the river.

Next comes the Adur, with the little port of Shoreham at its mouth, and Bramber Castle on a detached spur of the Downs guarding the northern gap. Finally there is the Arun, with Littlehampton, no longer a port but a flourishing holiday resort, and, upstream, the castle of Arundel, ancestral home of the Dukes of Norfolk, with the little town nestling under its walls, and the wooded slopes of Arundel Park rising almost from the end of its main street to one of the most open and windswept ridges of all the downlands.

A few miles to the west is the Goodwood racecourse, overlooked by the natural grandstand of the Trundle Hill, on which Stone Age man and later Iron Age man built fortified villages, and where the Romano-British citizens continued to live until well into the third century A.D. Here indeed historic interest and natural beauty are allied as nowhere else. It may well have been the inhabitants of the Trundle who moved into the lowlands to found the city of Chichester, which became one of the principal Roman towns, linked with London by the Roman road, Stane Street, which the wayfarer today can follow over the South Downs across the Weald, over the North Downs near Epsom, to the very outskirts of London. Few Roman roads are so well preserved as this one, few pass through such romantic and varied scenery.

The gypsy is a country type fast dying out in the south-eastern counties, but traditionally racecourses attract them and in the first few decades of the

DEW-POND ON THE DOWNS

In the South Down country of Sussex the art of making dew-ponds has been handed down from ancient times. The dew-pond is formed by scooping a hollow in the chalk and lining it with puddled clay. Thus the moist winds that blow over the downs condense on the colder surface of the clay and keep the pond filled even in the driest summers. So it is possible to water the sheep and cattle that range over the downs without driving them into the valley farmsteads or bringing water to the pastures by cart.

present century there were permanent gypsy encampments near Goodwood and also near Epsom in the North Downs. The gypsies may no longer camp on Epsom Downs, though there are still a few who ply their crafts in Surrey, especially in the Holmbury Hill district, and one may often come upon a small encampment on or under the Downs of Sussex. Gone are the times when begging was the gypsies' main prop of life. Nowadays they are skilled woodworkers, fashioning baskets and all manner of other things from the wood which they collect, and hawking their wares round the neighbouring villages. It is the men who make and the women who sell. And most of the women still carry with them on their expeditions the young baby traditional to their craft. The early life of any gypsy is certainly a much-travelled existence.

Look at a map of south-east England. You will see that the western boundaries of Surrey and Sussex make almost a straight line from north to south. This line is very nearly the dividing point between the central mass of the English downlands and the detached spurs which we call the North and South Downs. If we stand on the summit of Butser Hill, which is just across the Hampshire boundary from Sussex, we can see the North Downs

SUSSEX CRAFTSMANSHIP

Many counties retain a traditional style of farm cart that is still built, in spite of the growing tendency to uniformity over the country as a whole. Sussex crafts are especially resistant to influences that have stamped out the crafts of some parts of Britain. Sussex ironworking, for instance, remains as flourishing a rural industry as ever it was. This picture shows another phase of Sussex craftsmanship. The wheelwrights are putting the finishing touches to a distinctive kind of farm cart known as the Sussex wain or tug.

SUSSEX POTTER

The potter's wheel rotates anti-clockwise, while the craftsman shapes the clay with his fingers. He is working in a pottery at Rye, which was once an important town as one of the Cinque ports, but now is some two miles from the sea. Although small ships can still get up the River Rother to the town, today its main activities, apart from some local industries such as pottery, are concerned with agriculture and catering for the tourist trade.

going south and the South Downs going north, to join in the great plateau which stretches from Winchester to Salisbury Plain.

In these two counties, Hampshire and Wiltshire, there are several ridges, but there is not the same contrast between highland and lowland as there is in Surrey, Kent, and Sussex. The south of Hampshire is, of course, the continuation of the Sussex coastal plain, and here Portsmouth and Southampton, with their dockyards and shipbuilding and other heavy industries, owe nothing to the downlands, though they look northward to the downland ridges which dominate the skyline and southward to the downlands of the Isle of Wight. There is, too, the New Forest, land of broad tracks, traversing heather commons and pine woods.

For the rest, the scenic beauty and the rural life of both counties centre on the Downs. Winchester and Salisbury, the two county towns, both medieval places and cathedral cities, are also the market-towns to which come the farmers, shepherds, and peasants of the chalk hills and the downland valleys.

WINCHESTER FROM ST. GILES HILL

Winchester is the county town of Hampshire, and one of the most historic
cities of England. The town is identified with the Camelot of King Arthur and,
under the later Saxon kings and on into Norman times, it was the capital of
England. The cathedral, seen here, is dedicated to St. Swithun, the Saxon
bishop whose festival is celebrated on 15 July.

If you go to either of them on market-day you will see a cross-section
of the people whose life is spent in the midst of this typical English scenery.
They are small farmers for the most part, with all the independence of the
Kentish yeoman and something of the dour nature of the husbandman whose
work is in the grey Pennines. Not so many decades ago this was a great
sheep country and every farm had its flocks of thousands of head, which
grazed at will over the grassy hills, cutting it short as efficiently as a lawn-
mower. But a change has come over the face of the land, as anyone who
travels over the high road of Salisbury Plain can see for himself. The flocks
of sheep are fewer and sparer, and for miles on end the grass is rank and
uncropped. Though the plateau still invites the wayfarer to explore its
tracks on foot, it is no longer the rich sheep country that Nature intended.
Instead the land has been ploughed up to the higher slopes and here and
there fine crops of wheat, oats, or barley are harvested. Elsewhere the return
is poor, for the land is flinty, the climate of the upper slopes cold and damp,
and an exceptional season is needed to gladden the farmer's heart.

Though the highlands are poor, the valleys which intersect them are compensation. Where the Itchen and the Test flow southward from the Downs the land is rich, so, too, is the valley of the Avon in Wiltshire and its tributary the Wylye. On the north of the Downs another Avon, flowing westward to Bath and Bristol, waters a fertile plain which separates the chalk hills from the limestone of the Cotswolds.

Along these charming, winding valleys there is a picture of English agriculture at its best. Broad meadows flank the streams, where good head of cattle find pasture for eight months of the year. As the land rises, ploughland takes the place of the meadows and there are fine crops of vegetables and corn, interspersed with coppices and thickets rich in timber and undergrowth. Towards the skyline the typical downland pastures replace the arable fields. To the wayfarer who walks or rides up one of these valleys towards midday, under the summer sun, the contrasts of colour are greater still than the contrasts in scenic types. The water-meadows are always emerald green, the ploughed fields brown and grey, picked out with the white flints on the upper slopes, merging into the green of the hills, which is entirely different from the green of the water-meadows. Down by the river

LACOCK, WILTSHIRE

Lacock is a Wiltshire village near Chippenham, lying in the valley that separates the chalk downs from the southern range of the Cotswold Hills. It contains some of the finest examples in Britain of stone-built and half-timbered houses dating from the sixteenth and seventeenth centuries.

ALDBOURNE, VILLAGE OF WILTSHIRE

Among the Wiltshire Downs are many small villages, of which Aldbourne is
typical. A medieval settlement, it was once one of the chief centres of the
sheep-rearing industry that dominated the economic life of Wiltshire from
the earliest times. Many of the cottages grouped about the late Gothic church
date from the sixteenth and seventeenth centuries.

there will be some farmhouse or village nestling round its church, gleaming
white in the bright sun, for most of the cottages are flint-built and the
churches fashioned of local stone.

Of no county is it so true as of Wiltshire, in the words of Hilaire Belloc,
that the chalk country is "the meaning of that good land." For some who are
accustomed to the intimate beauties of hedged lanes and meadowlands the
Downs seem featureless because their beauty owes so little to the hand of
man, so much to the hand of Nature. But for the lover of the downlands
they are supreme in their proud solitude, perfect in their bold outlines, with
infinite variety in their very uniformity.

When the first tractors appeared on the rural scene, the hardy Wiltshire
farmers would have none of them. And they were right, because the extent
of land which they had to farm would not have justified the use of such
expensive machines when experiment with them was in its infancy. When
the tractors became reliable and their cost more reasonable, Wiltshire
farmers were swift to adopt them and today on all the larger farms the
tractor does the work which was formerly done by horses and sweat of
human toil. So, too, when the first combine-harvesters were introduced,
Wiltshire farmers would have none of them, and again for a very good

reason. Their arable lands were not extensive enough to justify the expense, but when some sort of co-operative use of harvesters became common, there was found no word of dissent from the yeomen of Wiltshire.

So the conservatism of Wiltshire folk is rather inherent in their land than in their own character, and if they are a little dour and abrupt, it is because the wealth and prosperity which has come to farmers from time to time in a richer, more fertile land has passed them by.

The Downs cover more than three-fifths of Wiltshire. The Vale of Pewsey divides them roughly into two parts and leads at its northern end towards the high slopes of Inkpen Beacon, rising nearly a thousand feet above sea-level and overlooking the plain of Berkshire. The Vale of Pewsey is a world of its own, but it is essentially a world of the chalk country. Here and there it is ten miles or more broad, but always dominated by the Downs on either side. Its farms are richer than in most parts of the county, its homes more prosperous, its villages larger, but always its pastures extend up the hillsides and its life centres on the downlands.

How great is the contrast in the far north-west of Wiltshire, where the traveller across the chalk comes to the edge of the Marlborough Downs and suddenly finds himself looking down into a wide valley picked out with trim hedges and elm trees and interspersed with thick coverts and orchards.

ON TOP OF THE WORLD

The scene is the Wiltshire Downs, unmistakable by reason of the exposed patches of chalk, the scattered scrubby bushes and the isolated larger clumps of trees. The activity is the reclaiming with tractor-drawn plough of this intractable countryside to prepare it for a crop of barley or oats. All through the centuries the chalk land has provided sheep-walks for vast flocks of sheep and it is only within the last twenty-five years that serious efforts have been made to reclaim the higher slopes of the downs.

RAMPARTS OF MAIDEN CASTLE

This is one of the largest and best preserved of the prehistoric earthworks of Britain. It is situated on the lower slopes of the Dorset Downs where they fall away to the valley in which Dorchester is set. The earthworks consist of treble lines of concentric banks and ditches surrounding an open space wherein was an Iron Age village over a hundred and fifty acres in extent. The photograph shows one of the entrances to the earthworks, which were originally perpendicular and surmounted by wooden palisades.

Nowhere in England is the contrast between the highlands and the lowlands more sudden or more certain.

Beyond Wiltshire the downlands stretch away into Dorset and there is a subtle change in their character, as the central mass once more breaks up into distinct ridges, comparable with the North and South Downs of Kent and Sussex. The traveller along the main road from Salisbury to Shaftesbury will mark this distinction, this gradual transition. First his road follows the Salisbury valley, then rises very gradually through Wilton on to a shelf which overlooks the harsh outlines of Cranborne Chase on his left. Not even an occasional clump breaks the regular contours of the Chase, which was one of the great hunting districts in medieval England. It drops away on the south to pleasantly wooded valleys in which nestle substantial villages like Tollard Royal.

At Shaftesbury the traveller comes to a high spur detached from the main mass of chalk hills. The town itself is at the very summit, so that whichever road you take out of Shaftesbury you must go down a steep hill. Perfectly placed for defence, Shaftesbury stands on the edge of its cliff, where one can well realize how it was that its strategic importance in England's story from the earliest time right up to the Civil Wars was second to none. No army advancing from the south-west could cross the hills except here, and a handful of men placed strategically at the summit of the pass would be enough to hold off a whole army. Its great coaching inns testify to its continued importance when every stage-coach between London and the south-western counties paused here for the night after struggling up the long steep hill from Sherborne or the much longer though less steep road from Salisbury.

What a view rewards the traveller from the edge of Shaftesbury cliff! Half of Dorset lies spread before his eyes and the whole of the long extension of the chalk, which is called the North Downs of Dorset and continues the line of Cranborne Chase.

Immediately beneath him there is spread the Vale of Blackmoor, which comprehends almost the whole of Dorset's rural wealth and is indeed one of the richest lands of southern England. He can pick out the scores of little streams which water its meadows and the elms and oaks which give diversity to its immemorial pastures. Beyond is the abrupt face of the chalk downs, which form an unbroken bulwark between the Blackmoor Vale and the sea, and are traversed only by the main road from Yeovil to Dorchester.

Dorchester itself, the county town, is the market centre for hundreds of villages which lie along the narrow valleys winding up into the hills from the parent stream of the Trent. Transport here is still undeveloped and many of the downland villages are served by only a weekly or twice-weekly omnibus, whilst even along the main road from Dorchester to Bridport there is only an infrequent and irregular service.

From Piddletrenthide to Cerne Abbas and Maiden Newton there are

THE OLD TOWN OF SHAFTESBURY
Shaftesbury is one of the largest of the hilltop towns of England. It lies on the fringe of Cranborne Chase and was a great coaching centre. The older part of the town straggles up Gold Hill, shown here.

THE VALE OF THE WHITE HORSE
The whale-back ridges of the Berkshire Downs, the fertile fields of White Horse Vale beneath them, and the rude outline of the running horse that gives its name to both the hill and the vale, are all seen in this magnificent

serried ridges which effectively cut off one valley from its neighbour, even though it be only two or three miles away, as the screes of the Lake District isolate one lakeland settlement from another which is only just across the hill. The main road from Dorchester climbs over the very summit of the hills before its steep ascent into Bridport, where in most winters the road is blocked for days on end with deep snowdrifts, and the view from the summit follows the ridge to the point where it goes down to the sea by Lyme Regis.

That is all of the western downs except for the lonely slopes of the Purbeck Hills which look across to the Isle of Wight and resemble the South Downs of Sussex far more than they do the limestone uplands of north Dorset.

Finally, to complete our survey of the southern downlands there is the no less fascinating off-shoot of the chalk which extends north-eastward from Salisbury Plain towards East Anglia, and which is called in turn the

ON THE BERKSHIRE DOWNS

panorama. The White Horse itself is certainly one of the oldest of the hill figures of England, its outline symbolic of speed and strongly impressionist. It is probably prehistoric in origin and may belong to the New Stone Age.

Berkshire Downs and the Chiltern Hills. As far as the point where it crosses the Thames at Goring, this downland ridge is in keeping with the character of all the downlands described. Its highest distinction is between Lambourn and Wantage, King Alfred's town, where White Horse Hill looks across the Thames Valley to the Cotswold uplands, and links, as it were, the downlands with the limestone hills of central England.

On the face of Uffington Hill is cut another of those figures of the chalk whose origin defies exact knowledge. This is the White Horse which gives its name to the valley beneath, a figure which most authorities accept as at least four thousand years old and one which was probably first cut in the chalk by the warrior herdsmen who built the ramparts of Uffington Camp on the summit of the hill. It may have been just the sign of their tribe, but more probably it was a symbol which had significance in their religion. Hereabouts fresh prosperity has come to the Downs from the many training stables about Lambourn which have made the area second in importance only to Newmarket as a centre of horse-breeding and horse-training.

Beyond the Thames rise the Chiltern Hills, and here the Downs have an entirely different character, for the beech tree, which takes so kindly to the chalk soil, is no longer an occasional feature of the landscape; rather it dominates it for miles and miles. The glory of the Chiltern beech-woods is in autumn, when the green turns to russet, gold, and brown. But the beech-woods have an added significance, for they brought a new kind of rural craft to the countryside, the craft of basket-making and chair-making, which flourishes extensively in most of the villages between the Thames and the main road from London to Aylesbury. Nowadays the craft has been largely superseded by a more organized industry, its centre in High Wycombe, but the woodman with his team of horses and the village craftsman in wood are still the most characteristic figures of the Chiltern Hundreds, a district which once harboured highwaymen who preyed upon the coaches and carriages which had to cross the hills from London to Oxford or Aylesbury.

Many of the Chiltern villages and small towns have beauty of architecture as well as charm of setting. Among the larger, Amersham and Chesham stand out, and farther north Berkhamsted, with its historic castle which guarded one of the main passes through the Chilterns in the Middle Ages.

END OF THE HARVEST

The Chiltern Hills are not all beech-wood and rolling commonland. Much of the area, especially that part which falls away to the valley of the Thames, is rich pasture-land, with occasional patches of cornfields, larger and more numerous since the Second World War, when an intensive campaign was inaugurated in the district to increase the acreage under the plough. This scene of fertile cornfields at the end of the harvest, when the crops have been safely stacked and only stubble remains, is in the beautiful countryside near Fingest in Buckinghamshire, where several long valleys reach up from the Thames Valley into the very heart of the Chilterns.

WATER END, NEAR GADDESDEN, HERTS

The Gade is one of several little rivers that rise in the high ground of the Chiltern Hills and flow down between chalk ridges into the valley of the Grand Union Canal. They give some of the most charming scenery in Hertfordshire and Buckinghamshire, well wooded and fertile, with pasture-land and ploughed fields alternating. They are the richest part of the downland heritage, and have a characteristic beauty of their own. This view, taken in the early spring sunshine, shows the park-like country fringing the Gade at Water End, between Hemel Hempstead and Gaddesden.

In the valleys that run down toward the Thames there are Fingest and Turville, both Norman villages, which have been rebuilt, it is true, but have scarcely changed their shape in nine hundred years.

Under the face of the Downs, toward Aylesbury, there is Wendover, which nestles precariously beneath the steep ascent of Combe Hill, and Aldbury, one of southern England's prettiest villages, built round a pond, beside which stand the medieval stocks and whipping post, and a famous old oak tree, which must be five hundred years old and may be much more. But these are only a few of the score or more which make Chiltern villages as distinguished in their own way as the villages beneath the Sussex Downs.

It is indeed a country of every-varying beauty, as attractive as any of the downland landscapes described here. Where the ridge continues by the Dunstable Downs above Royston and towards high-set Saffron Walden, the hills are lower, the views less extensive, but there is the same unchanging character of the chalk country, the same mixture of small farmhouse and trim village, the same hardy quality among the husbandmen and the same sharp contrast between the Downs and the plain beneath that we have seen wherever the chalk hills dominate the landscape.

237

COTSWOLD COUNTRY

Cotswold Country

THE Cotswold country is the very heart of England, a long tract of upland country in which the pulse of rural life beats most strongly. From the Bristol Avon in the south-west, the hills stretch north-eastward, undisputed monarchs of the landscape, as far as the Warwickshire Avon. On the west a high cliff, often exceeding a thousand feet above sea-level, falls abruptly to the valley of the Severn, and looks across the lowlands to the Welsh hills and the Malvern beacons.

From this abrupt edge there are some of the loveliest prospects in the whole of Britain, and some of the most thrilling cameos of scenic beauty; the checker-board pattern of hedged fields and square coppices recedes as the eye follows them to the silver loops of the broad Severn and beyond that to the rising wooded uplands of Herefordshire and Shropshire.

From the other side of the cliff to the south and the east the Wold falls more gently, almost imperceptibly, toward the valley of the Thames. Starting from the cliff you can walk for twenty miles or more in a straight line south-eastward and still be in the Cotswold country. It is a wold in fact as well as in name, a rolling upland plateau intersected with many a little stream and many a deeply eroded valley in which nestle the farmsteads and villages that give it much of its charm.

Such is the Cotswold proper. It covers about eight hundred square miles, every one of which has a fresh surprise for the country lover. It is uniform in character, yet ever different; it reveals change after change in scene, yet paradoxically it is ever the same, a joyous mixture which every Cotswold lover would recognize in a moment.

This tract between the two Avons and between the Severn and the Thames is held by some to be the Cotswold proper, but the Cotswold country extends much farther, northward and southward, for the Wold is only a small part of a long chain of limestone hills which cuts England in two and effectively divides the south-eastern half, which is all man-made like some vast garden, from the sterner and more rugged beauties north and west, which by comparison owe little to the hand of man.

From Dorset the range runs northward, and crosses the Avon near Bath, where the division from the Cotswold Hills is one of name only. North-eastward again from the Warwickshire Avon the razor edge is only rarely broken, and reaches across Northamptonshire and Leicestershire, and along the western borders of Lincolnshire, where it is known appropriately enough as the Cliff. Even that is not the end of it, though it is a long jump from the end of the Cliff across the Humber to where the range goes down to the sea above Whitby and forms the wide expanse of the North York Moors.

There is, however, something strange about this far northern extension of the Cotswold country. It is as though, as the hills stretched farther and farther to the north, they became more and more akin to the typical northern landscape, more rugged in their grandeur, less intimate, less certain in their appeal to the lover of the southern Cotswold. The hand of the north is upon them. Yet, in spite of that, they have a link with the main range of hills.

What is the factor which gives such a wonderful uniformity to such a wide and divergent area, covering so many counties? In a word, it is stone. It is the very native stone of which the hills are fashioned, the oolitic limestone which weathers to a mellow warm hue toning in perfect unison with the strong melody of the hills and valleys. It is a theme which has infinite variations, which is reproduced in the endless stone walls which take the

A DRY-STONE WALLER AT WORK

The craft of dry-stone walling is a traditional one, handed down in Britain since prehistoric ancestors built the lower storeys of their huts in this fashion. The Romans were masters of the craft, though their city walls were basically of rubble and cement. In all the stone districts of Britain, particularly in the Pennines and the Cotswolds, dry-stone walls are still being built. Although they have no cement or other adhesive material, these walls often last for hundreds of years without repair. Here a Cotswold stone-waller is placing the top layer of stones at right-angles to the wall itself, a finishing touch.

BURFORD—GATEWAY TO THE COTSWOLDS

The long broad High Street of Burford, lined with many old houses and cottages half-timbered and built in the characteristic Cotswold stone, makes one of the most pleasant street scenes in England. On the very fringe of the high Wold, Burford, which slopes down to the Windrush river, is an ancient and historic centre of the wool trade that brought wealth to the whole of the Cotswold country. The medieval stained glass in its church is some of the finest in Britain and there are still a number of old houses belonging to the time when this prosperous community was at the height of its fame.

place of hedges, in the Elizabethan manor-houses and farms, in the Tudor and Jacobean cottages (many of which are wonderfully preserved in the centre of the villages), in the towers and the walls of village churches and even in the modern dwellings, which are the visual sign of rehousing.

Throughout the Cotswold country the limestone is still today the principal building stone. Except on the very fringes of the wold, brick has never taken the place of stone, the unsightly villas of suburbia which mar every other part of the country here take tone from the landscape and mellow in an incredibly short time to form part and parcel of the rural scene.

It is stone, then, which gives the Cotswold country its unfailing grace, but it is as though man had gilded the lily, for this man-made grace is superimposed on a scenic backcloth which in its own way has no peer in England. The rolling contours of the hills, the broad backs which stretch as far as eye can see, the rhythmic rising and falling of the grassy slopes, the narrow winding valleys of such streams as the Windrush—all these stand high in the order of natural beauty.

It is Nature, too, who has determined through the centuries, as much as she does today, the pattern of rural life. Nature has endowed the Cotswold country with a soil and a climate which produce perfect pasturage for sheep. Historically, the Wold is one of the great wool-producing areas of Britain.

241

ROUNDING UP SHEEP ON CLEEVE COMMON

Sheep-rearing is still an important part of the Cotswold economy, even though
it no longer dominates the life of the people as it did when the medieval woollen
trade was at its height. Today the accent is on ploughed land and it is the higher
slopes of the Wold, particularly near the western escarpment, that are still
sheep-walks. Here shepherds on horseback and on foot, with the help of their
many sheepdogs, are driving the sheep to the valley for the annual dipping.

Even today, when the importance of sheep is diminishing, Gloucestershire,
Northamptonshire, and Leicestershire are among the greatest sheep counties.
Because it is a sheep country pre-eminently, the villages have stayed small,
for the rearing of sheep takes far less labour than the working of arable land,
and the real unit of rural life has remained the manor-house or manor-farm.

Here, then, is another cause of unity, the unity which affects not only the
scene but the spirit of the people, who, generation after generation, have gone
about their daily tasks, their whole craft and skill devoted to a finer and still
finer breed of sheep. Not that the villages need call on the outside world for
supplies, for they are nearly all villages of the valleys and near the streams
there are thousands of precious acres which can be ploughed.

Where the valleys widen there are occasional herds of cattle in the lush
meadows, but cattle-rearing is not, and never can be, the first pride of the
Cotswold villages. They look to the uplands and to the spacious sheep-walks.
In times of crisis the ploughshare has ravaged the sheep-walks in an effort to

produce more grain for the country's need, and the Cotswold soil has responded nobly to this new call upon its resources, but when the time of crisis is over the fields return to their primeval grass, close-cropped by sheep.

This bounty of Nature and this traditional craft of the Cotswold people have contributed another important, though man-made, feature of the landscape—the number of magnificent fifteenth-century churches, some of them among the finest in England, which date from the time when Cotswold sheep brought great wealth and prosperity to the village communities, and when for a hundred years or more the Wold ranked with East Anglia as one of the two richest parts of England. Then every field that could be was given over to sheep, every farmhouse was a factory, manufacturing woollen cloth by the hands of its womenfolk, while its menfolk tended the flocks.

The lofty towers of the churches beckon the wayfarer across the hills and the contemporary stone houses of the merchants who collected and distributed wool and woollen cloth stand as memorials to this, the first of Britain's

STOW-ON-THE-WOLD

One of the chief modern tourist centres of the Cotswold country, Stow-on-the-Wold is an ancient town and market centre that still retains a medieval appearance enhanced, as in the case of all the Cotswold towns, by the uniformity and excellent weathering qualities of the local stone used for building. In this photograph the old (the posting-house) and the new (the office of a bank) are side by side yet give little impression of discordance.

many industrial revolutions. Burford, Northleach, Stow-on-the-Wold, Moreton-in-Marsh, Winchcomb, Chipping Campden—those are just a few of the centres which were then most flourishing and which, though now they are dwarfed by the nineteenth-century growth of the valley towns, like Cheltenham and Gloucester, are still prosperous market-towns, changing little in size or shape or appearance with the centuries, as vital and vivid today as they were five hundred years ago.

But the nineteenth century brought another industrial revolution to the Cotswold country, though mercifully not to the central part of the range. The grace that man had added in stone, men seemed likely to destroy with iron; for iron is the mineral resource of the Cotswold country. Though the existence of ironstone has been known since Roman times, it is only since the growth of the Midland industrial belt in the last century that its economic

CHIPPING CAMPDEN

With Northleach, Chipping Campden was one of the two great centres of the medieval wool industry. It retains today many fine houses that reflect the prosperity of those times and a church which is one of the most magnificent in all the Cotswold country. Here in the background is the 120-ft.-high tower of the church, a splendid example of the Perpendicular style of Gothic. In the foreground is a group of almshouses founded by Sir Baptist Hicks, who was Sheriff of London in 1613 and a great benefactor of Chipping Campden.

COTSWOLD STONE QUARRY

All over the Cotswold country stone is quarried today as much as ever it was. It remains, with ironstone, one of the two most valuable natural resources of this countryside. Here at a quarry near Stanway in Gloucestershire can be seen the great depth of solid stone that underlies the rolling scenery. Vast slabs are blasted away from the quarry face and trimmed on the spot to the more manageable shapes and sizes shown here. Then they are carted from the quarry and dressed for use in building, while the fragments are taken separately and used for road dressings and many other purposes.

importance has become great. Because much of the wold is within easy reach of the Midland industries, transport of the iron has been easy and the iron has gone to industry rather than industry going to the iron. The latter would have been an irreparable tragedy. It must have wrecked the Cotswold heritage of beauty as surely as the blast-furnaces of Yorkshire and the cotton towns of Lancashire have despoiled the scenic beauty of the Pennine foothills.

As it is, the ironstone mines or quarries are seldom conspicuous, though here and there in Northamptonshire the tall chimneys, the surface works and the slag-heaps of the ironworks are eyesores which can be seen for miles around. But more often than not the ironstone is quarried and carried away by road or rail to distant factories, and the only scars on the Cotswold's beauty are an

THE VIEW FROM SHENBERROW HILL
In the time before recorded history there was an encampment on the spot
from which this photograph was taken. What is now the famous Vale of Evesham was then uninhabited forest-land; now it is one of the most fertile vales

occasional quarry, which, once its working life is over, soon becomes grass-
covered and merges once more into the all-embracing landscape.

Partly it is the very sparseness of the population which has prevented the
growth of industry near the ironstone quarries, for labour is always one of the
most important factors in the setting up of a new industry, and in the Cotswold country, even in the towns which lie at the foot of the Wold, there is no
reservoir of labour and little to induce the townsman to migrate.

So, the industrial communities in the Cotswold country are few and far
between, and are scarcely an integral part of the pattern of life. There are
ironworks a few miles from Melton Mowbray, to which workers come by
cycle and car and omnibus from villages many miles away, but the villages
they live in are rural villages and they themselves have never taken on the
mien of Britain's industrial millions. Rather it is the reverse. The Cotswold
country has need of more and more rural workers, for in the last hundred
years the number of workers on the land has steadily diminished and now
when harvest-time comes round the farmer must depend, to a far greater
extent than in most parts of Britain, on casual labour to bring in his crops.

If we think of the central part of the Wold as that part of the country
which is bounded on the west by the Severn and the Warwickshire Avon,
on the south by the Wiltshire Avon and the upper reaches of the Thames, on

ON A NORTHERN SPUR OF THE COTSWOLDS
in England. At the left, on the long line of the Malvern Hills which flank the
northern side of the vale, can be seen Dumbleton Hill; on the right is Bredon
Hill. Behind, in the far distance, are some of the mountain peaks of Wales.

the north and east by the main road from Stratford-on-Avon to Banbury and
Oxford, then we have a rough triangle of countryside which bears comparison
for its manifold attractions with any district of the British Isles of comparable
size, and which certainly yields to none in its wealth of lovely villages, sequestered valleys and lonely hillsides.

As in the downland country of the south-east, rural life chiefly centres
on the small market-towns; but to the south some of the hill villages look to
Bristol, in the west to Gloucester and to Stratford-on-Avon, and in the east
to Oxford. These are the great centres of communication and include among
them, especially Bristol, all the industrial life which the last century and a half
have contrived to bring within fifty miles of the Cotswolds.

The main ridge of the Wold runs northward and north-eastward from a
point about ten miles from Bristol. Unlike the chalk downlands, which owe
so much of their diversity to the occasional river valleys which intersect them,
for the whole of the fifty miles that this ridge is within the Gloucestershire
boundaries it is unbroken by any considerable stream. All the rivers flow
southward and eastward into the valleys of the Avon and Thames, and the
escarpment is a real watershed in the fullest meaning of the term. It is only
when we come near to the Warwickshire boundary that we find a few tributaries of the Avon cutting deep combes into the northern escarpment.

For the most part, therefore, it is a continuous cliff, which rises with surprising abruptness from the Vale of Severn. Near its southern extremity, where the Vale of Severn is known as the Vale of Berkeley and the romantic ruins of Berkeley Castle guard the strategic road beside the river, the hills are often wooded. In one of their folds lies Stroud, a small manufacturing town of no mean importance, the exception, as it were, that proves the rule of the Wold's escape from industrial development. But Stroud is no typical manufacturing town. Indeed, it is unlike any other, and stands to Cotswold sheep as does High Wycombe to Chiltern timber. In the heyday of medieval prosperity, Stroud existed only as a market-town where the wealthy merchants carried on their rich business. But as the age of machinery drew on, competition from northern mills began to be severe, the local rural industry of weaving and cloth-making became centralized in Stroud, and right up to the present day it has remained the chief centre in England of broadcloth-making.

THE HISTORIC WOLDS

Like Bath, Stroud is built up the hillside, and its few factory chimneys are dwarfed into insignificance by the frowning faces of the hills. There is an old-world atmosphere about this famous Gloucestershire town which makes it a real part of the Cotswold scene as surely as romantic villages like Bibury or Stow-on-the-Wold. It is the first sign of work, other than the toil of the land, the traveller will find after leaving behind him the suburbs of Bristol. These stretch almost to Chipping Sodbury, which is in the very foot-hills of the Cotswolds, while near-by Badminton Park, one of the most gracious expanses of parkland in all England, is no more than an enclosed section of the Wold, as indeed are all the parks in the Cotswold country, for where there are trees Nature gives a park-like quality to the landscape, which needs no artifice of man to make it a park in name as well as in fact.

The road rises steeply from Stroud's sixteenth-century town hall to the breezy expanse of Minchinhampton Common, which looks across the valley to Painswick Beacon, one of the highest points in the whole of the Wold. Away to the east wooded parklands lead to Cirencester, one of Gloucestershire's most historic centres and one of its most charming market-towns.

Cirencester breathes the very spirit of the Cotswolds. It has been a centre of the sheep country since the Roman town of Corinium stood on its site, where two great roads met, one the mighty Fosse Way, the trunk road between the south-west and the north-east of England, the other which connected the farthermost settlements in the Welsh Marches with the busy Roman towns of Wiltshire and Hampshire.

Nearly two thousand years ago "Ziren," as the local people call it, became a centre of commerce and the clearing house of the many Roman villas which were dotted over this part of the Cotswolds. It never lost its importance and its history is the epitome of the history of Cotswold towns. Though the Saxons razed it to the ground in the sixth century, it rose again from its ashes to become a place of fresh importance under Norman rule, with a castle and an abbey, of which there is still a single gateway standing.

248

THE CLOISTERS OF GLOUCESTER CATHEDRAL

Gloucester is today, as it always has been, the chief business and commercial
centre of the Cotswold countryside. It lies on the banks of the Severn only a
few miles from the escarpment of the hills. Its cathedral is especially famous
for its late fourteenth-century cloisters, formerly part of the abbey, which
are the finest in England, each walk being 150 ft. long and 12 ft. wide.

The parish church is a memorial to its long history and to its medieval prosperity. It contains many signs of its Norman foundation, while its wonderful tower, more than a hundred and sixty feet high in all, and so heavy that it must be propped up by giant buttresses, is in the tradition of the great churches of England, built and enriched from fortunes made in the woollen trade, and dates from the first half of the fifteenth century. All who approach Cirencester, from whatever direction, must be struck by the grandeur and the noble proportion of this great church, but few probably realize that it is larger than at least three English cathedrals and that it is one of the largest parish churches in the whole country.

Only a few miles away to the north, under the shadow of Chedworth Wood, there is another historic place of pilgrimage which links naturally with the romantic history of Cirencester. This is the Chedworth Roman villa, one of the most perfectly preserved of its kind and a veritable lesson in the culture of an age which many regard as uncivilized. The Roman villa was a self-contained entity, the equivalent of the medieval manor, which it resembled in many ways, for it had its own farm, its own workshops and its own rural industries. Here the wealthy Roman merchants set up their establishments and used the labour of the British peoples, who gladly accepted the protection of Rome. Fully sixteen hundred years ago, if the ruins are any guide, the prosperity of the Wold must have been as great relatively as at any time in its history, its standards of comfort and way of living scarcely less attractive than in the present day.

It was the accident of a landslide which preserved the Chedworth "villa," for the hillside collapsed on it when it was still comparatively recently

MEDIEVAL
DOVECOT

In the Middle Ages a stone-built dovecot adjoined almost every large farmhouse and manorhouse. A number of these old buildings survive, such as this one in a farmyard near Minster Lovell. Often the dovecot has been reconstructed and now serves a useful purpose as barn or storehouse. Others are retained as curious relics of a past age, when doves were kept, not as now for ornament, but for the reason that when weather or other circumstances made the hunting of animals for meat impossible the dovecot acted as a reserve larder.

TURNPIKE HOUSE

Marshfield is in the extreme south of Gloucestershire near the border of Wiltshire and on the old road from Bristol to Chippenham. The photograph shows that dry-stone walling, even here on the very fringe of the Cotswold country, takes the place of the traditional English hedge. The house, which is on the site of the east gate of Marshfield, is an old turnpike house, once the home of the official collector of tolls from users of the road in the first great road-building era of modern England. The receipts from the turnpike were used to pay for the upkeep of the road.

built and there it lay buried until modern archaeologists excavated it.

It was a courtyard house, two storeys high, solidly built from local stone, with its upper storey of wattle and daub. There were workshops along one side of the courtyard, the living-rooms along another. The living-rooms were not just utility chambers, but were lavishly appointed, with paintings on the walls and tessellated floors carrying beautiful work designed from themes of mythology and pure imagination. The whole establishment was centrally heated by an elaborate system of flues, the furnace no doubt fed by the timber which in those days covered most of the valleys of the Cotswolds. Corinium was the market-town to which this, and hundreds of other villas like it, looked in the same way as the surrounding villages look today to Cirencester.

One of the loveliest drives over the Wold is along the Fosse Way from Cirencester to Stow-on-the-Wold, and on either side of this road are some of the most beautiful of Gloucestershire villages. First there is the valley of the Coln, which actually rises in the hills above Cheltenham, very near the source of the Thames at Seven Springs, which is only a few miles from the steep road into Gloucester from Birdlip Hill. No one in search of beauty should seek the source of the Thames. He will find nothing but a notice and a weedy pond, as unromantic a beginning of Britain's greatest river as one could possibly imagine. Rather will he find beauty in the valley of the Coln, where the villages are lovely, and Bibury, which lies where the road from Cirencester to Burford crosses the river, is one of the loveliest villages in England.

As in many other Cotswold villages, the river runs down the main street, but the great distinction of Bibury resides in its Elizabethan manor-house,

ARLINGTON MILL, BIBURY

Bibury is on the River Coln, which, before the use of modern fuel, powered
a number of mills, mainly built of the local Cotswold stone, ranking among the
prettiest of a typically English kind of building. Arlington Mill, shown here,
is on the edge of the village and is now in the care of the National Trust. In a
countryside that has many lovely villages, Bibury was picked out by William
Morris as the most beautiful in England.

in the three-arched bridge which spans the river, and the gabled Tudor
cottages of Arlington Row.

The next lovely valley to be explored is that of the Windrush, which
waters the countryside about Burford and flows down between the hills
towards the Thames. Burford itself is famous for the stained glass in the parish
church, but that is only one facet of its ageless charm. Its old inns, its many
Tudor cottages and its steep tree-lined main street combine to make it a most
distinguished Cotswold town.

Higher up the river are Upper and Lower Slaughter, the latter distinguished by its many foot-bridges across the stream which divides the road
from the cottages. There is design in Lower Slaughter and quaintness and
genuine beauty and, above all, in spite of its tourist attractions it has never
become spoilt and the roads which lead down to it have not been widened.

If only the same could be said of its more famous neighbour, Bourton-on-the-Water. That, too, might rank with Britain's loveliest villages. But, alas, the motoring age has almost ruined its loveliness, the road to it is vastly "improved," the original village is almost lost in a number of new houses which, unlike most Cotswold buildings, have not yet toned with the landscape. One feels that its fame as "Venice of the Cotswolds" has robbed it of its own particular fascination without bringing to it one whit of the beauty of that other Venice across the sea.

Downstream from Burford is Witney. Not truly of the Wold (for here the hills flatten out into the broad lowlands of the Thames Valley about Oxford), it is yet more really the "gateway" to the Wold than Burford, although the latter proudly claims that title! If you travel from Oxford on the high road to Cheltenham, once you are past Witney you feel you have crossed the threshold of a new world. The road rises gently to the windswept downs and the first of the stone walls makes its dramatic appearance.

Witney resembles Stroud in that it is primarily a market-town and only secondarily a centre of industry. Witney's traditional industry is a very famous one, for Witney blankets are almost as much a household word as Wilton

THE ROLLRIGHT STONES

The Rollright Stones are a group of three prehistoric monuments that stand near the edge of the Cotswolds above the village of Great Rollright in Oxfordshire. This view shows the battered and worn remnants of the great stone circle known as the King's Men. Like all the other circles of the Stone Age it was probably a temple connected with sun-worship.

carpets or Stilton cheese. That is another link which the town has with the Wold, for it was, of course, the Cotswold sheep which provided the raw material for the blanket factory.

The Evenlode is a scarcely less distinguished river than the Coln or the Windrush—nor are its villages any less lovely or sequestered. It rises within a few miles of Stow-on-the-Wold and takes a winding but generally southerly course through Evenlode itself and on to Kingham and Charlbury. There is nothing special to say of these places; indeed in that very fact lies part of their attraction. They are just typical of the best of Cotswold architecture set in the midst of typical Cotswold scenery. Could any man desire more?

TREES OF THE WOLD

Near the Evenlode the word "wychwood" occurs more than once as part of a place-name—Shipton-under-Wychwood, for instance. This recalls the time, many centuries ago, when large tracts of this part of the Wold formed a forest where the wych-elm predominated. It is, in fact, the only district of the Wold traditionally wooded. Now all that survive to give the name substance are a few small coppices and thickets and one larger wood in which, if truth be told, the wayfarer will have to look hard to discover either the wych-elm or the wych-hazel. The trees of the Wold in the present century are chiefly the beech and the fir, particularly the latter, whose hardy roots "take" easily in the rather thin soil-covering of the uplands. Wide areas are, however, almost as treeless as Dartmoor or Cranborne Chase, though, as in the case of those other two, the valleys are well wooded enough. There the trees are the common English lowland ones, conspicuous among them being the oak, the ash, and the chestnut, with the lime a more recent but always welcome addition to the company, its palest green contrasting well with the evergreens.

The quiet peasant life of the Cotswold farmers and villagers has contributed in no small measure to the strength and variety of the country's folk-lore. Romances are woven round everything the origin of which is not clearly visible. Fairy glens and pixies' holes and devil's jumps are common enough as local descriptions of some of Nature's more remarkable freaks of landscape. It was, however, when the people tried to explain the many links with prehistoric man existing in the Wold that the development of folk-lore was most prolific.

Beside the lonely road which runs from Stow-on-the-Wold toward Banbury there are three prehistoric monuments, within a stone's throw of each other. They were set up by Stone Age man nearly four thousand years ago. One is a "stone circle," a complete circle of tall standing stones (though some have been knocked down and a few used for road building). This, a kind of miniature Stonehenge, was probably a temple in honour of the sun god. The second is more certain in origin and purpose. It consists of the slab-like stones which were originally the chamber of a burial mound, once covered in earth which, through the lapse of time, has been eroded and washed away, leaving the stones naked to the sky. This must have been the last resting place of the chief of a tribe, or perhaps of its high priest. The third monument is a single

A GARGOYLE FROM WINCHCOMB CHURCH

Winchcomb, one of the oldest towns near the Wold, was the site of a Saxon abbey. The present church of St. Peter was begun in 1490 and so is one of the later medieval churches. That explains the wonderful series of gargoyles which appear in the clerestory and aisle roofs, comparable with the gargoyles of Thaxted Church in Essex. This one represents a winged man in pain.

standing stone, of which even today nothing is known for certain, though it is a fairly safe guess to hazard that it is a stone commemorating some great man of the tribe or some great victory won. Thus through all phases of civilization has man commemorated great men and great events for the sake of posterity.

So even with the help of the archaeological research of the twentieth century, we can only approximate to the truth concerning this most complex and famous group of monuments which are known as the Rollright Stones, after the village of Great Rollright near-by. To the citizens of an earlier and less learned age they defied rational explanation. It is easy, then, to appreciate how legends grew up round them and were passed down by word of mouth from generation to generation.

THE LEGEND OF THE ROLLRIGHT STONES

This is the outline of a legend which has often been recorded with many variations. Long, long ago, it seems, a tribal chieftain planned to become king of all England. He was encamped on this bare ridge of the Wold, together with his knights and a company of soldiers. Now it chanced that he met a witch who promised him that if he really craved to be king of England he should fulfil his wish if only he could see the village of Long Compton (no difficult feat, since Long Compton lies just beneath the ridge in the valley towards Stratford-on-Avon). But, said the witch, let him think carefully before doing this, because failure meant death.

The chieftain, it seems, was no coward, for, undeterred by the warning, he stepped out briskly toward the edge of the hill. Just at the moment when he was about to descry the village in the valley, the witch (fulfilling the second part rather than the first part of her prophecy) turned him to stone, and there he stands today, the King Stone, a permanent memorial to the proverb that pride has a fall.

While this was going on, the prince's knights were whispering together plotting to usurp the king's rights. The witch was shocked at this exhibition of perfidy and turned them to stone likewise. There they stand today, the second of the monuments described, known far and wide as the Whispering Knights of Great Rollright. This left the company of soldiers without a leader. They could think of nothing to do except to turn brigands and prey on the countryside. The witch felt she could not allow this, so she turned them also to stone—and so the stone circle is known as "The King's Men."

So far we have barely touched on the real show-places of the central Cotswold. These are Winchcomb, Stow-on-the-Wold, Broadway, Chipping Campden, and Moreton-in-Marsh, not forgetting Chipping Norton, though this latter is more in the nature of a market-town pure and simple. Each of these has an illustrious history and retains many fine buildings in keeping with its historic heritage.

Winchcomb has been a place of importance since Saxon days. It lies just under the hills only a few miles from Cheltenham. Of the famous abbey which flourished for several centuries until the dissolution of the monasteries not a stick or stone remains, but the lofty-towered parish church, chiefly built

XVII. THATCHED COTTAGES AT GREAT TEW, OXFORDSHIRE

XVIII. NAUNTON-IN-THE-VALE, A VILLAGE OF THE COTSWOLDS

XIX.　BATHFORD HILL, NEAR BATH, SOMERSET

in the Perpendicular style, will remind the wayfarer of two other great Cotswold churches—those of Cirencester and Northleach. Its collection of grotesque gargoyles is one of the finest in the country—in itself worth a visit.

Stow-on-the-Wold, by contrast, as its name suggests, stands on some of the highest ground in the very centre of the hills. Like Shaftesbury in Dorset, it is approached, whichever way you come, by a long ascent. Its fine market-place is surrounded by stone buildings, many of them in the finest Cotswold tradition. There is an air of departed glory about Stow; in the Middle Ages it was one of the great centres of the woollen trade and it would not have you forget it, but it is still proud and stately even though its wealth today is chiefly derived from tourists who come in large numbers to visit it.

ARCHITECTURAL BEAUTIES OF THE COTSWOLDS

Broadway and Chipping Campden are separated by only four or five miles of hill-country. The former lies just inside Worcestershire, the latter across the county boundary in Gloucestershire. Broadway, like Stow, is a place of atmosphere. It consists of a single long, wide main street straggling up towards the lofty summit of Broadway Hill. Its stone houses are old and mellow, its coaching inns large and wealthy-looking. All the best periods of English architecture are represented here, from the sixteenth century to the present day. So it is at Chipping Campden. The latter has added beauty in some still older buildings dating from the late fourteenth or early fifteenth centuries, and in some of the finest examples of Georgian architecture modified to the Cotswold style. The town hall, the market hall, the vast parish church, the incomparable row of old almshouses—those are only a few of the highlights of one of Britain's most fascinating small towns—just too large to be a village, but not nearly large enough to be called urban.

Finally, Moreton-in-Marsh, though geographically a town of the plain, fully preserves the tradition of the Wold with its numerous old stone houses, fine church, and ancient inns. Though it can boast less that is remarkable than Campden, it has no need to blush, for it has grace and a restful tranquillity and a great wealth of mellow beauty.

The Oxford canal, which follows roughly the course of the highroad from Oxford to Coventry, marks a clear-cut boundary between the two great divisions of the Cotswold country. It is a far more complete division than any change in the contours or characteristic scenery would seem to warrant, but the wayfarer travelling in a general north-easterly direction, while noting the change, might find it difficult to define.

What then is this significant but hardly perceptible change? It is nothing in Nature, and yet it affects the very essence of the scene. In a word, it is the stone walls. In the central Wold round Stow and Broadway every upland landscape is bounded by the grey-stone walls—dry-stone walls in the tradition bequeathed two thousand years ago by the Roman masons. Beyond the Oxford canal they cease, their place being largely taken by hedges in the manner of the typical English landscape. Their absence makes all the difference in the world to the country scene. Here and there they appear again—round

Aynho and Croughton, for instance, which is well on the way to Buckingham —and when they do, it is almost with a shock that we realize we are still in the Cotswold country and so by inference identify the stone walls as the salient feature of the Cotswolds proper, the one individual feature which above all others distinguishes them from every other district of England.

Apart from this one difference there is little change in the nature of the country, which goes on and on in an infinite succession of rolling hill and dale across the Oxfordshire boundary into Northamptonshire. The villages are stone-built, the churches just as noble, the generous coppices and woods still diversify the scene, and there are many lofty view-points rising above the general level of the hills and rewarding the wayfarer who climbs them with panoramas as wide and varied as from the peaks of Gloucestershire and Warwickshire.

The ordnance map shows these peaks all within a dozen miles as the crow flies—Priors Marston 662 ft., Arbury 735 ft., Newnham 658 ft., and Borough 653 ft. Those are just four of the highest points on the almost continuous ridge which preserves the line of Broadway Hill and Edge Hill. The last of the four rises steeply behind the little town of Daventry, its bold outline broken by the incredible array of masts and meshing which is the B.B.C. Daventry transmitting station. Here is a new rural industry, or rather a link between

BY THE DIKLER BROOK

Go in what direction you will from high-set Stow-on-the-Wold, you must drop into the valley of one of the several streams that diversify the scenery of this part of the Wold. The Dikler Brook, seen here, is one of the most graceful. It rises near the summit of the hills above Chipping Campden and flows down a steep wooded valley into the Windrush. At this point, only a mile from Stow-on-the-Wold, Upper Swell Mill, gleaming brightly in the winter sunshine, is almost surrounded by mature timber. The stunted willows growing by the brink of the river are a feature of the Cotswold valleys.

SNOWSHILL, GLOUCESTERSHIRE

Six miles from Winchcomb, almost directly under the slopes of Broadway Hill, Snowshill is one of the many villages that nestle in the folds of the Cotswolds where they fall away to the Severn Valley. The trim grouping of church (in this case an old one completely rebuilt less than a hundred years ago), manor-farm, and scattered cottages, is typical of all these Cotswold villages.

modern mechanical civilization and rural life. It is a symbol of the new in the midst of the immemorial and unchanging, as significant in its own way as the increasing tendency for farm labourers to own motor-cycles which take them swiftly and cheaply to the synthetic attractions of town life.

Whatever the cause, there are many parishes in this very rural part of Northamptonshire in which the population has dwindled since the turn of the century. That is, of course, a national problem of rural England rather than a local one; but it is one which is felt most in the lovely agricultural districts such as the Cotswold country. In the rural areas near the big towns, such as the downlands of London's countryside, there is the same drift from the country to the town.

Here in the midst of hundreds of square miles of unbroken country, where an expedition to the nearest big town is a long day's adventure, the case is very different. If the son of the soil leaves his job on the farm and seeks work in the town, there his home has to be. He uproots himself from all the ties of home and village. He scarcely ever returns. So the pattern of life is slowly changing, and the chances are, if the wayfarer meets the rural worker wending his weary way homeward at the close of the day's work, that he will see an old or oldish man with relatively few years left to him of active work.

As we drive or walk through the old villages which lie between the crest of the hills and the valley of the Ouse we may be struck by the outward and

COMPTON WYNYATES

There are many magnificent manor-houses in the Cotswold country, especially where it extends north-eastward into Warwickshire and Leicestershire. Compton Wynyates is one of the largest and best-preserved of the medieval manors. It lies four miles from Shipston-on-Stour and is the seat of the Marquess of Northampton. The present buildings, though restored, largely date from Tudor and Elizabethan days. The fantastically shaped chimneys, the half-timbered gables and the stone facade, the square-headed porch and the irregular square-headed windows date from the sixteenth century.

visible signs of this dangerous trend. If we visit the local inn, which remains essentially the village club, there will be few young men to welcome us; pitifully few children will be playing in the village; the vicar may tell us that he has not had a wedding for a twelvemonth. We may well wonder whether even the new cottages, smartly built of Cotswold stone, like their centuries-old neighbours, which are appearing in increasing numbers as part of the post-war drive for rural rehousing, will be inducement enough to hold those few of the younger men and women who remain.

Perhaps the very beauty of the villages palls on those who have dwelt in them all their lives. But certainly there are very many which are uncommonly lovely. There are Moreton Pinkney, and Canons Ashby, Farthingstone and Great Everdon, Preston Capes and Newnham. If we say that none of them has any special claim to distinction, we are praising the high level of their attractions rather than detracting from the individual charm of any one of them. They each have a pleasant church of local stone, an old manor-house and a varying number of old cottages, some thatched and some stone-roofed. Above all, the country-lover who seeks out each of them in turn will necessarily have seen some of the loveliest of the country and some of its most arresting viewpoints before the winding lanes bring him to his destination.

A grand feature of all the Cotswold country is the wealth of gated roads which give motoring or cycling a fresh intimacy with the spirit of the land; in this part of the Northamptonshire uplands these gated roads have become green lanes or tracks, perfect for walking yet retaining beneath the grass a firm surface which prevents them becoming impassable through mud in winter. The only traffic which disturbs their calm today is the occasional farm wagon going from farmyard to village. Some of them go on for mile after mile, often athwart the ridges so that they rise and fall with a bewildering succession of scenic change which takes in every kind of country from sheep pasture to woodland and ploughed field.

These green tracks and tiny roads are at their best in the countryside which lies between the Daventry-Northampton road and the crest of the hills which here follow a nearly straight line from Daventry to Market Harborough. From the tiny village of Dodford, itself only just escaping the turmoil of the A5 highway, yet rich in lovely examples of the sixteenth- and seventeenth-century builders' art, two such open ways extend, one northward to Norton, the other westward toward Daventry. Both are as fascinating as any. From Heyford another runs north to Brington, which is on the fringe of the tree-studded expanse of Althorp Park, approached by one of the noblest avenues in

EARTHWORKS ON PAINSWICK HILL

On the highest part of the Wold where it sweeps north-eastward above the valley of the Severn there is a series of ancient hill fortresses, the entrance of one of which is shown in this photograph. They all consist of ramparts and ditches surrounding what must once have been a village or settlement, and they probably date from the early Iron Age. The banks, which were once perpendicular, have been partly levelled by weather over a span of more than two thousand years. From Clifton Down above Bristol to Bredon Hill nearly a dozen of these ancient camps have been found.

all the Midlands; yet another extends for nearly three miles north from Long Buckby, high-set centre of a fine stretch of rolling hills.

It would be futile to list more of them. The wayfarer must discover them for himself with the simple help of the one-inch ordnance map, on which they appear as "white" roads often defined by dotted lines from which he can infer that they are unhampered by fence or hedge. There is no better way of exploring this typical part of rural England than by following the course of these roads from village to village, from farm to farm.

It is a far cry from the heart of the Cotswold country round Stroud and Broadway to the wide-spreading wolds of Leicestershire. Yet they are part of the same range of hills and there is a definite unity of scenic and architectural character between them.

Uppingham, which lies just off the Wold in Rutland, smallest and most intimate of the English shires, is as much a town of the stone belt as Chipping Campden or Stow-on-the-Wold. Its countryside is certainly less well known, but no less colourful, no less gay and carefree in summer and no less awe-inspiring in its loneliness in winter. Here, as in the Northamptonshire uplands,

CAUDLE GREEN, GLOUCESTERSHIRE

The small farmhouses and hamlets add enormously to the beauty of the Cotswold valleys. In this picturesque group are all the elements that go to make up the typical Cotswold scene. There are the stone-built farmhouse with its trim garden, the stone walls, made of the selfsame Cotswold stone as the farmhouse, and the rich woodlands that rise from the floor of the valley almost to the summit of the hills. There is Cotswold stone everywhere, for many of the byways and lanes are surfaced with chippings, so that the colour scheme of the whole landscape is in keeping with the predominant colours of Nature.

THE STROUD COUNTRY

Stroud is one of the largest towns in the Cotswold country and one of the principal centres of the cloth trade in the west of England. Yet a mile away from it, as this photograph shows, the countryside is totally unspoilt, the rolling hills cultivated and planted with rich woodlands—the entirely characteristic appearance of the Cotswold country, which is like no other part of England. In this picture is Rodborough Castle, a castellated mansion.

there are hedges for the most part and there is something lacking of the uniform warmth of the true Cotswold grey houses. But there are some stone walls, too, and stone-built manor-houses and villages, the same wide sheep pastures on the upper slopes, gracious parklands and wooded dales in the combes, and fine arable land in the valleys which are watered by dozens of little rivers.

For the traveller by road the highway from Leicester to Uppingham catches the spirit of the whole countryside. Rising quickly out of Leicester it reaches the Wold at Houghton, drops down into the village of Billesdon and then rises again to cross the plateau to Belton and Uppingham. For the wayfarer on foot there are paths and tracks just off this road which follow in general the ridges from east to west; for instance, there is that long green track which leads from Ridlington above Belton to Launde Abbey, and then crosses a stream to reach the high road at Tugby. But that is only one of the many scores of green tracks and faint paths which make the Leicestershire Wold a veritable walkers' paradise, as well as the most famous riding country in all England, whether for riding to hounds or for hacking.

The "cliff" of the Wold—the steep face where it faces north and west—is less well-marked here than it is farther south in the Cotswold proper, or than it is northward toward Lincolnshire. Rather the Wold is a wide undulating plateau with many deep valleys eroded out of it and many broad-backed

A COTSWOLD MEET

The Cotswolds have always been great hunting country. "The Hunting Shires," and particularly Leicestershire, fall largely within the belt of limestone country that forms the Wold, and the famous hunts that meet in the Melton Mowbray, Uppingham, and Oakham districts all range over a little-known extension of the Cotswold Hills. This scene was photographed near Painswick in Gloucestershire, where the beauty of the Wold is at its finest, and wooded valleys and steep hills alternate in swift succession. The house in the background is built of the light-coloured freestone, one of the Cotswold stones, that is still quarried in the district and still used for building new houses.

ridges running parallel with each other and dividing one long sequestered valley from the next.

The hills cross into Leicestershire from Northamptonshire near Market Harborough, a pleasant market-town and one of the great centres of fox-hunting. There are many Georgian houses here which hark back to the time when foxhunting attracted wealth to a town just as industry does today, and a seventeenth-century half-timbered market hall, the upper part of which was originally the grammar school.

From Harborough the Wold spreads northward past Melton Mowbray and then north-eastward toward the Lincolnshire boundary near Grantham. Its towns are few and far between. There is, of course, Melton Mowbray itself, which rivals Market Harborough for its foxhunting fame, and has won fame the world over not only for its sporting distinction but for its Stilton cheese industry and its pork pies. Like so many other towns in the Wold, too, its small wool-spinning industry, which was flourishing until recent years, is a reminder of the time when wool was the staple of the Cotswold dwellers.

For the lover of architecture, Melton has added distinction on account of its parish church, which is sometimes claimed to be the loveliest parish church

264

in the country. It is definitely the most magnificent of Leicestershire parish churches and is a rare example of the Decorated style of architecture at its best, though the clerestory and the tower more strictly belong to the later period of the Perpendicular style.

There is, too, Uppingham, second town of Rutland, and the site of a famous public school which, on a small scale, gives this little place an air of learning akin to the great university cities. Though Uppingham can claim with reason to be a town of the Wold, Oakham, a few miles to the north, lies in the Vale of Catmose. But it deserves a place in any story of the Wold because the vast area of rural country which it serves is so largely wolden country.

There is the same old-world sequestered air about Oakham as there is about Uppingham, and many stone buildings heighten the impression of a Cotswold town. Its central square has changed little since the late Middle Ages, and near-by are the butter-cross, the original market-place, a fine medieval church, which is almost as noble in its proportions as the church at Melton Mowbray, and the substantial ruins of a castle which is not really a castle at all, but was a late Norman dwelling with magnificent banqueting hall. It was built at the end of the twelfth century by a descendant of William the Conqueror's Master of the Farriers, whose badge of office was a horseshoe, which is incorporated in the heraldic device of the county of Rutland. So it is appro-

THE ROOF OF THE WOLD

Here is the view from Cleeve Hill, more than a thousand feet above sea-level, the highest point in the whole of the Cotswolds. Below and to the left the wooded valley of the Severn stretches away toward Worcester and Evesham, a land of fair promise that never disappoints. In the foreground to the right, as far as eye can see, the main ridge of the Cotswolds fades into the distance. It consists of rich grass-land, over which flocks of sheep still range.

priate that the castle of Oakham should contain, as it does, the finest collection of horseshoes in the world.

Of the hundreds of villages which nestle in the heart of the Wold, every one has some feature or other of interest, some special charm and beauty. But no single one stands out in the way in which, for instance, Lower Slaughter or Bibury do in the southern wold. Most are quaint old-world villages right off the beaten track, the very names of which are scarcely known to most wayfarers. Who has even heard of Burton Overy or Carlton Curlieu, or of Owston or Somerby? These are only a few that stand out in memory.

Farther north the native ironstone has set a mark, however slight, upon the face of the countryside. The great ironworks at Asfordby stand alone, but they are a dominating feature of the landscape for miles around, and there is the feeling of industry in the air as far as the high ridge above Old Dalby, most beautifully set of all the Wold villages, in a tree-girt rounded hollow looking north toward the green fields and coverts of the Vale of Belvoir.

Here we must bid farewell to the Cotswold country; for though the hills go on through Lincolnshire, stretching northward a long finger to the Humber

LOWER SLAUGHTER

On a tributary of the Windrush, Lower Slaughter is only two miles from its more famous sister village, Bourton-on-the-Water, and is no less beautiful. The stream runs through the village between road and cottages and widens into this natural pond by the old stone-built mill, the wheel of which can be seen in the centre. Even here in the valley the buildings are of local stone.

MINSTER LOVELL

Although on the fringe of the Wold less than three miles from Witney in Oxfordshire, Minster Lovell is in the true tradition of Cotswold villages, built almost throughout in stone of the typical mellow Cotswold kind. Here is the historic group of fifteenth-century church and the ruins of the famous manor-house. This is one of the oldest manors in the Cotswold countryside and was held by the Lovell family from Norman times until the end of the fifteenth century. The last holder of the manor was involved in the revolt of Lambert Simnel, and thereafter the building fell into decay. In the foreground are the ruins of the great hall, now scheduled as an ancient monument.

estuary and encompassing Lincoln itself on two sides, this is not true Cotswold country, though it has many features in common with it. But the ridge is much lower, though its face is abrupt to the west (whence comes the name of the Cliff), in contrast with the wolds of Lincolnshire, which do not belong to the wold country at all, but are a part of the chalk downs.

Here and there the wayfarer will find a stone wall, here and there a stone-built village. Many of the old buildings in Lincoln itself are fashioned from the local stone, the limestone which gives the whole of the Cotswold its supreme unity. But for the most part hedges and ditches are in place of the stone walls, and brick and timber has been used in village architecture as much as the native stone. The landscape, the villages, and the people will all remind us of the wolden country of Gloucestershire and Oxfordshire, but on all is stamped a distinguishing mark, the pride and the individuality of Lincolnshire itself, the county which truly links the north of England with the south.

267

THE GEORGE HOTEL, GLASTONBURY

This is one of the most ancient houses in Britain now used as an inn, rivalling in that respect the George Inn at Norton St. Philip, also in the county of Somerset. Built about 1475, this hotel was originally a pilgrims' inn built by Abbot Selwood at the same time as the abbey of Glastonbury was enlarged.

268

The West Country

To many the West Country is merely a place in which to spend one's summer holidays—ideal holidays, warm and sunny, with kindly seas and extravagant sands, where no one ever hurries and the natives drawl their words into lullabies, where trains saunter through miles of apparently uncharted country, and roads delight to twist and turn in a bewildering maze of uncertainty.

The West Country is much more than that. It is England as she was before the Industrial Revolution turned her into one vast engineering shop, mechanizing the people and making the countryside merely a huddle of houses. There are towns in the West Country, of course, and coal pits and factories, but the workaday needs of life manage to hide themselves discreetly amidst trees and undergrowth, and the towns each have a character of their own, a factor sadly lacking in the large industrial areas.

As a whole the West Country is mainly agricultural, though the counties, like the towns, vary in character. Somerset, with its fir-crowned hills, hidden combes and flourishing farm-lands, merges gently into the red soil of Devonshire, aptly called the Orchard of England. Here the natives, wrinkled or rosy as apples according to their age, justify the description. Even the flocks and herds take their colour from their surroundings, for the local sheep-dip gives to the sheep the same rich russet hue of the soil, and Red Devon cattle are famous the world over.

The Duchy of Cornwall is a country in itself. The Cornishman considers himself a race apart, looking on the neighbouring counties as foreign land. Natives still talk of "going over to England" when a visit to Devonshire is contemplated. They had a language of their own, now unfortunately fallen into disuse. It has been said that Cornish fishermen could understand the speech of a Breton fisherman when they met on the highway of the sea, when other folk would be completely at a loss.

Along the great Atlantic sea-route came strange settlers, bringing with them new ways of life and burial, building enormous temples and circles of stone in which to worship their gods. Lost and scattered as the remnants of ancient worship are today, they still retain that same aura of mystery with which they were surrounded in those faraway days of which we know so little.

Faced with these huge monuments, seemingly too large to have been placed there by human means, and nourished by unwritten tales repeated by word of mouth through countless generations, little wonder that the Cornishman has inherited a mystic outlook on life. His folk-tales are full of giants and of the Herculean feats of simple men, of pixies who live in out-of-the-way

SCILLY ISLES
(25 miles from Land's End)

BRYHER · ST MARTIN'S
TRESCO
Hugh Town · ST MARY'S
ST AGNES

LUNDY ISLAND

Morte Pt · Ilfracombe
Braunton
Bideford Bay
Barnstaple
Hartland Pt
Bideford

Bude Bay
Bude · Holsworthy

Boscastle
Okehampton
Tintagel Castle · Launceston · Lydford

Padstow
BROWN WILLY
BODMIN MOOR
Callington · Tavistock
BODMIN · Yelverton
CORNWALL
Saltash Bridge

Newquay
Perranporth
St Austell · Looe · Plymouth
Fowey
Redruth · Truro
Mevagissey
LONGSHIPS LIGHTHOUSE
St Ives · Camborne
EDDYSTONE LIGHTHOUSE
Falmouth · St Mawes Castle
Penzance · Helston
Land's End · St Keverne
ST MICHAEL'S MOUNT
Mounts Bay
Mullion Cove · Lizard Pt

BRISTOL CHANNEL

Portishead

Clevedon

River Avon
Bath

Weston-super-Mare
Rock of Ages

Bridgwater Bay

Cheddar Gorge

MENDIP HILLS

Frome

Devils Cheese Wring

Minehead
Watchet
Burnham

Wells

Bruton

Lynton
Dunster

EXMOOR

DUNKERY BEACON

Nether Stowey

Glastonbury

Castle Cary

Templecombe

BRENDON HILLS

QUANTOCK HILLS

SOMERSET

Dulverton

South Molton

Bampton

TAUNTON

Wellington

BLACK DOWN HILL

Tiverton

Crewkerne
Chard

Yeovil

Crediton

Honiton
Axminster

DEVON

Powderham Castle
EXETER
Sidmouth

Moreton Hampstead

Exmouth

Lyme Bay

DARTMOOR
Widecombe

Dawlish
Teignmouth

Newton Abbot

Buckfast Abbey

Totnes

Torquay

Brixham

Dartmouth

Kingsbridge

Salcombe
Start Point

Scale of Miles
0   5   10   15   20   25

WEST COUNTRY

KYNANCE COVE

One of the most famous of the Cornish coves, Kynance lies beside the Lizard promontory facing the unhampered waves of the Atlantic Ocean. It is the action of this stormy sea that has eroded the rocks into such fantastic shapes and left isolated fragments jutting out of the sand in wild but beautiful patterns. There was a time when Cornwall boasted that it had a cove for every holiday-maker. Though today many of the Cornish coves are much frequented in summer, there are in all over two hundred sandy inlets around the coast, many of them tiny beaches reached only by steep cliff paths.

places, and "knockers" who haunt the mines. The Cornish litany: "From ghoulies and ghosties and things that go bump in the night, Good Lord deliver us," had a very real meaning for the Cornishman not so long ago.

The Cornishman has two sides to his character. On the one hand we find the mystic, a lover of music and the arts, gentle and dependable, on the other there is the hard-headed man of business, eager to drive as hard a bargain as can be managed—a love of barter inherited from the past.

The life of the Cornishman is a constant war against Nature. The tin-miners worked under wellnigh impossible conditions to wrest the precious metal from the earth. Quarrying, when faced with enormous blocks of granite, is no light task. The stony and often unfertile land makes farming a test of endurance, while the fisherman has to face frequent storms, especially dangerous on a coast of which the granite cliffs give magnificent scenery but few safe landing places.

St. Patrick was a Celt, and it is in man's religious fervour that we find the

Celtic strain in full flower in the West Country. Like a flame spread the teaching of John Wesley. The first meeting house of the Methodists was in Bristol, and in a grass-covered amphitheatre at Gwennap in Cornwall, where he preached when over eighty years of age, his followers still meet every Whitsuntide. Few villages are without at least one chapel, which by its straightforward appearance, matter-of-fact architecture and unadorned interior attempts to defy the influence of the ancient village church, which, however, still retains the love and reverence of the simple village folk.

Cornwall has, unfortunately, the reputation of having "a shower for every day, and two for Sundays," but that is true only of the moors, where rain is frequent and mists a nightmare to the cautious traveller. Mendip, too, greedily clutches at every passing rain-cloud, but in the lowlands warmth and sunshine are the general rule.

The sea that so nearly surrounds the peninsula of Cornwall (it is only six miles across at its narrowest point) is partly to blame for the heavy rainfall, but, to atone, it gives to the West Country the most temperate climate in the British Isles. Owing to the vagaries of the Gulf Stream the temperature

IN THE LORNA DOONE COUNTRY

The valley of the Weirwater lies under the high slopes of Exmoor in Somerset. This view is at Careford, where the Weir and Chalk rivers unite, and looks eastward towards the summit of Porlock Hill. It is in the heart of the Lorna Doone country, for ever associated with R. D. Blackmore's novel of that name. It is a landscape of narrow valleys between heather-covered hills, the last home in England of red deer and, with the New Forest, of the wild pony.

LOOKING ACROSS BIGBURY BAY
The south coast of Devon is one of the loveliest parts of Britain's coastal beauty. This view near Stoke Point, looking across Bigbury Bay, has all the qualities that make this coastline so famous. The varied contours of the cliffs, distinguished by their bright-red colouring, like all the South Hams of Devonshire, the occasional wooded combe which goes down to the very edge of the sea, and agriculture on the cliff top, make the coastline attractive.

varies in different places, Torquay having an average temperature one degree above that of Plymouth, less than thirty miles away.

The West Country is a paradise for flowers, both wild and cultivated. It is said that over a thousand varieties of wild flower are to be found in Cornwall alone. The casual observer revels in the lovely blue of the chicory and wild hyacinth, while the diligent botanist searches the nooks and crannies of Cheddar for Alpine plants and the rare Cheddar pink.

In the small towns hydrangeas flourish where, in the north, housewives would be scrubbing the flagstones at their front doors. Hedges of gaily coloured fuchsias survive the winter and, in February, wild snowdrops carpet both woods and spinneys; wild daffodils cover many meadows, and bulbs of every description herald the spring in an abundance only exceeded in the Scilly Isles. The marketing of bulbs is one of the local industries, and special trains wait to carry them to the homes of winter-weary townsfolk.

In the extreme west fig trees and palms give an exotic appearance to town and village, while the graceful tamarisk grows with its roots practically in the sea. Seals sport in the waters and porpoises practise their strange gymnastics. Sharks, dolphins, grampuses, and whales have been sighted off the shores of Cornwall, and puffins turn their reddish-brown beaks to the setting sun.

The scenery of the West Country is more varied than that of any other part of England. The eerie caves of Cheddar and Wookey, the rock-strewn

Cheddar Gorge, the desolate heights of Mendip, the heather-painted slopes of Exmoor and the dominating tors of Dartmoor are as Nature conceived them. The fertile valley of Taunton Dene and the chequered pattern of hedge and field are man's contribution to this land of infinite variety. The apple orchards are a joy to the lover of beauty in the spring and a temptation to the passer-by in autumn.

The coastline is as varied as the country itself. Stretches of sandy beaches, demure little bays, imposing harbours, and broad river mouths add to the interest of its gigantic rocks and precipitous headlands. There are many little coves and inlets on the northern coast that challenge any but the surefooted to visit them, so steep is the pathway leading down.

Tintagel, with its ruined Norman castle literally split in two, is by courtesy called King Arthur's Castle, a name which might more rightly be given to the earthwork near-by.

Bedruthan Steps, about seven miles from Newquay, is not named from

TINTAGEL, CORNWALL

The north coast of Cornwall is for ever associated with the legends of King Arthur and his Knights of the Round Table. King Arthur appears in the chronicles of Geoffrey of Monmouth and was a Romano-British hero who defeated the advancing Saxons, withstood their advances for many years and then retreated to the mountain fastnesses of Wales and Cornwall. Tintagel has always been particularly linked with these legends, and the castle shown here, now in ruins, is traditionally supposed to have been one of the British king's last strongholds. In fact, there is no evidence to establish so early an origin, the only certainty being that there was a monastery in Saxon times.

TEIGNMOUTH: FISHERMEN'S VILLAGE

In Devon and Cornwall, as also in the south-east of England, a number of ancient fishing villages have become modern holiday resorts. But in many of these, as in Teignmouth, fishing remains the staple industry that goes on winter and summer irrespective of the influx of visitors. This photograph shows the fishermen's houses, with a number of fishing boats drawn up on the cobbles. Some of these boats do double service—for coastal fishing proper and also for a day's rowing and fishing combined.

the steps a kindly council has provided, but from the massive rocks on the shore that formed convenient stepping-stones for the giant Bedruthan in the days when giants seem to have formed a large proportion of the Cornish population. It is a majestic bay, with caves that can only be visited when the tide permits. Clovelly, too, has steps leading to the beach; in fact, the road is merely a succession of steps, down which patient little donkeys carry goods and passengers to the shore.

Lynton, perched on the top of an almost perpendicular hill, overhangs the little fishing village of Lynmouth, where the East and West Lyn join the sea. The wooded valleys of the twin rivers and the rugged mountainous hills give to Lynmouth the reputation of being the most romantic and beautiful of Devonshire villages.

Sand, which once engulfed the little church of St. Enodoc, forms ideal bathing places in the bays on the north coast, but the more popular holiday places are on the south coast. Exmouth provides music and entertainment, the river and an unbroken stretch of sand for its summer visitors. Torquay and Penzance, with their array of continental flowers and shrubs, similarly offer a

276

charm of their own. Teignmouth, Dawlish, Seaton, and Sidmouth are typical seaside resorts. Gaily coloured cliffs hem in many charming little bays and combes towards Land's End where the green slopes and distant hills give to the scenery a beauty that must cheer the hearts of all who linger in their shade.

As a contrast, the few towns on the Bristol Channel have discovered that scenery has little to do with popularity. Both Burnham and Weston-super-Mare cater for those who prefer amusement and entertainment, though Burnham, with its sands, is a paradise for the small child. Minehead has placed its old fishing town under the care of North Hill, where smugglers' cottages are built into the rock, and the old pier stretches rather forlornly into the sea. Bude and Newquay each manage to provide both scenery and entertainment and the little fishing villages go about their business in the calm, serene way of all who find a living in the deep waters, though St. Ives has also catered very effectively for artists and sightseers.

For the earnest holiday-maker the heights of Dartmoor and Exmoor have a strong fascination. Here walking is free and varied, if not easy. Glimpses of wild life rarely seen elsewhere are an added interest to the majesty of the scenery. The lordly buzzard, rare falcon, and gently coloured merlin all make their homes there. The ill-mannered raven is rarely seen, though known to be present. The Cornish chough, into whose dark little body the

ENGLAND'S MOST SOUTHERLY POINT
The Lizard Point, Cornwall, is the most southerly part of the mainland of Great Britain, a fact reflected in its extraordinarily mild winter climate. Here the land is broken off in jagged pinnacles and sheer cliff faces, as shown in this photograph looking towards the Lizard across Housel Bay. The Lizard lighthouse is in the centre of the picture, which also shows how the land is cultivated to the very edge of the cliffs; the area of cultivation is clearly marked by the lighter tones of the cultivated fields, which are separated by stone walls.

soul of King Arthur was said to have passed, is practically, if not quite, extinct. The moors are also a gathering-place for nearly all the familiar British birds, both migrants and residents.

The little wild ponies belie their reputation, for they seem as tame as ponies should be. People living on the fringe of the moors spend a lot of time chasing them out of gardens and barns as if they were neighbours' chickens! The red deer roams the hills of Exmoor and, like the fox, is a joy to the huntsman and the despair of the farmer. The harmless, lumbering badgers live their uneventful lives as they did even before man came to take possession of the land. The ubiquitous rabbit burrows its way in bank and spinney, with the murderous polecat, weasel, and stoat to keep their numbers down.

It is chiefly from the earth that the West Countryman obtains his livelihood. The tin-mines of Cornwall were worked on a commercial basis during the Bronze Age. In 445 B.C. Herodotus speaks of the "Tin Islands," or Cassiterides, probably meaning Britain. Today the tin-mines are practically derelict owing to the difficulties of transport and the competition of foreign trade.

Slate quarries add their drab, depressing colour to the scene, and many

DARTMOOR FOOTPATH
Characteristic of the high moorlands of Dartmoor, this photograph is of a scene on a hillside overlooking the valley of the Dart. There are innumerable narrow paths, such as the one seen here, that climb round the hilltop covered with a scrubby growth of grass and heather. There are, too, slabs of granite from which the earth covering has been washed away. It is this eroded granite that composes the striking feature of Dartmoor scenery known as tors. The stone wall, also shown in the photograph, s made of granite fragments. Dartmoor is in fact the most easterly of four granite outcrops, of which the other three are Bodmin Moor, Land's End, and the Scilly Isles.

SOMERSET SCENE

Exmoor covers much of the countryside of western Somerset and North Devon, but Dunkery Beacon, the highest point, is inside the Somerset border and some of the finest of the moors and wooded valleys are in that county. This view shows the village of Allerford in the hinterland between Porlock and Minehead, with the Horner woods in the background. A feature of Exmoor scenery is that some of the highest and most magnificent parts of the country are within a few miles of the sea, for Exmoor ends in high cliffs, which are at their finest between Porlock and Minehead.

of the buildings in Cornwall, if not completely covered with slate, have their roofs made of it. Huge curving walls of granite show where man is for ever taking this sturdy stone for his own use, either for building or for road-making.

The mining of china clay is an important industry at St. Austell, about a dozen miles from Truro. The large, white glistening heaps of refuse, looking like Saracens' tents in the distance, are a landmark for miles around. The clay, or to give it its more familiar name of kaolin, is formed from the felspar found in highly decomposed granite, which, in some places, is so soft that it can be dug with a spade to the depth of twenty feet. The Carclease mine, from which St. Austell obtains the clay, was originally worked only for tin. It was a Plymouth Puritan who, in 1765, discovered the value of the china-clay in the mine. Whether he would have approved of it being used to powder my lady's wigs, as the clay from the Dresden mine was at first, is another matter. The clay from St. Austell is sent chiefly to the potteries, though it is also used in other places for glazing paper and dressing calico.

SOMERSET PEAT AND CORNISH CLAY

Historically the china-clay industry ranks in Cornwall with tin-mining and granite quarrying. In recent years china clay has become by far the most important raw material of the south-western peninsula. The special quality of Cornish clay is that it makes a white china of a purity which no other material from any part of the world can match. On this account it has become a valuable commodity for export as well as for home use. The right-hand photograph was taken at the Hendra pit at St. Dennis, but St. Austell remains the chief centre. Peat is cut on the moors near Glastonbury. On the barrow shown in the left-hand picture six blocks, each about twenty-eight pounds in weight, can be carried. The peat blocks are being laid out in rows to dry.

In Devon and Somerset, where the red sandstone and the limestone are found, the land is the most fertile in England. Apart from root crops and the more familiar grain, Indian corn or maize, sugar-beet, teazles, and flax are grown, their unexpected foliage causing great confusion to the townsman. When ready for cutting, Indian corn is a majestic plant. It is mainly grown in England as fodder for cattle, and not for the well-known corn-cob of American cookery books.

Sugar-beet is now being grown in increasing quantities in the West Country. It is a profitable crop, for, after the sugar has been extracted, the remaining pulp makes excellent fodder for cattle.

The clay regions of North Devon and Somerset are not as fertile as the limestone districts. There the rearing of cattle, sheep-grazing, and the raising of young stock prevail. On the moors the farmer has the right of pasturage and free turbary, or cutting and carrying turf for fuel, a privilege that has outlasted many centuries.

Whole areas of peat are to be found in the marshy districts around Glastonbury, where the cutting and drying of this sphagnum moss is a summer industry. It is first cut into square blocks, which are sliced into three and built into conical heaps, called rockies. The bricks are laid so that the air can freely circulate to assist in the drying process. Peat, being rich in humus, has been found to make excellent manure and, if mixed with soil and sand, is equally good for raising seeds.

The manufacture of woollen cloth, introduced to the West Country by an Italian in the reign of Queen Elizabeth, is not as important today as it was when Tavistock kerseys, or lengths of closely woven woollen cloth, were a household possession and dunsters the stock-in-trade of the packman, although there are still cloth-mills at Frome, Tiverton, and Wellington. Axminster carpets, once so famous that the Sultan of Turkey paid a thousand pounds for one, are no longer made at Axminster, but at Wilton, near Salisbury, where the industry was removed in 1835.

Home life is more than a tradition in the West Country, where every cottage is surrounded by a miniature market-garden, and allotments flourish. The women are never idle and take their share in earning the family wage. They are to be seen round the Yeovil district carrying large sacks of dressed skins to stitch into gloves in their own homes. Collars are pressed into shape and finished by the workers' own firesides around Taunton. Hand looms are to be found in many a house, not only in cottages. Osiers lean stiffly against walls in and around the marshy districts of Sedgemoor and Athelney, waiting to be made into baskets. They have been grown around Athelney from time immemorial—long before King Alfred distinguished himself by burning the housewife's cakes! Fat shiny pillows for the making of lace are still found round Honiton and Beer, but in many cases the bobbins are still, the fingers that wove the cobwebby lace are at rest. Nets are made in cottages by women as well as on the seashore by fishermen, and the hurdle-maker is met in the fields, sheltered from the wind and the rain by a prehistoric type of hut.

CHIVELSTONE, SOUTH DEVON

The South Hams of Devonshire is that part of the county that lies between Dartmoor and the coast. It is a countryside of rolling hills distinguished by the bright-red colouring of the Old Red Sandstone, a colouring that appears in the ploughed fields, as it does in the fabric of churches and many of the houses. It is a land, too, of narrow hedge-girt lanes such as that shown on the left of the photograph, winding up the hillside to the distant farm. The church is characteristic of the sandstone churches of South Devon, many of them marked by tall fifteenth-century Gothic towers.

SOMERSET RURAL INDUSTRY

Many of the manufacturing industries of Britain have retained their traditional sites, in spite of the flow of most heavy industries to the industrial area around the coalfields, particularly in the Midlands. An important example is the industry of glove-making associated with Yeovil in Somerset. Gloves have been made there ever since the first glove was invented. The photograph on the *right*, taken at Reckleford factory, near Yeovil, shows the finished articles being inspected before dispatch. In many parts of Somerset, particularly in the low-lying central area, including Sedgemoor, where there are numerous streams lined with willows and alders, rural wood-crafts are still carried on. The basket-making workshop seen in the photograph on the *left* is at Athelney, and the picture shows how the straight withies are fixed to the base of the basket and other withies are woven round them to form the sides.

It is perhaps in the fields that one meets the real craftsman. Iron hasps and hinges on field-gates often show the pride the village blacksmith takes in his work, even if the spreading chestnut tree is absent. The skilful thatcher, who makes of untidy bundles of straw or reeds a tidy, warm, and lovely roof to house and cottage alike, also thatches the ricks in the farmyard or meadow. The hedger and ditcher slashes and bends saplings and young trees to his design without cutting off one of his own limbs with his murderous hook— an ever-present wonder to the onlooker. The ploughman who drives a straight furrow over the uneven field is as much a craftsman as is the man who drives a pen over a ledger, and not everyone can milk a cow! In fact, every farm-worker is a craftsman.

Life in the West Country centres round its market-towns, both large and small. On market-day sheep and cattle pervade the roads from an early hour on their way to the market, where the voice of the auctioneer will later on compete with the complaints of the beasts and the barking of sheepdogs.

Farmers and shepherds from surrounding villages congregate round the cattle pens, prodding the animals and discussing the affairs of their own world, while their wives spend happy hours in the shops.

In many towns the actual market is held some distance from the centre where the market-hall is situated. Market-crosses, or, as they are locally called, butter-crosses, under which the country woman spreads her home-grown product of butter, eggs and poultry, are a feature of most of the smaller market-towns. Often built centuries ago as preaching crosses, arcades were added as the weekly market grew in importance. At Shepton Mallet, on the borders of Mendip, the old shambles, or stalls, still stand under the shadow of a highly decorated and restored fifteenth-century market-cross. The stalls are narrow, roofed with mellow russet tiles, and are thought to be even older than the cross itself. Dunster, near Minehead, possesses a yarn market that is unrivalled, both for its picturesque appearance and historical interest.

Cheddar, too, has its butter-cross, the arcade having been added in the reign of Henry VII. In summer Cheddar somewhat resembles a fairground, with stalls and booths catering for the tripper and sightseer, but when they

THE GEORGE INN, NORTON ST. PHILIP
One of the oldest inns in Britain, the building that is now the George Inn was built in the thirteenth century and was licensed in the fifteenth century. Since then many alterations have been made to the fabric, but the main entrance, shown here, and the tracery of the lower storey windows probably date from medieval times. The George Inn has added fame in legend as the reputed headquarters of the Duke of Monmouth during the rebellion of 1685.

have departed it is a quiet little town sleeping peacefully at the foot of its famous Gorge, where tier upon tier of magnificent rocks rise to a sheer height of 450 ft. from the roadway. Cheddar's written history stretches back to Saxon days, when kings hunted in its forest.

To visit Cheddar caves, though specially lighted and made easy of ingress, is a strange and eerie experience. There are stalactites spreading like gaily coloured curtains, and pools of water and enormous caverns. Ferns that have never seen the light of day cluster round the electric lights a thoughtful owner has placed for the benefit of visitors. Cheddar, as everyone knows, is famous for its cheeses, although their manufacture is not confined to Cheddar, as they are made in other parts of the county. Wookey Hole, about five miles away, is even more eerie. Here the still waters of the River Axe reflect the ancient Witch of Wookey, a block of stone roughly shaped by Nature into the form of a woman, and round which centre many legends.

DUNSFORD, DEVONSHIRE

This charming village is in the valley of the Teign below the slopes of Dartmoor and in the midst of the fertile loveliness of Devonshire. The gay whitewashed cottages with their thatched roofs are typical of this part of Devonshire. So, too, is the church, an ancient edifice dating back to Norman times and rebuilt and enlarged in the fifteenth century, which was a time of great prosperity for South Devon. The tower is characteristic of the smaller late Gothic towers, the counterpart in the west of the more magnificent examples seen in East Anglia and the Cotswold country.

ON THE QUANTOCK HILLS

The Quantock Hills cross Somerset from north to south parallel with the ranges of Exmoor and at their northern end overlook the sea, just as Exmoor does. They show the same magnificent mixture of wooded valley and heather-covered hilltop traversed by long tracks, some of them in use since medieval days. Vast flocks of sheep range over the high ground. In this picture some of these are being rounded up near Bicknoller Post, an isolated part of the moors.

Of the many lovely buildings in the West Country, the cathedrals must take pride of place. Although Exeter Cathedral is considered by many to be the finest, it has not the dignified setting of Wells Cathedral. The more modern township of Exeter has encroached almost to its heavily sculptured west door—or the taxicabs have. Wells Cathedral, on the other hand, has contrived to keep its medieval surroundings and stands, serene and alone, amidst buildings that have altered little for centuries. Four gateways lead through the ancient wall which encloses the Cathedral Green. Two, known as Penniless Porch and the Bishop's Eye, were built by Bishop Beckington, the city's greatest benefactor, during the fifteenth century. The Palace has been described as a perfect example of a fortified medieval house, though a portion of it dates from the eleventh century. On the moat, fed by the streams that gave their name to the city, swans still ring the gatehouse bell for their daily bread—a trick taught over a century ago by the daughter of Bishop Eden to the swans then frequenting the water.

Although Bath Abbey is not strictly a cathedral—the bishop's throne being at Wells—it ranks amongst the cathedrals of the west. It stands on the site of an earlier church built by John de Valula, of Tours, physician to King Rufus. John rose to fame by concocting an ointment that soothed an obscure skin disease on the royal hands. With the money he bought the city of Bath, and transferred the bishopric from Wells to Bath, an action that caused a heated controversy for well over a century between the rival cities. Finally, in 1245, the see was united under one bishop.

Thanks to the emptiness of Henry VIII's treasury and the self-centred desire on the part of his officials to bring as much money as they could to fill it, few abbeys or priories exist in the West Country that are not in ruins. Others, like Montacute and Woodspring, have been converted into farmhouses and private residences, but of the many only scattered stones or their names remain, traditionally or in Domesday Book.

Of the ruins Glastonbury is the most sacred. The Chapel of St. Mary, or

THE ROYAL CRESCENT, BATH

Bath was a spa in the days of the Roman occupation, when the healing properties of the waters were well known and many beautiful buildings were erected around the springs. Modern Bath dates from a revival of interest in spas in the eighteenth century, when many of its present buildings were erected to the designs of the Woods, father and son. In spite of considerable damage by enemy action during the Second World War, it remains the supreme example of eighteenth-century architecture and town planning in Britain. The Royal Crescent is one of the loveliest creations in the late Georgian style.

POST BRIDGE, DARTMOOR

The "clapper" bridge over the Dart at Post Bridge, Devonshire, is one of several ancient bridges in the Dartmoor area. How ancient these bridges are no one knows for certain. They consist merely of slabs of granite thrown across rough piers, and at one time it was thought that they derived from prehistoric times. Certainly they are the kind of bridge one would expect prehistoric peoples to build and are in fact the only kind that would be open to them to build. A more recent theory is that they are medieval packhorse bridges.

St. Joseph as it is sometimes known, stands on the site of the ancient wattle church, believed to have been built by Joseph of Arimathaea, soon after the Crucifixion. The present chapel was built by Henry II.

There are few churches in the West Country that are not worth a visit, for they tell the story of the countryside. A Saxon font, probably rescued from a neighbouring farmyard, speaks of an earlier church, rebuilt in Norman days. Spacious aisles and windows, carved rood-screens and ostentatious tombs of generous benefactors appeared during the Middle Ages until, after long years of neglect, the smug prosperity of Victorian days was responsible for the many disastrous "restorations," the painted pews, and overhanging galleries that are the despair of all lovers of antiquities.

Much has been done to restore the churches in their ancient glory, but there is still much to be done. At Poughill, in Cornwall, two immense paintings, of St. Christopher bearing the Christ Child over a stream, have been repainted, clearly following the lines of the medieval artist. They are well in view from the door to enable the traveller to obtain the saint's blessing without even entering the church. This tiny, fifteenth-century church, with its massive door, is a treasure-house of carvings, both on the beams of the roof and bench ends, perhaps the finest in the West Country.

To the generosity of medieval wool-traders are due many of the larger and dignified churches in the smaller towns. Tiverton Church is perhaps as fine an example of a wool church as any, with the local trade commemorated by fat, squat little woolsacks carved in stone, and a ship to tell of oversea trade.

Houses vary in character as much as the scenery does in the West Country. In Somerset, where stone is plentiful, whole villages are built of the softly gleaming stone from the Ham Hill quarries, or the more dignified limestone from the district around Bath. Both are delightful when the sun shines, but are apt to be depressing when the sky is overcast. Cob walls and thatched roofs make of every Devonshire village a living fairy-tale, while granite and slate give to the Cornish landscape that hard, matter-of-fact appearance in tune with the lives of its inhabitants.

VILLAGE COMMUNITIES AND CRAFTSMEN

Although the buildings may differ, life in the villages has altered little since the Saxon thane set up housekeeping in the neighbourhood. The manor-house takes the place of his scattered homestead. Common-land may be enclosed, but a few fields still show where the peasant tilled them in rotation over a thousand years ago. Where the squire, or lord of the manor, has not been overwhelmed by taxation, or the difficulties of finding sufficient labour, he still takes an active interest in his property. His dependants live in his cottages and work at their various trades for his benefit. Woodmen, game-keepers, the estate carpenter and gardeners, grooms, and stable boys find plenty to do, while farmers and, occasionally, millers provide food sufficient for the whole community.

The West Country has every reason to be proud of its manor-houses. Many date back to medieval days, others show the ostentation introduced into Merrie England during the reign of the Virgin Queen. Imposing mansions glory in the classical outline beloved by such architectural giants as Inigo Jones and John Thorpe, who attempted to make of the gentle, undulating landscape an echo of the Greece and Rome known to the ancients.

But the real charm of the West Country lies, not in its magnificent mansions, but in the smaller, comfortable houses built during early Georgian days. Many stand, literally, with their steps on the pavement, others can only be glimpsed through beautiful wrought-iron gates—or could until the Second World War took toll of so many lovely things and transformed them into guns.

The charm of the country cottage has been extolled by many who pass through the West Country villages. Picturesque they certainly are, with latticed windows hiding under thatched gables, Tudor drip-stones and flower-bordered cobbled paths. They delight the artistic, horrify the hygienist and cause despair in the heart of the tidy housewife. There are too many delightful villages in the West Country to attempt to enumerate them. Perhaps Selworthy, on the fringe of Exmoor, is the best known—at least to photographers. Standing around its village green and overshadowed by walnut trees are seven perfect Tudor cottages, with thatched roofs, chimneys rising from the ground and bulging bread-ovens spreading into the gardens. Monta-cute, near Yeovil, has been described as the perfect village and an example for the town planners of today to follow. It is mostly built of Ham stone and has an ancient priory, now a farmhouse, a fine church dating from Norman days, and the perfect Elizabethan mansion built by Sir Edward Phelips after the design of John Thorpe. It remained in the Phelips family for three centuries, but now is in the wise and kindly care of the National Trust.

XX. CHURCH LANE, LEDBURY, HEREFORDSHIRE

XXI. CHURCH STEPS, MINEHEAD, SOMERSET

The Welsh Marches

THE Marcher counties of Cheshire, Shropshire, Herefordshire, and Monmouthshire, together with that part of Gloucestershire which lies west of the Severn, are all in England but they all look towards Wales, in scenery and tradition. Go where you will, you will not find any place more typically Welsh than the mining villages of the Forest of Dean round Coleford and Cinderford.

Most people think of the Wye as a river of Wales. It is, too, in its upper reaches near its source on the sides of Plinlimmon, but for most of its length it runs through country which is geographically part of England, yet it never loses its Welsh character. Lower down toward the sea, from Symond's Yat to the ancient walled town of Chepstow, the scenery is as un-English as you could imagine, so unlike the quiet pastoral countryside of western England that the traveller almost invariably believes himself to have reached Wales when he comes to the Wye Bridge at Monmouth.

There is a very good reason for the Welsh traditions, at least of the southern Marcher counties. These were the cockpit of the fighting between the English and the Welsh from the Middle Ages until the time of the Union. Most of the people of Monmouthshire and part of Herefordshire were found on the side of the Welsh chieftains. That fact in turn was a legacy of the spirit of intense hatred and bitterness born in the people when the Fitzhamons were Earls of Gloucester, and other Norman families held sway in the great fortress towns of western England, pillaging and plundering the Marcher counties and keeping some semblance of peace only at the point of the sword.

The misdeeds of the Norman-French overlords were exaggerated in tradition as the actual memory of their undoubted cruelty faded. Yet near-contemporary records prove that they brought fire and pillage into the homes of peaceful and industrious citizens.

Just as there is a line of castles stretching across the counties of South Wales, so there is a line of castles athwart the communications between England and Wales in the Marcher counties. Many of the castles have disappeared entirely, not even picturesque ruins being left to remind the wayfarer of times past, but others are in good repair, as are the walls of some of the medieval towns. These include Newport, Chepstow, and Monmouth in the south; Hereford, Ludlow, and Shrewsbury; and Chester in the north.

The traditions associated with these castles are very different from those of South Wales. If you read local histories or talk with knowledgeable antiquarians, you will find that they stand for the oppression of the Marcher earls and the misery these "foreign noblemen" inflicted on the people. That is in contrast with the castles of South Wales, which are remembered chiefly as symbols of resistance and of the long struggle which Welshmen waged to deflect the English from their conquest.

Let us take a brief tour together, northward from the estuary of the Severn to the estuary of the Mersey, so as to comprehend in our journey the spirit of the people as well as the varied beauties of the countryside in which they live. We will start our tour at Newport, with its medieval castle beside the slow-running river and busy streets crowded with people, and lined with shops which vary from local Welsh-sounding names to the great multiple stores which we find in almost every large town of Britain.

This is an appropriate start for any tour of the Welsh Marches, because it accents the link between them and Wales itself. To Newport come the people of some of the mining valleys such as Ebbw Vale. What place could be

CHEPSTOW CASTLE
Chepstow Castle was first a Norman fortress, one of the castles from which the Earls Marcher ruled over the territory which is now Gloucestershire and Monmouthshire. In the fourteenth century the castle was extended and re-modelled. Most of the present ruins date from that time. In the later Middle Ages Chepstow was one of a string of fortresses which stretched from Gloucestershire to the Pembrokeshire coast and which were the strongholds of the English in the constant guerrilla warfare with the native Welsh. This part of the ruins is Henry Marten's tower. Henry Marten, one of those who signed King Charles's death warrant, was prisoner here for twenty years.

ON THE BANKS OF THE WYE

Photographed from the ferry which crosses the Wye at this point, the white-washed cottages and houses of Symond's Yat are set off by the dark green, almost black, mass of foliage which cloaks the cliff rising to the summit of the Yat rock which overhangs the horseshoe bend of the Wye at the point where it enters the plain of Hereford.

more Welsh than Ebbw Vale? It comes with a shock of surprise to many to find that Ebbw Vale, together with places like Abertillery and Pontypool, are all in England. How many times has one read statements such as "typical Welsh mining valleys like Ebbw Vale"? Of course, such statements are misleading geographically, but they have a power of truth in them.

From Newport, with its modern look partly concealing its age-old tradition, let us travel across country to Chepstow at the mouth of the Wye. Here is a place that looks as old as it is. It has a magnificent embattled castle built precariously on a high cliff overhanging the broad stream of the Wye, a steep street running up from the river to a high point where one of the ancient gates marks the line of the medieval walls of Chepstow. Though there is bustle here and much 'traffic passing by the old buildings (and some modern buildings, too, taking the place of older houses and shops), the voices of the people betray our nearness to Wales. It is a place of romance and charm and historic memories.

Next let us journey up the Wye as far as Monmouth. That will prove as lovely and as interesting a journey as we shall take anywhere in England. It matters not whether we go by the left bank or the right bank. If we have the time we shall do both by going upstream through Tintern and coming back again on the other bank through the outliers of the Forest of Dean. The road from Chepstow leads out of the old town and passes the race-course, cutting across a narrow neck of land and going back to the very bank of the river, which it follows all the way upstream, crossing it after Tintern but never leaving it by more than a few yards. The road bends and twists. It is never straight for a hundred yards and every bend reveals a fresh vista, a fresh insight into the green and lovely beauty of the river. There are hanging woods in plenty climbing up the steep cliffs from the river's brink to 500 ft. Sometimes the road passes through them so that they blot out the view of the river. The interlacing branches form a tunnel in which, on the brightest day, the scene is darkened.

THE BEAUTIFUL RUINS OF TINTERN ABBEY

Down goes the road toward Tintern, with a wonderful view of the abbey ruins in a meadow beside the river. Is not this one of the most beautiful of English abbeys ? Can you think of another which combines such entrancing beauty of architecture with such a lovely setting ?

This is where a party of monks came to found a settlement far from the strife of towns, far from the temptations of peopled cities. First they built huts of wood and a little wooden church. Then they tore down the wooden fabric of the chapel and started to build an edifice in stone that would be a glory to the name of God. How well they succeeded we can still judge. When all that was done with the toil of their own hands and the sweat of their own brows, they set to work to reconstruct their living-quarters in stone, sparing neither time nor trouble, nor money, to make the whole worthy of its purpose.

As the centuries went by and more and more patrons added to the wealth of the monastic orders, they embellished the buildings further, so that many of the abbey churches, including Tintern, are nearly as beautiful, nearly as elaborate, as the great parish churches and cathedrals. Tintern Abbey has become a show-place to which, on account of the beauty of the surroundings as much as for its own sake, come thousands of trippers by car, bicycle, and motor-coach. In spite of it all, its atmosphere is still one of dignity and magnificence, an atmosphere which, you feel, nothing in this world can ever mar or destroy.

The scene changes after Tintern. The valley of the Wye broadens a little. In place of the hanging woods there are ploughed fields and green pastures and the swelling hillsides, kindly and welcoming. There is no less loveliness but less grandeur.

When you come to Monmouth and enter by the Wye Bridge you have reached another town as typical in its own way of the Marcher counties as is Chepstow. Not so beautiful in itself, it looks lovely from any viewpoint on the hills around. Perhaps its most intriguing sight is the ancient Monnow Bridge at the other end of the town, where there is still the medieval toll-house on the hump of the bridge.

For the rest, there is a broad High Street and the memories of Britain's historic past in names such as Agincourt Square, the Beaufort Arms, and many

RUINS OF TINTERN ABBEY

The walls of the nave of the abbey church are nearly intact. The fine west
window is in the Decorated style.

293

WOODWORKERS OF THE MARCHER LANDS
In the woodlands of the Wye and Severn valleys the wood-craftsman yet
flourishes. The photographs above show a boy spokeshaving ladder rungs and
a trug- or basket-maker at work.

others. Cannon in Agincourt Square lend a falsely martial air to a town as
peaceful as any you will find.

The main part of our journey has been up the west bank of the Wye.
Our return to Chepstow will be well to the east through Coleford. So we shall
pass through a sizeable part of the Forest of Dean, that strange and contradictory tract of woodland and common which conceals within itself some of the
pleasantest places in the Marcher country, and only a mile or two away some
of the worst blots on its landscape. A coalpit and slag heap may be only a few
hundred yards from untrodden woodland, brightened in summer with tall
foxgloves and traversed by leafy, unfenced tracks and roads which might be
hundreds of miles from the nearest industrial settlement. At one moment you
are in the middle of a modern industrial town like Cinderford. Five minutes
later by car or half an hour on foot, you are in primitive forest-land where the
charcoal-burner and the woodworker carry on their medieval crafts by
methods which have changed but little through the centuries.

It is all surprises. Everything is other than it seems. Even the Speech
House, which used to be the combined parliament and law courts of the
forest folk, is now an hotel. In the tourist season some of the roads are busy,
but a hundred yards away from them the sound of passing traffic is blanketed
by the thick woods, and you might be miles away from the nearest motor-car.
You can easily get lost in these forest-paths. The old tracks are confused with
modern woodmen's paths. The right way is seldom the obvious one, which
too often ends abruptly at a clearing, where only the trunks of the magnificent
trees remain to show what was here before tree-fellers got to work.

Then again, what was open common-land twenty years ago is now an

294

impassable plantation of fir trees; for the Forest of Dean is one of the areas which is being afforested under the auspices of the Forestry Commission. In beauty, the fir plantations are a poor second to the primeval forest-lands but no less useful for future generations. There are a few small settlements here and charcoal-burners' huts, ancient cottages in which forest folk have lived for three hundred years or more. In the mining towns, in contrast, the houses are all very modern, and if not so grey as the homes of the Welsh miners they have little of beauty in their long, even rows and monotonous vistas of red brick.

Next let us follow together the course of the Wye upstream from Monmouth. The river takes us quickly northward into Herefordshire. The first few miles are the most beautiful. It flows in a narrow valley until it comes to the great horseshoe bend round Symond's Yat, a beetling craggy eminence, half covered in thick woods. Climb to the top of the hill and you will come to a small area clear of the woods from which the winding valley of the river is spread out before you, and hundreds of square miles of lush plain of Hereford-

VALLEY OF THE WYE

Here the Wye between Symond's Yat and Monmouth cuts a course through densely wooded hills. Here and there rocky outcrops break through the wood-lands where the valley closely resembles Dovedale in Derbyshire. There is the same mixture of steep, wooded cliffs and occasional bare rock-faces for contrast. This photograph is taken from one of the Seven Sisters rocks and looks upstream toward Symond's Yat. On the right of the picture is the railway which hugs the river bank nearly all the way to Monmouth. On the other bank a footpath extends from Symond's Yat to the outskirts of Monmouth.

shire. Go to the very edge and you will look down on the river hundreds of feet below you, coiling like a serpent round the high cliff, and, from this great height, looking for all the world like a silver ribbon tempting the wayfarer to savour at closer quarters the essence of its beauty.

The valley of the Wye itself above Symond's Yat, and of its tributary, the Monnow, is kindly, rich agricultural country in which the husbandman reaps a fine reward for his work. The same is true of the country to the east as far as the Malvern Hills which hem in the plain of Herefordshire and divide it from the Vale of Severn.

Apart from the city of Hereford there are only a few small towns in the county, like Leominster, Bromyard, and Weobley, and, of course, Ledbury. These are all market centres and they are distinguished by many features of architecture common to this and the more northerly counties of the Marches. First among these characteristics is the intensive use of timber in medieval and later buildings. Nowhere in Britain will you find the art of half-timbered

THE BRIDGE AND CATHEDRAL OF HEREFORD

Hereford Cathedral was founded at least by the year 700, though nothing of the original Saxon building survives. The graceful central tower is one of the few large towers raised in the first half of the fourteenth century, but it is built on a Norman base. There are fine examples of the Romanesque style and of all periods of Gothic in various parts of the fabric. One of the most ancient maps in the world, the Hereford Mappa Mundi, is preserved in the cathedral. This was drawn before the fourteenth century. There is also a medieval chained library, thought to be unique in England.

HEREFORDSHIRE BEACON

The Malvern Hills divide the Vale of Severn from the rolling country of
Herefordshire. One of their highest points is Herefordshire Beacon, here seen
in sharp relief against the skyline. On its summit are clearly shown the banks
and ditches which are all that remain of an ancient British fortress town,
similar to the many that have been found in the south of England.

building so well developed. It is most perfect perhaps in Cheshire, but only a
little less so in Shropshire and Herefordshire.

Of the places mentioned, Weobley and Ledbury are the two most
distinctive in this respect. The latter has an old timber market-house and an
old inn, half-timbered throughout and beautifully preserved. Here in Herefordshire the black-and-white half-timbered work is comparatively orthodox,
but northward in Shropshire and especially in Cheshire the art was developed
into what was known as magpie architecture, the timber facing being used as a
medium for decoration which took the shape of fanciful forms and designs
covering the whole facades of houses and public buildings. Houses like
Moreton Old Hall are typical of the art, which had its finest expression
between the sixteenth and eighteenth centuries.

Hereford itself is a gracious city, with a mellow cathedral overlooking the
Wye. Inside the cathedral you will find one of the earliest maps of the world,
the Hereford Mappa Mundi, now restored and refurbished after its wartime
period of seclusion. In one of the main streets of the city you will see a lovely
Jacobean house now used as a museum, and furnished throughout in the
Jacobean style of furniture, a gem of its kind, and one of the most perfectly
restored houses of its age in Britain.

Now we come to Shropshire. This is one of the least known and one of
the most beautiful of the English counties. Its great charm is its scenery,

THE CASTLE AND BRIDGE OF LUDLOW

Ludlow is one of the many historic towns of Shropshire built beside the wide
flowing Teme and protected since Norman times by a castle constructed on
a bluff that rises sheer from the river's bank. The castle, which was built at
the end of the eleventh century, was one of the strongholds of the Earls
Marcher, who earned an unenviable reputation for the rigour and cruelty
of their rule over the people of the Welsh Marches and eastern Wales.

though all that we have said so far about the people of the Marcher counties
applies equally to the countryfolk of Shropshire. On the whole, it is a prosperous county well endowed by Nature and well tilled. The River Severn cuts
across it and divides the high ground of the south-west from the lower ground
of the north and east. It has one large town in Shrewsbury, another largish
and mainly modern town in Wellington, a small but intensely historic town in
Ludlow, and, for the rest, only a number of small market-towns and
numerous quiet villages.

Shrewsbury was one of the fortress towns of the Earls Marcher. It is still
full of old buildings and combines to a remarkable degree the air of a bustling
modern market centre and of an ancient and attractive place.

Ludlow more nearly approximates to one's idea of a medieval town.
There is the ancient stone bridge over the Teme which still carries the main
road, so narrow that buses and heavy vehicles generally have difficulty in
making an approach. Two of the old gates remain; and substantial ruins of the
castle, which is set romantically on a sheer bluff overhanging the river. Above

all, Ludlow retains several of the narrow thoroughfares virtually unchanged in the last three hundred years, so narrow that the old houses leaning slightly inwards almost meet in their upper storeys.

In spite of this wealth of historic interest, it is to the hills that you will be attracted most. The hills of Shropshire have something of the mountainous districts in them, but they are infinitely more placid and quietly beautiful than the mountains, yet more impressive than the southern downlands. Church Stretton is one of the favourite centres. The little town lies in a narrow valley called Stretton Vale, its newer houses clinging to the steep hillside.

North and south the sharply etched massive back of the Long Mynd forms the skyline. Just as the valley of Llanthony goes deep into the heart of the Black Mountains in Monmouthshire, so the Cardingmill Valley cuts a narrow and precipitous way into the Long Mynd, revealing ever-new landscapes of beetling crags and smooth green slopes. The summit of the Long Mynd is covered in heather stretching for miles in an unbroken blanket.

Across the valley, a complex and more beautiful group of hills rises abruptly. Caer Caradoc, Hope Bowdler, and other smaller hills are traversed by numerous paths and tracks leading up the valleys and across the hilltops, and there are enough rocks exposed near the summits to give a real impression

BRIDGNORTH, SHROPSHIRE

Here are the "low town" of Bridgnorth and the graceful bridge which spans the Severn. At this point the great river of the west runs through a valley which is rapidly narrowing. The hills rise steeply from its banks and the "high town" is connected with the riverside by a lift. Bridgnorth has long been a centre of the carpet-making industry.

of mountainous country. The loveliest of all the paths climbs up a gulley between Hope Bowdler and Caer Caradoc and crosses a high pass to the village of Cardington beyond. That comparatively short path—not much more than four miles in length—gives in swift succession a sight of almost every type of English scenery; first, the cornfields and pastures of Stretton Vale, then the rich woodlands of the gulley, followed by the rank grass and bare rocky slopes of Caer Caradoc, and finally a hedge-girt lane running between the farm-lands that fall to Cardington. Add to that a panorama which stretches in every direction, northward as far as Shrewsbury, westward to the Long Mynd, and eastward toward Wenlock, and you have an uncommonly dramatic walk or horseback ride.

"Toward Wenlock"—that sounds another note which will remind you of lovely scenery and varied countryside. It will remind you of Wenlock Edge, that long and almost unbroken ridge which stretches from Wenlock across the county to a point near Craven Arms, a ridge that is so well wooded that it is almost forest-land, a ridge which rises abruptly from the plain on the north-west and falls gently into the undulating country of the Severn valley.

Finally, in the south of the county there are the isolated peaks of the Clee Hills, Titterstone Clee and Brown Clee, which give an impression of far greater height than they actually possess, because of the level fields that surround them. North of the Teme, where the county adjoins central Wales, the Forest of Clun is a steep country with many high hills and deeply shadowed valleys, yet not a forest in the sense of being thickly wooded, but rather in the sense that it was one of the tracts of land set aside in medieval days to be a "forest" or hunting preserve.

In the north of Shropshire, where a detached spur of the Welsh county of Flint abuts into the Shropshire Plain, there is a famous beauty-spot called Ellesmere Lake, hard by a little old market-town of the same name. There is something so singularly English about this place and the countryside surrounding it that it almost deserves a chapter on its own. The placid waters of the lake are surrounded by green lawns and gracious woodlands and the grounds of a magnificent classically designed mansion. There are swans on the lake, and it is exactly like a picture of southern park-lands, with more of Kent or Sussex about it than of the Welsh Marches.

The little town of Ellesmere, too, might have stepped straight out of rural Suffolk, with its air of quiet detachment and rustic simplicity, its small and pleasant square, its few half-timbered houses. Even that is not the end of the story. Go which way you will from Ellesmere, you will find narrow hedged

THE SHROPSHIRE HILLS

The highlands of Shropshire are a grand mixture of heather-covered hills with outcrops of bare rock on some of the summits. This view is looking down the Cardingmill Valley, a narrow defile which runs into the heart of the Long Mynd, near Church Stretton. In the middle distance is the fertile wooded country of Stretton Vale and beyond, from left to right, the sharp ridge of Caer Caradoc and the more rounded summit of Hope Bowdler. A pass between the two leads to the village of Cardington.

WELSH ROW, NANTWICH

The fine Georgian-style houses on the left, with black-and-white half-timbered buildings lower down the street, and the square, solid tower of the parish church behind, make up some of the characteristic charm of Nantwich, which is itself typical of many Cheshire towns. Famous for its modern brine baths, Nantwich was one of the centres of the Cheshire salt industry, which may have originated as early as Roman times and which for centuries brought trade and commerce to a part of the country which was otherwise solely agricultural.

lanes winding through fertile countryside in which there is as much ploughed land as pasture, and in which you feel yourself transported in spirit to the quiet lands of the south. It is only the outline of the Welsh mountains to the west, visible in nothing but exceptionally clear weather, which reminds you that you are near wild Wales, only a few miles from some of the wildest and roughest landscapes of Britain.

For a few miles near Overton, the Dee forms the boundary between Shropshire and Denbigh. It is a wide and quiet river here, but you can look up it towards the Vale of Llangollen and see the narrow gap in the distant but clearly visible blue hills of Wales. You have a much greater sense of the imminence of austere beauty here than in any other part of Shropshire.

The last of the Welsh Marcher counties, Cheshire, is a strange mixture. Some of it is very English. It would be difficult to think of a more English town than Crewe or of people more typically English in their speech and character than those who live and work there. When you come near to the Welsh boundary, for instance at Malpas, you feel yourself to be very near the Wales of the Welsh, and if you cross the Dee the transition is quite sudden.

When you reach Wrexham you know you are in the midst of a Welsh community. Nowhere is the transition more sudden, nowhere the contrast more remarkable.

There are beautiful landscapes in Cheshire, and there are dull patches, where industry is vigorous, in which you will find it hard to rediscover the loveliness of the landscape. Then again, the north-east of the county looks toward Manchester, and though your typical inhabitant of Altrincham or Stockport will say proudly: "I live in Cheshire," it is sometimes hard for the outsider to see where Manchester's satellite towns and suburbs end and where Cheshire begins.

As if to underline the mingling of these two worlds apart, the Mersey river forms the boundary for miles between Cheshire and Lancashire. Warrington is in Lancashire. Cross the river and you are in Cheshire. Runcorn is in Cheshire, but cross the river and you are in Widnes, which is very Lancashire.

The truth is that all this wedge of country, from the foot-hills of the Pennines westward through Manchester to the estuary of the Mersey, is industrialized, the Manchester Ship Canal forming a link between the merchants of Manchester and the port of Liverpool. It does not seem to mean very much except in local tradition on which side of the waterway you happen

STAUNTON, IN THE FOREST OF DEAN

The quiet, often deserted, village street lies only a few yards from the main road which connects Monmouth with Gloucester. Like most of the ancient villages of the Forest of Dean, Staunton is stone-built, its rather drab colouring lightened by the bright green of the wooded hills which rise on every hand. It makes a complete contrast with the modern coal-mining towns and villages which mar the beauty of the forest in other parts.

to live. Few southerners distinguish clearly between Liverpool and Birkenhead, yet Birkenhead is one of the proudest towns of Cheshire, Liverpool of Lancashire.

Cheshire, on the fringe of its industrial belt, has something which Lancashire has not: a quiet pastoral undulating peninsula called Wirral, between the estuaries of the Mersey and the Dee, a happy hunting ground for country lovers from industrial Cheshire and from Liverpool alike.

The farther you go from Birkenhead and Wallasey the more closely you approach the true feel of the Welsh Marches, until you come to Chester, which has all the fascination and all the historic memories of a city which has seen every civilization come and go, and which has again and again stood as a bulwark for the forces of order against rebellion and frenzied hate.

We can do no better than end our outline tour of the Welsh Marches at this ancient city. We shall walk through its crowded streets and see today the many links which it has with its long history—the cathedral, the walls, the old houses, the black-and-white timbered fronts, the strange shopping thoroughfare called the Rows, and hundreds of others. We shall reflect that here is a place which was not new in the days of the Roman Province in the first century, A.D., but then for the first time reached a position of eminence. For the Romans it was a bulwark against the wild people of Wales, and one of the headquarters of one of their permanent garrisons.

Its noble and illustrious cathedral testifies to its medieval prosperity. In

MONMOUTH FROM THE HILLS

Monmouth, the county town, straddles the River Wye between that river's two most famous reaches. Above the town is Symond's Yat and the wooded slopes where the Forest of Dean overhangs the river, below is the narrow gorge which leads to Tintern and Chepstow. On every side of Monmouth there are well-timbered hills which give glimpses across the valley to the compact little town, marked afar by the tall Gothic spire of the church.

THE OLD HOUSE, HEREFORD

This magnificent half-timbered building in the very centre of Hereford dates
from the seventeenth century. It is used as a county museum and has been
furnished throughout in the style of its period.

the Middle Ages we find it still a walled town. The Roman foundations of its walls were built up into new battlements and a fine castle added to give it greater strength. We find it, in the traditional Marcher way, a centre of English rule, strongly defended to overawe the Welsh, its barons administering cruel and effective justice, its wealth increasing apace as it became the market centre for the whole of the fertile country of Cheshire. And we find it still in the thick of the fighting in the great Civil War which devastated Britain.

What a tale of blood and slaughter for a city so essentially peaceful! Peaceful it is today, however busy and prosperous, and peaceful it has always been, you would think, when you walk in the cathedral close. It is only when you come to the walls that you are reminded of its turbulent past. In its romantic mixture of old and new, and its varied memories of peace and war, it somehow epitomizes the spirit of all the Marcher towns and cities. It is the very essence of a countryside which is half English and half Welsh, with something of the beauty and spirit of both.

TEWKESBURY MILL AND HALF-TIMBERED HOUSES

Tewkesbury is a typical small town of the Welsh Marches, a place of importance since early medieval days, with an abbey church that is almost entirely Norman. The town is set on the banks of the Avon in the midst of the Vale of Severn. By the riverside there is an old mill, the scene of episodes in *John Halifax, Gentleman,* and a number of half-timbered cottages and houses dating from the sixteenth and seventeenth centuries.

Round the Coasts

FISHING is one of the traditional industries of Britain. It is traditional in the sense that there were fishermen round the shores of Britain before there were men working on the land. Many thousands of years before the birth of Christ, prehistoric man was established in settlements round the coast; fish was his staple diet, eked out by the flesh of wild animals which he hunted.

It is a tradition which has been maintained ever since; the peoples who have dwelt in Britain, primitive or civilized, have never been able to dispense with the wealth that resides in the seas. Since medieval days there has been a story of continuous development. First it was the individual fisherman who sailed in his coracle-like boat to catch the food to feed himself and his family. Then fishing became a craft and fishermen, singly and in groups, with improved methods and improved boats, were able to catch enough fish not only to feed themselves but to distribute among their neighbours and receive other goods in exchange.

It was really the beginning of fishing in the commercial sense, when fishermen began to design nets and catch fish by dragging the nets through the water in the wake of their boats. Craftsmen developed the means to make the mesh of the nets even and of such a size that all the fish large enough to be useful for food were retained while the small useless ones were let through the mesh. This, too, was a means of conserving supplies, which were not inexhaustible, for the small fish thus escaping were usually young fish which would grow and serve for food months or years afterwards.

Small rowing boats were exchanged for larger sailing vessels and in time sail gave place to steam. When the modern era of the steam-trawler and steam-drifter began, fishing became an industry of nation-wide importance supplying the inhabitants of the great industrial towns as well as the coastal towns with a reasonable proportion of their food.

Through all these phases the men carrying out the work were the same, in the sense that fishing is one of the most conservative industries in the world and fishermen come from the same families for generation after generation. Father teaches son and son's son. In the nineteenth and twentieth centuries there has been a drift from the fishing settlements, as there has been from the countryside at large, to the industrial towns; but enough have remained to carry on the craft and develop it, especially since the financial rewards for successful fishermen in the modern era are comparatively large.

Side by side with the commercializing of the craft, the true village fisherman, plying his own boat, making and mending his own nets, has continued

START POINT, DEVONSHIRE

This aerial view of Start Point and the South Devon coastline looking north shows at once the beauty of the coast and the charm and fertility of the South Hams of Devonshire, a district, limited inland by a line from Tor Bay to Plymouth Sound, covering about 240 square miles. The rocky promontory with the lighthouse at its end is one of several between Plymouth Sound and the estuary of the Dart. They are all jagged and inhospitable, the terror of sailors in times gone by.

to thrive. The steam-drifters and trawlers are confined with few exceptions to the large fishing towns, from the Moray Firth to the south coast of England. But every sheltered bay conceals its fishing village. All along the coasts, in the west as well as the east and south, fishermen continue to gather their harvest whenever tide and weather permit. Not only that, but they find a ready market for their wares.

A great deal of the wealth of the fishing industry derives from the herring, whose shoals are found principally in the North Sea, moving south as the season progresses. Most of the great fishing ports from Aberdeen to Grimsby and Lowestoft owe their rapid development to the wealth of the herring shoals. The same is true of the fishing ports farther north, especially the ports of Caithness and the Moray Firth.

There are many interesting traditions associated with this single phase of the industry. For many generations it has been customary for the labour required to gut, cure, and pack the surplus fish to be recruited from Scotland. The Scottish fisher girls are a legend in all the east-coast towns. Year after year the same "girls" report for duty (from families of inland as well as coastal towns) and move south with the herring shoals, finding accommodation for a few weeks in each of the big towns. Traditions inevitably die hard and this is one which still lives on, though more and more local labour is recruited and the number of Scottish "girls" who regularly make the trip is decreasing every year.

The east-coast ports are fortunate in that the herring has never failed them, though inevitably some years bring a far richer reward than others. But other parts of Britain's coast have not been so fortunate. The pilchard used to be to the south-western peninsula what the herring is to the east coast. The pilchard fisheries were centred in Devon and Cornwall, where the whole prosperity of village after village depended on a good return of pilchards in their season. For reasons that have never been explained, the pilchard began to desert these waters at the turn of the century. Since then, rich catches have never been made and the prosperity of the Cornish fishing villages has declined

BERWICK-UPON-TWEED

The ancient and historic border town of Berwick-upon-Tweed, the estuary of the River Tweed, and the hills of Northumberland, where they merge into the southern uplands of Scotland, are shown in this aerial view. The central of the three bridges shown is a modern concrete construction; in front of it is the James VI Bridge, ten of its fifteen arches visible. Behind is the railway viaduct that carries the main east-coast line from London to Edinburgh.

more and more, though it returned to some extent between the two world wars owing to the annual influx of holidaymakers and the money they brought to spend in these industrially undeveloped regions. Since the Second World War there have been signs that the pilchard would return in force, though the shoals have never matched those of the prosperous years of the late 1800s. At least pilchard fishing, which almost died out, is once more established as a live industry, even though as yet its returns are poor.

The south-western peninsula is pre-eminently the Celtic England of tradition, so it is not surprising to find here surviving ways of fishing which have been forgotten in most other districts. In at least one small bay in Cornwall a vast net is stretched from headland to headland at high tide so that as the tide recedes the fish who are on the landward side of the net are caught in it. The net is owned communally by a number of families, who are jointly responsible for keeping it in repair and drying it.

Another interesting facet of Britain's fishing industry is the way in which small-scale fishing goes on side by side with urban development and the growth of holiday resorts. Perhaps Hastings, in Sussex, gives the most startling example of this contradiction. Modern Hastings is a seaside town as divorced from seafaring as any could ever be, but tucked away under the cliff is the Old Town and on the shingle foreshore the visitor will see now, as centuries ago, nets laid out to dry, and fishermen at work tending their nets or their boats; the old fishing village nestling under the hill is virtually unchanged by the

A LANDMARK OF THE DORSET COAST
The limestone and granite cliff of Portland Bill is a well-known landmark jutting out from the coast near Weymouth and dividing the sheltered waters of Weymouth Bay from the stormy exposed beaches along the coast. The photograph shows the beginning of the Chesil Bank, a long shingle beach that stretches north-westward from Portland Bill toward Abbotsbury. It is a freak of Nature in that the pebbles that compose it grow steadily larger from north-west to south-east, becoming small boulders as Portland Bill is approached.

THE FISHERMEN LAND THEIR CATCH

Folkestone is one of the most ancient of the fishing towns of southern England. This scene in the harbour is repeated almost every day as the fishermen land their catch and seagulls are attracted by the smell and sight of fish. In the background are a number of the fishing boats, some of them operated by companies, and others still in the ownership of individuals.

rapid growth of the neighbouring town. It is almost as great a surprise as it is to find fishermen's nets drying on the promenade at Southend-on-Sea.

Those are scenes which are duplicated in many different parts of the country. Even vast towns like Brighton and Scarborough still have their fishing communities, where the fishermen often eke out their living by hiring their boats to the holidaymakers.

As though to underline these strange contradictions, the tendency all round the coasts is for the individual fisherman to disappear. The individual trawler-owners of the Scottish coastal towns once had a reputation very much like that of the yeoman-farmers of Kent. They were conservative and prosperous, the backbone of social life in the eastern ports. It is only within the last half-century that the big fishing companies began to put these "yeomen" out of business, usually by buying them out and leaving them in command of their own boats. So the personal touch of the owner-captain is disappearing, together with the personal interest in the welfare of the workpeople, just as the same quality is disappearing from the land with the break-up of the larger estates. Even so, there seems no dearth of men to seek service with the fishing companies, and the only potential threat to this prosperous industry is a decline in the size of the herring shoals. Certainly there are not lacking prophets who base their sad premonitions of decline on the undisputed facts that the North Sea fisheries have been over-fished and that international control of trawling and drifting leaves many loopholes for evasion.

If the craft of fishing is ageless, so are the village settlements in which the fishing families live. Excluding the large fishing towns of the east coast and a few of the west like Fleetwood and also the south-coast fishing towns which have become holiday resorts, there are still thousands of villages almost untouched by time, unspoilt, quiet, and sequestered. Very many of them in the south and west were founded by the Saxons, many along the east coast were founded by the Viking invaders who harried the Saxon kingdoms. Almost all of them were founded by the time that William of Normandy crossed the Channel and defeated Harold at Battle.

All that was necessary as a site for one of these early medieval settlements was a tiny natural harbour or a good beach on which the fishing boats could be drawn up clear of the tides and the storms. For early settlers like the

ON THE BEACH AT BEER

Under the chalk cliffs of Beer Head, most westerly point to which the chalk hills extend in England, fishermen are drawing up their boats on the Hard with the primitive "machine" of tradition. This is a windlass, which is manually operated by means of long poles inserted into the hub. In recent years a number of power-operated windlasses have been introduced on various parts of the coast to draw the fishing boats up above high-water mark. The "power unit" is often a discarded motor-car engine.

DEVON'S NORTH COAST

The north coast of Devon stands high in the order of scenic beauty, especially between Ilfracombe and Lynton, where the uplands of Exmoor reach almost to the sea and the hills are broken off abruptly in towering cliffs and tiny landlocked bays. This view is taken from the slopes above Combe Martin and looks eastward toward Lynton. The cliff beyond the narrow inlet is known as the Great Hangman.

Saxons a clear stream running into the sea was an added reason for building their homes there. Fresh water was always a problem for medieval people and a near-by stream offered an inexhaustible supply.

A nearly landlocked bay was an ideal place in which to found a fishing village, for thus a natural harbour was provided and inshore fishing was possible within the bay itself in rougher weather than would permit of the boats putting out to sea. Where the coast is rocky or much indented, as in the south-western peninsula and along the west coast of Scotland, the villages take tone from their surroundings and have a picturesque quality which hundreds of artists have sought to capture and which today is the delight of every amateur photographer.

Villages like Mevagissey or Polperro, Mullion or Port Isaac, spring to the memory as among the loveliest that Britain can show. The individual buildings of each may not be architecturally exciting in every case but there is a certain inevitable beauty of composition which follows from their situation. They cling, as it were, precariously between sea and cliff. The cottages hug the strand and straggle up the hillside, often rising in terraces or, as at Clovelly, strung out up the steep hill on either side of the "road" which rises in steps to the cliff-top.

All these villages are in Devon and Cornwall, but there are others in

STAITHES, YORKSHIRE

There are a number of small fishing villages along the coast of the North
Riding of Yorkshire nestling under the abrupt cliffs in which the North York
Moors end at the sea. Several of these fishing communities were founded by
Vikings and have prospered for more than a thousand years, some, for instance
Whitby, revealing their origin in their names, others, such as Staithes, shown
above, having no visible link with it.

different parts of the country no less fascinating, villages like Robin Hood's
Bay in Yorkshire, Kirkton of Slains in Aberdeenshire, or Ullapool on one of
the north-west lochs of Scotland. In Wales, too, which few think of as a fishing
country, there are many pretty coastal villages, especially round the rocky
coast of Pembrokeshire and the shores of Cardigan Bay, where the wayfarer
may still find fishermen putting to sea in their traditional coracles.

Many country lovers choose a fishing village as a holiday centre. It is a
choice which no one would criticize—no one, at least, to whom the fascination
of the sea is known. Many who have spent holiday after holiday at one of the
larger seaside resorts can have no idea of the peace and quiet which is still to
be found in hundreds of the smaller fishing towns as well as in the fishing
villages themselves.

There are many who voice the opinion that the British countryside is
spoilt, that in it the wayfarer can never get far from the madding crowd or
from the noise of traffic on the main roads. Those who know their Britain

really well are aware how incredibly untrue this statement is. So with the coastline, a cursory glance at the map and a superficial knowledge of a few districts suggest, perhaps, that there is development everywhere, that the modern increase in holidays and commercial traffic has brought every place within reach of everyone, with consequent devastation to what was once beautiful and peaceful. That is just as untrue as the alleged spoliation of the countryside. A few fishing villages have become popular holiday resorts, and hotels have been established. A few others, to which good roads lead from near-by larger towns, are thronged in summer with day trippers. But there is not the least need to choose these, for they are only a few among very many. Hundreds of coastal villages, like the greater part of the coastline itself, remain completely unspoilt, places where the wayfarer can find simple accommodation and live a simple life in close communication with the people whose chief interest as well as livelihood is bound up with the sea.

Let us take together a swift journey in imagination round the coast, beginning our tour in the far north of Scotland. The first thing that will strike us is that the coastline is infinitely longer than we might have thought. It is about eight hundred miles from the north coast of Scotland to the south coast of England in a straight line. It must be twice that distance following the line of the coast, with its many inlets and estuaries.

From Cape Wrath to Duncansby Head there are well over a hundred

PEMBROKESHIRE COAST

There is much in common between the scenery of the Pembrokeshire coast and that of Cornwall, a similarity that goes further than scenic likeness, because many of the settlers along the Pembrokeshire coast came originally from Cornwall, and many of the Pembrokeshire coastal villages have Celtic names and a population largely derived from Cornwall. Solva, set on a creek of St. Bride's Bay, is one of the most ancient of these villages and one of the most attractive. Its only industry, as it has been through the ages, is fishing.

LOCH NEVIS, INVERNESS-SHIRE

Almost entirely surrounded by mountains, Loch Nevis, which means literally Loch of Heaven, extends fourteen miles into the interior of Inverness-shire opposite the Isle of Skye. At the mouth of the loch stands Mallaig; at the head there are mountains rising to more than 3,000 ft. above sea-level.

miles of coastline so unspoilt, so lonely, that any who have never visited this remote part of Britain can have no idea of its grandeur and solitude. A single road closely follows the sea, making a wide detour round the various lochs and especially Loch Eriboll, which cuts fifteen miles or more into the mainland. Thurso is the only place of any size, but there is a score of fishing villages from Eriboll itself to Tongue and Port Skerry.

The whole life of the people who dwell here is centred on fishing and the very small-scale farming which is possible in this region. Though the land is unfertile and the climate a comparatively cold one, there is plenty of sunshine in the summer months and there is added compensation in the wealth of rare wild flowers and bird life. Though the fisherfolk are poor, they are hardy and determined, many of them being descended from the Scandinavian invaders who overran much of the Scottish coast in the centuries immediately preceding the Norman occupation of England.

The east coast of Scotland is more kindly than the north, the villages are nearer to each other, more prosperous and on the whole larger. The country of the hinterland, too, is more hospitable and at least south of the Great Glen a prosperous agriculture in the coastwise fields goes hand in hand with the fishing industry. In Caithness and Sutherland, between the relatively big fishing ports of Wick and Tain on the Dornoch Firth, there is nothing larger than a village, though many of them are pretty villages showing signs of the easier life which the people live compared with that of the villagers of the north coast. There is a village at the mouth of every stream which runs down to the North Sea from the highlands of Caithness and Sutherland. Three of them, Helmsdale, Brora, and Golspie, hard by the romantic ruins of Dunrobin Castle, have a more than local fame, and deservedly so, for they are interesting alike in their situation and in their local history of struggle to win wealth from the sea. Still prosperous, they are fine centres in which the true country lover can explore on foot some of the lesser-known valleys and glens of the eastern Highlands. The fortress of Dunrobin Castle dates from the eleventh century. Some remnants of the older structure have been incorporated into the present modern building, which is the seat of the Duke of Sutherland.

The story is the same all the way down the east coast of Scotland. The

A SCOTTISH SEA-LOCH

The whole of the west coast of Scotland, from Cape Wrath in the north to the Firth of Clyde in the south, is deeply indented by long sea-lochs very similar to the fiords of Norway. These lochs reach in many cases thirty or forty miles into the very heart of the mountains, which often rise precipitously from their waters. Fishing villages are found where there is a narrow strip of level land beside the loch. This photograph shows Loch Carron, which for many miles lies beside the road to Skye. In the foreground is the village of Plockton, in the background Applecross and the Torridon Hills.

farther south we come, the nearer we reach the obvious marks of twentieth-century civilization, with ever-larger towns—Peterhead, Aberdeen, and Montrose; but even as far to the south as Angus the majority of the coastal places are very small towns or villages.

The coast which faces the Moray Firth is a great centre of the modern fishing industry; towns like Cullen and Banff have behind them a long tale of achievement and prosperity, reflected in the fine houses which grace their central squares and main streets.

There is a real air about these Scottish fishing ports, an atmosphere which is uncommonly attractive and as different as can be imagined from the bustling activity of the fishing ports of eastern England. Perhaps the most charming town of them all is Stonehaven, on the coast of Kincardine, a sizeable place which nestles round a fine natural harbour, with tall cliffs and a rocky coastline stretching north and south, and one of the finest castle ruins in Scotland, Dunottar, on the cliff-top a few miles to the south.

That is only one of the larger and more attractive places. Bervie, Johnshaven, Findon—they are all attractive in their own way, all beautiful places between cliffs and sea and all, curiously enough, easily accessible by rail and road. Yet the number of visitors who go to them is few and the effect these

CULLEN, BANFFSHIRE
Cullen is one of a string of small fishing towns on the coast of Scotland facing the northern North Sea. It lies between Buckie on the west and Portsoy on the east. Like a number of other fishing towns on the Moray Firth, it is a royal burgh and has had a continuous history of quiet prosperity since the coastal districts of Scotland were first colonized.

ON THE ISLE OF MULL

Mull is one of the largest of the islands that lie off the west coast of Scotland. Its coastline is deeply indented by lochs and bays. Just as there are fishing villages along the lochs of the mainland, so there are ancient fishing settlements by the shores of the lochs of Mull. Many of these, like that shown above, are very small, some of them consisting of little more than half a dozen crofter-fishermen's cottages, whitewashed and single-storeyed, and with thatched roofs. Owing to the poor quality of the ground in these parts the crofter is often compelled to supplement his income by fishing.

visitors have on their natural beauty and their unsophisticated charm is negligible.

Western Scotland is very different from the east in almost every way, but it has at least this one thing in common with it, that it contains scores of unspoilt seaside places, although generally speaking, the traditions they inherit are diametrically opposed to those of the east. All down the coast of western Scotland the land is invaded by numerous sea-lochs cut into the hinterland between the peaks of the mountains.

The fishing villages are set along the banks of these lochs, often in surroundings of magnificent scenery. They are mostly tiny straggling places where fishing is still the craft of the individual and there are only small boats unequipped for putting out into the open sea. A few of these places, like Ullapool, have become well known as centres for exploring the highland country, but their fame has altered them very little. By virtue of the long distances involved from any centre of population and the absence of rapid means of transport, relatively few visitors can penetrate to them, though here and there a big hotel has been built and one or two of the old Scottish castles have been transformed for this purpose. Accommodation is still very limited and fishing remains the chief industry of the people. In this respect the

CRAIL, FIFESHIRE

This Scottish royal burgh is one of the many fishing towns of the east coast of Scotland, facing the Firth of Forth between Fife Ness and Kirkcaldy. These are generally smaller and less ancient in origin than the fishing towns that face the Moray Firth, but are no less prosperous, while many of them during the present century have been developed as holiday resorts, owing to their relative nearness to Dundee and the industrial towns of the Scottish Lowlands. The stepped gables seen in a number of the cottages are duplicated in very many of the ancient towns and villages of eastern and southern Scotland.

villages of western Scotland are different from some of the most famous of Cornwall, where catering for holidaymakers has become an integral part of the rural economy.

From the shores of many of the lochs, as in the case of the fiords of Norway, which they so closely resemble, the mountains rise sheer from the water's edge and have precluded colonization at any period of history. The villages of west Scotland are not only isolated from the rest of Britain, but each is isolated from the other except by sea. The sea, therefore, is the traditional means of transport between one place and another. It is often a hundred miles' journey to reach the nearest village overland, though it may be only six miles away across the mountains as the crow flies.

Ullapool, Lochinvar, and Strome Ferry are three of the most famous in the north-western highlands, and Ballachulish is one of the most attractive of the more southerly coast of Argyllshire; but dozens of others whose names are almost unknown are equally fascinating and equally remote. The Argyllshire coast inevitably comes to some extent under the influence of Glasgow and the industrial places of central Scotland, which have given rise to the growth of modest resorts like Oban. Even here development is controlled and it is easy to visualize the fishing town that was in the holiday resort of today.

Nor is the coast of the extreme south-west of Scotland without its coastwise villages, especially in Ayr and in Wigtown round the rocky shores of Luce Bay, hemmed in on the one side by the Mull of Galloway and on the other by Burrow Head. Here the village settlements are more numerous because communications are better, and a fine coast road commanding magnificent vistas over land and sea connects them one with another.

THE CHANGELESS CHARACTER OF SEAFARERS

So virtually the whole of the coastline of Scotland is rich in the lore of the sea and in fishing villages that delight the eye of the country lover and rouse the interest of the antiquarian and historian. There is additional interest on account of the fact that in these remote places the people who live by the sea and draw their living from it have not changed very much through the ages. They are in most cases the descendants of the original settlers, perpetuating in their physique and character the special qualities which have made the Celtic and Viking peoples conspicuous in the story of the racial strains contributing to the British people.

The coast of England and Wales is not so remote as that of Scotland. Communications by road and rail are easier. There is not the same sense of great distances, nor, in fact, are there the same distances to be covered between one village and the next or between a village and the nearest market-town. Above all, the nearest industrial town is rarely a hundred miles from any point on the coast; this has produced during the last century a degree of fusion between the life of town and that of village which is unthinkable in the wild and remote districts of north and west Scotland.

The erstwhile fishing village has all too often become the small holiday resort, with large houses being built about the turn of the century to accommodate an increasing number of visitors. In a few cases the small fishing village has become the modern watering-place and holiday centre. Then, as we have seen before, only the core of the old village remains side by side with the large modern town, continuing an independent existence by virtue of the determination of its people not to be absorbed by a new and strange way of life and the need, too, to continue drawing a livelihood from activities more permanent than that of catering for holidaymakers.

In spite of this growing tendency towards fusion of elements in the population which are so incompatible—a fusion which none could argue was beneficial to the British race—there are still numerous villages which, owing to many factors, have not yet felt the full impact of industrialized civilization. The railway cannot go everywhere. The growth of road transport is too recent yet to have effected any major revolution, especially as a good part of the era of easy road transport has been at a time when building labour was required for nationally more urgent purposes than increasing the size of coastwise villages.

Moreover, some of the villages are built on sites which defy the builder to increase their size beyond a certain limit. If Clovelly were to be "developed" it would mean a new town on the cliff-top and there are many others straggling up a steep hill where new building would be uneconomic if not impossible.

So though it may take a little searching for the country lover to find the coastal village of his dreams in England, yet his search will be rewarded if he looks in the right place. The north-east coast is relatively untouched except near the great river estuaries, where Newcastle, Hartlepool, and Hull have thrown tentacles across virgin country to near-by seaside villages. The coast-

CHURCH COVE, CORNWALL

To many lovers of the English countryside, the coves of Cornwall seem the most beautiful parts of the long coastline. This view shows Church Cove, Gunwalloe, near Helston, its tiny beach of sand and shingle hemmed in by jutting promontories. The turbulent water that boils over the half-hidden rocks, and the dark forbidding escarpment of the cliff, provide a striking contrast with the fertile fields, which reach to the very edge of the cliffs.

BAMBURGH CASTLE, NORTHUMBERLAND

One of the great fortress mansions of the north-east coast, Bamburgh Castle
has a history that extends over almost nine hundred years. It was one of the
castles raised by the Normans as a safeguard against uprisings of the peasants,
and the square keep, or inner fortress, can be seen slightly left of the centre
of the picture. The castle was dismantled after the Civil Wars, and, except
for the keep and parts of the great wall, the present buildings are modern
and contain a library of some fourteen thousand volumes.

line of Northumberland at least is in the main so rocky and bare and at the same
time so far from the great centres of population that it is little more changed
than is Scotland. Bamburgh and Alnmouth and Amble are as quiet and pretty
as anyone could desire. Bamburgh, nestling under the walls of its great castle,
is still in appearance a medieval feudal village.

North Yorkshire, too, is charming in every way. Here the coastline is less
rugged than in Northumberland but scenically not less impressive, especially
where the North York Moors come down to the sea and are broken off in tall
cliffs fissured with deep ravines down which short swift streams follow their
brief but lovely course to the sea.

This is Viking country. The people of villages like Staithes and Robin
Hood's Bay are, many of them, descended directly from the Scandinavian

invaders who sailed here in their long ships in the ninth and tenth centuries. The town of Whitby came into prominence as a medieval fishing port, a big centre in centuries gone by with a famous abbey whose ruins are still on the hill above the harbour, the ancient centre, too, of the jet industry for which the Yorkshire coast is famous. Whitby, like Rye and a few other places in the south, though a town, has all the attributes of a village, and though a holiday resort has none of the noise and bustle of the great seaside holiday centres.

The same is true of Bridlington in lesser degree, for here the fishing port is still as busy and important as ever it was. Scarborough, a few miles away, is pre-eminently a holiday town with few signs of its former greatness as a medieval port protected by its castle.

The coast of Lincolnshire scarcely lends itself to picturesque villages, for the sand-dunes of the shore are backed by the "Marsh," an expanse of level country stretching away as far as the rolling country of the wolds. The seaward landscape is not unlike that of Romney Marsh, the beauties of which

HOLY ISLAND, NORTHUMBERLAND

Holy Island, or Lindisfarne, can be reached from the mainland across the sands at low tide, though the road is covered at high tide. A monastery was established on it early in the seventh century by St. Aidan. Later St. Cuthbert became head of the monastery and it was from Lindisfarne that Christianity was spread through the north of Anglo-Saxon England. In Norman times a new Benedictine priory was established and ruins of the church survive. The main building crowning the natural eminence is a castle built in the sixteenth century and restored by the late Sir Edwin Lutyens.

ROBIN HOOD'S BAY, YORKSHIRE
In beauty of setting this little Yorkshire fishing town vies with the famous villages of Devon and Cornwall. Of its inhabitants, many are direct descendants of the Viking adventurers who sailed to England during the ninth and tenth centuries. Their hardihood and perseverance is shown by the crops that are grown, despite salt sea winds, on fields reaching to the cliff edge.

lie hidden and usually impress themselves on the visitor only after a long stay.

It is easy to recognize that the sea has receded, for the villages are often half a mile away from the outermost of the dunes and go down to the seashore only where new building has increased them in the last fifty years or so.

If the beauty of the Lincolnshire coast is disappointing, East Anglia (surprisingly, because of its relative nearness to London) retains many villages of character as well as beauty. That is especially true of the line of villages along the coast of north Norfolk, one of the famous stone belts of England, where the characteristic building material is cobblestones, which form the fabric of many of the churches and farmhouses as well as of the fishermen's cottages.

In the Middle Ages many of these places, such as Blakeney and Cley,

325

were vastly more important than they are today. They were ports with a large coastal trade, which has gradually disappeared with the recession of the sea and the silting up of their harbours. But the little harbours of Wells and Blakeney are a joy to behold, even though the craft they handle today are mainly small sailing yachts and fishing-boats.

The stretch of marshes which intervenes between the old cliff line and the sea is a sanctuary in which many species of wildfowl have found safety. A goodly expanse of the marshes is now preserved for this purpose. It is an eerie but beautiful coastline, traversed by one of the most exciting coast roads in all Britain, which, between Wells and Sheringham, reveals at every twist and turn a fresh panorama, each one more attractive than the last, with a wide diversity of woodland, cornland, and pastureland reaching to the edge of the low cliffs.

As much as the sea has added to north Norfolk it has taken away from the coast of east Norfolk and Suffolk. It is here that cliff erosion has become a very real problem which the ingenuity of man has not resolved effectively. It is sad to realize that some of the ancient fishing villages and ports have disappeared completely "down cliff," notably the ancient port of Dunwich, which finally disappeared within the memory of the oldest inhabitants. The town hall of Aldeburgh, which used to be the centre of a flourishing fishing town and port, now stands upon the promenade, with a small but pleasant modern town added.

The coast of Essex is a surprise and delight, for this is the country of the "eastern estuaries." The seaward places which actually face on the sea are mostly modernized towns, of which Clacton and, inside the Thames Estuary, Southend, are the two largest. But most of the coast of Essex paradoxically is not sea-coast proper but faces on to the broad estuaries such as those of the Colne, Blackwater, and Crouch. Just inside these estuaries there are old fishing towns and villages which have escaped modern development and

DESOLATE NORTHUMBERLAND COAST

The Northumberland coast varies from rocky cliffs and windswept head-lands to low alluvial land highly industrialized. There are few parts of the British coast wilder and more desolate than the part that lies between Holy Island and Alnmouth. Only a few miles south there are coal-mines under the sea at New-biggin. Farther south still there are the industries of Tynemouth. Here the natural beauty of the coast remains.

BEACHY HEAD, SUSSEX

The South Downs end at Beachy Head as the North Downs end at Shakespeare's Cliff by Dover. Here the bare chalk is exposed in a headland that shelters the town of Eastbourne. The sea is constantly eating away the soft fabric of the chalk, undermining it and forming caves.

remain altogether charming. Brightlingsea in the estuary of the Colne, one of the ancient centres of the oyster fisheries, is among the most famous.

Farther up the Colne, Wivenhoe, a quiet place centred about the church which used to be a landmark for mariners plying their craft up the river to Colchester, is another attractive little town with small shipbuilding yards, and today, like most of the other estuary towns and villages, scores of sailing yachts moored off its waterfront.

The greatest centre of yachting is Burnham-on-Crouch. Attractive though it is, the wayfarer may well feel that it has grown out of touch with ancient seafaring tradition. Perhaps the most attractive of all the estuary villages is Bradwell, which is inside the estuary of the Blackwater. Bradwell Quay is its proper name, to distinguish it from its sister village, Bradwell-on-Sea, half a mile away, hard by the Saxon chapel of St. Peter on the Wall, which is on the site of one of the Roman fortresses built to defend the coast against the early Saxon invasions by the Roman Count of the Saxon Shore.

MODERN HOLIDAY CENTRES

England's south-east coast is the most disappointing for the seeker after villages or even towns recognizable as descended from the simple fishing towns and villages of yesterday. This is partly because the south-east coast has always been the site of the ports of entry from the Continent and shipping has been the preoccupation of any and every place which has a harbour. Fishing, of course, was carried on in the old Cinque Ports and their satellites, but shipping on a big scale was the mainstay of their livelihood. Far more devastating than that is the proximity of the south-east coast to London, with the consequent expansion of places along it into holiday centres.

Almost the same is true of Hampshire, for with Portsmouth and Southampton and Bournemouth each stretching out in either direction almost the whole coastline is absorbed by them and their satellite villages. But there is one exception, that is the creeks and inlets of Chichester Harbour. Here there is one of the prettiest and most historic of all England's fishing villages, Bosham, which is in Sussex and proudly retains the air of a place which has been important since Saxon days and the life of whose people has always been centred on the sea.

The farther we go toward the south-west tip of England, the more nearly unspoilt is the whole countryside and the sea-coast in particular. Through the whole length of the southern coastline of Dorset, Devon, and Cornwall there are less than half a dozen really big towns such as Weymouth, Torquay, and Plymouth. The thought of industrial cities grows more and more remote, and so the number of casual visitors grows fewer as we go farther west. This in turn has prevented the building of many new houses, while the physical character of the coast, particularly of Devon and Cornwall, indented as it is, predestines many fishing villages along it to survival.

There is added fascination in this coast because of the variety of the cliffs, with their ever-changing colour and form. The most westerly of the chalk cliffs of England reaches the sea in Dorset, where White Nothe shines

CLOVELLY, NORTH DEVON

Clovelly is the most picturesque of the many fishing villages that line the north coast of Devon and Cornwall. Its main street is cobbled, and so steep that it is ascended and descended by steps. The whole village is built on the sides of the cliff, to which the many houses, old and new, cling precariously. At the foot of the steep slope are a small beach and fishing harbour.

brilliantly in the afternoon sun and dominates Ringstead Bay; to an observer on this bay there stands out also Osmington Mills, which is one of the many villages along this coast which specialize in winning lobsters from the sea. There is a reminder of the chalk hills, too, near Lyme Regis, itself a small fishing port of considerable charm.

Farther west the colours of the coastline deepen, where the famous red hills of Devonshire come down to the sea and make the coastal scenery of Babbacombe Bay among the most striking in Britain.

Some of the villages of the Cornish coast are so beautiful that they have attracted numbers of well-known artists as residents. Some of these have founded "schools" of painting for people associated with one or other of the villages. Lamorna is one of the most famous, Mousehole another. But there is scarcely a village along the Cornish coast, be it Mevagissey or Fowey, Looe or Porthcurnow, which has not been immortalized on the canvas of one or another of Britain's modern artists.

The north coast of Devon and Cornwall is very different. The scenery is grander and rougher. The winds are stronger. Somehow there is less of the peace of the English Channel about it and more of the vigour and anger of the Atlantic Ocean. The fishing villages, though scarcely less numerous or less interesting, are somehow less picturesque except for two or three like Port Isaac and Clovelly, which straggle up the steep cliff-side. Others, more numerous than in the south, have been vulgarized by modern development and, although still charming places, lack the seclusion of the South Devon and Cornish villages. Such are Lynmouth and Ilfracombe, and Newquay and St. Ives. But there remain Boscastle and Lynton, Combe Martin and Morthoe, and many others less well known.

THE COAST OF WALES

Finally, when we cross the Bristol Channel to the coast of Wales, once we have gone far enough west to escape from the industrial complex near the South Wales coalfield, we are in a land where the fishing villages remain totally unspoilt. Though their number is less than around the coastline of the south-west peninsula, they resemble them in that they, too, are the strong-holds of Celtic tradition, even though it may be less self-consciously preserved.

Pembrokeshire is curiously English in some of its ways, but the England which it resembles is the Celtic England of the south-west, not the Anglo-Saxon England of the Midlands and south-east. Round this coast there are many secluded coves reminiscent of Cornwall's landlocked bays.

And so up the coast of Wales there are infrequent but always character-istic villages, among them Aberdovey, at the mouth of the Dovey estuary, and Barmouth, at the point where the Barmouth estuary meets Cardigan Bay. There are others round the Pwllheli peninsula, where the wayfarer will find a peaceful scene and a quiet beauty comparable with any part of the British coast. He will find, too, just as deep and concentrated an interest in the sea and just as keen a memory of fishing lore as anywhere.

MEVAGISSEY, CORNWALL

The cottages of this famous fishing village are as typical of Cornwall as are the houses of Crail (page 320) of east Scotland. The stone-built lower storeys, the weatherboarding, and the narrow street, have not changed for three hundred years or more.

Folk-lore Calendar

JANUARY

New Year's Day

THIS is a public holiday in Scotland following the traditional Hogmanay celebrations on New Year's Eve. The ancient First-footing custom is generally observed throughout the north of Britain. A dark man makes his way from house to house to bring the local inhabitants good luck. In villages in the West of England, the Wassail Bowl is shared among neighbours for a similar reason; its ingredients include old ale, sugar, toast, grated nutmeg, and roasted crab-apples. The word "wassail" comes from the Old English "wes hal," meaning "be thou whole," a form of greeting.

Feast of Epiphany, or Twelfth Night

THE Feast of Epiphany, on the twelfth day after Christmas, 6 January, commemorates the visit of the Wise Men, or Magi, to Bethlehem. A special service is held at the Chapel Royal, St. James's Palace, on this day. Until the reign of George III the sovereign always attended in person. Today the King is represented by two Gentlemen Ushers of the Royal Household, who make the offerings of gold, frankincense and myrrh on behalf of His Majesty. The gold is in the form of golden sovereigns, the value of which is distributed to aged poor. For centuries Twelfth Night was celebrated on the liveliest scale all over Britain, as it marked the official end of the Christmas revels. In many places it is still believed to be unlucky to remove the season's decorations either before or after this day.

Wassailing the Apple Trees in
Somerset and Devon

THIS interesting custom is generally practised round about Old Twelfth Night, 17 January. One of the best-known ceremonies is held at Carhampton, near Minehead. Farmers and villagers visit the orchards to toast the largest trees with cider, after which shots are fired through the branches to drive away harmful spirits. Wassailing is a survival from remote pagan times, when it was practised to invoke the help of good spirits for producing bountiful crops.

Hood Game at Haxey, Lincolnshire

ONCE a year, on 6 January, the male villagers struggle for the "hood," a long roll of canvas, which is thrown among them outside the churchyard. Whoever manages to carry it off to a certain inn is rewarded with a shilling. Tradition ascribes the custom to Lady Mowbray, who, centuries ago, was riding to Haxey Church when her hood was blown off by the wind. Twelve men struggled to pick it up for her and, impressed by this gesture, she gave a piece of land, still called the "Hoodlands," which was to provide the money for hoods for the annual game.

Carnival of Up-Helly-A at Lerwick, Shetland Isles

ON the last Tuesday in January a long torchlight procession, a survival of an ancient Norse festival, is headed by men clad in Viking armour. They drag a model of a Viking galley through the streets and launch it ceremoniously from the waterfront. When the crew leave the ship, blazing torches are thrown into it and the vessel goes down in a blaze of flame.

FEBRUARY

Commemoration of the Purification

CANDLEMAS is a Christian festival in commemoration of the Purification of the Virgin Mary, 2 February, and is traditionally celebrated in churches with lighted candles. At Blidworth, Nottinghamshire, on the Sunday nearest the festival, the most recently baptized infant is carried to St. Mary's Church where, following its re-dedication at the altar as the representative of all children, it is rocked in a cradle placed within the sanctuary. Candlemas superseded an ancient pagan festival held on this day, and at one time many secular outdoor customs were observed. One which survives is the ceremony of Hurling the Silver Ball at St. Ives, Cornwall, which takes place on the Monday following Candlemas. An hour before midday the mayor throws the ball among the crowd gathered outside the town hall, after which it is hurled around the town for the next sixty minutes. Whoever is holding the ball at noon returns it to the mayor, who gives him a reward.

St. Valentine's Day

ST. VALENTINE, 14 February, was an early Christian bishop martyred in Rome in the third century. The date of his death happened to coincide with the great Roman love festival of the Lupercalia, when youths and girls indulged in revelry and feasting on a grand scale. It was the custom for young Romans to draw lots for girl partners, and for lovers to send tokens to one another. Hence the associations with St. Valentine's Day. For centuries afterwards men used to send presents or bouquets to the ladies of their choice on this day. Valentine cards, in lieu of gifts, first appeared about the beginning of last century and became most extravagant in sentiment during late Victorian times, but the custom is not now often observed.

SHROVETIDE

SHROVE TUESDAY is the day preceding Lent and the seventh Tuesday before Easter. In the Middle Ages, when the Lenten period was observed with strict fasting, on this day people attended confession to be shriven of their sins. The rest of the day was then devoted to outdoor sports. Cock-fighting and hen-slinging have happily died out, but some of the harmless games are still carried on.

Street Football

THE origin of the street and field games of football which for centuries have taken place in various parts of the country at Shrovetide is somewhat obscure. At Chester-le-Street, Durham, for instance, though no authentic record can be found, it is maintained that the game was actually played by Roman soldiers—Chester-le-Street, as its name implies, was a Roman camp. On Shrove Tuesday each year several hundred men and youths took part in a game of football in the main street. The centre of the street formed the dividing line and the team on whose "field" the ball was at 6 p.m. was proclaimed the winner. When, with the introduction of large plate-glass shop windows, the game became a rather serious matter for tradesmen, the custom was discontinued.

At Sedgefield, Durham, the commencement of Shrovetide football dates back to the ninth century, when the tradesmen building the parish church played the local farming fraternity. This has continued year by year since. The game is commenced at 1 p.m. by passing the ball through the Bull Ring on the village green, after which it is thrown into the air. It is concluded by the ball being lodged in either of the alleys or goals, i.e., the site of the old North End pond being the farmers' "alley," and the "Springs" in Spring Lane being the tradesmen's "alley." The person securing the ball after it has been "alleyed" and again passing it through the Bull Ring retains possession of it and it becomes his own property.

The village of Corfe Castle, in Dorset, is the scene of a Shrovetide football match in connexion with the annual visit of the Purbeck Marblers, when new Freemen of the Ancient Company of Marblers and Stone-cutters of Purbeck are enrolled in the Town Hall. The match usually takes place, at the end of the more serious business, in the Middle Hawes, a kind of common, and in the street, and is a preliminary to the walk across Newton Heath down to Ower Quay to pay the landowner a pound of pepper as rental for keeping open the right of way. Purbeck marble was shipped from Ower Quay probably as far back as the thirteenth century, and, although the practice was discontinued about two hundred years ago, the peppercorn rent is still paid and the game of football still takes place on the heath.

Until the outbreak of the Second World War, teams of from two to three hundred players for a game of football in the meadows adjoining Alnwick

Castle, Northumberland, were drawn from neighbouring parishes. The practice of playing in the streets of the town was discontinued in 1818. The ball was provided by the Duke of Northumberland as lord of the manor.

Hurling Match at St. Columb, Cornwall

THIS follows the pattern of the football matches, but a special wooden ball, slightly larger than a cricket ball, is used. The match is played between the Town team and the Country team, and the "goal-posts" are roadside stones about a mile on either side of the town. The lucky player who takes the ball to his own goal gets a reward and is afterwards carried shoulder-high through the streets. Hurling was once a popular pastime all over the British Isles, but it survives only at St. Columb and St. Ives on Candlemas Day.

Pancake Bell at Olney, Bucks

PANCAKES were originally made and eaten on Shrove Tuesday to use up fats not permitted during Lent. The "Pancake Bell" (a medieval survival) is still rung from many churches; at Olney it is even now the signal for housewives to compete in a frying-pan race to the church door, where they serve their hot pancakes to the ringers.

MARCH

St. David's Day

ST. DAVID, patron saint of Wales, whose festival is observed on 1 March, was born about A.D. 530. He founded many churches throughout the Principality, including the predecessor of St. David's Cathedral, in Pembrokeshire. He is said to have led an army of his compatriots to victory over the Saxons, and to have persuaded them to wear leeks in their caps during the battle as a mark of patriotic distinction. It has become customary for soldiers of the Welsh regiments to wear leeks on St. David's Day, 1 March.

St. Patrick's Day

THE patron saint of Ireland, St. Patrick, who lived during the fifth century, is commemorated on 17 March. For thirty or forty years his mission extended over the greater part of that country. The green shamrock leaf, which St. Patrick is said to have used to illustrate the mysteries of the Holy Trinity, was adopted as the national emblem of Ireland.

Tichborne Dole

FOR the past eight centuries a dole of flour has been distributed by the lord of the manor to his tenants in the Hampshire village of Tichborne. Each man receives one gallon of flour, and women and children get half a gallon each. The custom has a curious origin. Tradition says that before the first Lady Tichborne died she begged her husband for a piece of land to provide poor villagers with a dole of flour each Lady Day, 25 March. Plucking a burning faggot from the fire, he declared he would give such land as she might crawl around before the faggot burnt itself out. Lady Tichborne managed "with the help of Heaven" to encircle twenty-three acres on her knees and the land is still known as "The Crawls."

EASTERTIDE

Maundy Thursday

AT Westminster Abbey, the Lord High Almoner, in the absence of the King, distributes specially minted silver Maundy Pence, together with monetary gifts, in lieu of provisions and clothing formerly given in kind, to as many aged pensioners as there are years in His Majesty's age. The ceremony is attended by the Yeomen of the Guard of the King's Bodyguard. In bygone times, English sovereigns always washed the feet of the poor in memory of Christ's act before the Last Supper, but this was discontinued after James II's reign.

Good Friday

TWENTY-ONE sixpences for that number of aged widows are placed on a tombstone in the churchyard of St. Bartholomew's, Smithfield, London. The widows kneel to pick them up and are given a further half-crown and a hot cross bun. The charity is several hundred years old.

Ever since medieval times boys of the village of Midgley, Yorkshire, have dressed themselves in weird costumes and acted a short comic play based on the legend of St. George and the Dragon. The name Pace Egg, by which the ceremony is known, is a corruption of Pasch, *pascha* being the Latin of the liturgical term for Easter.

Egg-rolling at Preston, Lancashire

THE early Christians adopted the egg to symbolize the meaning of the Resurrection, and in bygone times eggs were blessed at the Easter services and used as holy gifts. At Preston, on Easter Monday, school children take part in a ceremony during which hard-boiled eggs (painted in bright colours) are rolled down a steep grassy slope. The winner of the game is he or she whose egg survives without cracking. The ceremony is said to be symbolical of the rolling away of the stone from the mouth of the sepulchre as related in the Bible.

The Biddenden Dole

DATING back to about 1135, the Biddenden Dole originated with a bequest made by the Biddenden Maids, Siamese-twin sisters, Eliza and Mary Chaulkhurst, who were born joined together at the hips and shoulders. The sisters lived joined in this way for over thirty years, until one of them was seized with a fatal illness. The other twin survived only a few hours and in their will the sisters left their property to the poor of Biddenden. This property included about twenty acres of land, upon which now stands the Old Workhouse, the remainder consisting of allotments and a smallholding

BOTTLE-KICKING MATCH IN PROGRESS AT HALLATON

called the Bread and Cheese Land. The rent from this property enabled the trustees to distribute on Easter Monday one pound of cheese and two four-pound loaves of bread to every poor parishioner.

Since 1907, when the Charity Commissioners formed a scheme to consolidate this trust with other Biddenden charities, the scope of the Chaulkhurst dole has been extended to include gifts of money and fuel, and to provide nursing facilities and medical treatment for the sick and needy. Since the Second World War it has been necessary to substitute tins of cocoa for the cheese.

Hare Pie and Bottle-kicking at Hallaton, Leicester

THIS ceremony is probably the modern form of a pre-Christian Saxon festivity. After a church service a hare pie is cut and distributed at the rectory. Then on Hare Pie Hill teams representing the villages of Hallaton and Medbourne push and kick a small cask of beer, striving to get it over the river boundaries on either side. The village which is twice successful keeps the "bottle" for the year and the rector of the parish stands the victors drinks of beer, which is partaken at the ancient Hallaton Butter Cross.

Hocktide at Hungerford

THIS festival is of very ancient origin and is said to go back to the time of

337

HUNGERFORD TUTTI-MEN AT HOCKTIDE

King Alfred. The town was originally part of the Crown property attached to the dukedom of Lancaster and the earldom of Leicester, but all the rights, franchises, and privileges were eventually confirmed to the town by Queen Elizabeth. On Hockney Day, or Hocktide, the Second Tuesday after Easter, is held the Court Leet at which the Hocktide jury elect their officers for the following year, and all the old charters are confirmed. While the jury is thus engaged the Tutti-men perambulate the ancient borough with staves decorated with flowers, demanding a coin from the male residents and a kiss from the females.

Oranges and money are scrambled for by the children, who look upon the event as an annual holiday. The Constable's Luncheon takes place at midday and is attended by all the jury, officials, and other commoners, and visitors, both invited and uninvited, are always given a hearty welcome. The fishing rights for which the town is so famous were granted to it by John o' Gaunt in addition to the other rights and privileges held by the commoners from a much earlier date.

Easter Tuesday
HUGE buns, called "Tuppenny Starvers," are distributed on Easter Tuesday by the rector to choirboys and children of St. Michael's Church, Bristol.

338

The origin of this custom is unknown, but it is thought to date from the days when the poor people ate black bread, and a special distribution of white flour was made as an Easter gift.

APRIL

All Fools' Day

THE custom of playing practical jokes on 1 April has given rise to that day being known as All Fools' Day or April Fools' Day. The origin of the custom is uncertain, but some authorities believe it to have arisen from a Roman celebration, at one time universal, which took place each year at the time of the vernal equinox. Though in ancient times 1 April appears to have been observed in Great Britain as a festival, it was not until early in the eighteenth century that the practice of making April Fools became general.

St. George's Court at Lichfield

ST. GEORGE was adopted as the patron saint of chivalry and of England in the reign of Edward III. St. George's Day, 23 April, is observed with special services in churches and the banquet of the Royal Society of St. George is held. At Lichfield the Court of St. George (originating about 1500) is held in the Guildhall to elect high constables and other officials, and absent jurors are fined one groat, equal to about fourpence. Afterwards the toast of the immortal memory of St. George of England is honoured.

MAY

May Day

TRADITIONAL customs in various parts of England are observed to herald the return of flowers and blossom. May Queens are crowned with ceremony, usually on the first Saturday in May at Elstow, and Northill in Bedfordshire, Knutsford, Cheshire, and Hayes Common, Kent, among other places. At Oxford, on May Day, boy choristers take part in a sunrise service in Magdalen College tower, and this is followed by morris-dancing in the streets. On the first Saturday in May, children at Abbotsbury, Dorset, make five or six garlands of flowers, which they take from house to house when they make a collection for their funds. The garlands are afterwards placed on the war memorial.

Hobby-horse Parade at Minehead

SEAMEN of Minehead maintain this custom, observed on 1, 2, and 3 May, which is considered to be a survival of the ancient festivals with which, all over Europe, the coming of summer was celebrated. The Minehead hobby-horse consists of a wooden framework, thickly covered with ribbons of all colours, which a man carries on his shoulders, his body being draped in a cloth, painted all over with vari-coloured circles. His head is covered by a grotesque mask, surmounted with a tall cap, also decked with ribbons. The horse has a long tail, to which in former days a cow's tail was attached, and attendants with a drum and musical instruments play a traditional folk-tune, while the "horse" prances through the streets, collecting "largesse" from onlookers.

Helston Furry Dance

THE furry dance held at Helston, Cornwall, on 8 May is a survival of a pagan festival in honour of the spring goddess. One of Britain's oldest customs, the dance has survived at Helston for nearly two thousand years. The furry dance is led by the town's most recently married couple, and the revellers follow the band down the High Street, waltzing in and out of shops and houses on their way.

Ascension Day

ASCENSION Day, or Holy Thursday, is the fortieth day after Easter, and commemorates the Ascension of Christ. Several customs are still observed on this day, though not all are of Christian origin.

Dressing the Wells at Tissington, Derbyshire

THE clergy visit the five village wells and bless them in turn. A few days previously boards have been erected behind each well and these depict biblical texts worked in flower petals, leaves, and mosses pressed on to wet clay. This is called "well-dressing." The custom is a survival of pagan water-worship (one of the oldest religious cults), widely practised by our early ancestors, who attributed divine powers to natural springs and wells. It was adapted for Christian purposes in later times, but the Tissington well-dressing dates from the time of the Black Death, when the continued purity of the village springs saved the inhabitants from the plague that ravaged near-by places. Their descendants have blessed the wells to this day.

Beating the Bounds

IN many towns the custom of beating the bounds is observed every Ascension Day. This is a survival from the Middle Ages, when officials of every town and parish were charged with perambulating the boundaries once a year to see these had not been encroached on. Boundary posts and landmarks were beaten with long canes by boys who accompanied the officials—afterwards the boys were beaten, too, to impress upon them the importance of their duty. London choirboys still beat the bounds of the Temple and the Tower. At Lichfield, Staffordshire, the bishop and other cathedral dignitaries parade the bounds of their great church and the close once a year.

Penny-hedge Planting at Whitby, Yorkshire

ON the morning of the eve of Ascension Day the "penny-hedge" of stakes, withies, and brushwood, strong enough to withstand three tides, is planted in Whitby harbour. This curious custom is reputed to be an act of penance

BEATING A BOUNDARY MARK OF THE TOWER OF LONDON

instituted by an Abbot of Whitby in the twelfth century, but its origin is almost certainly much earlier.

Oak-apple Day

THE escape in 1651 of Charles II after the Battle of Worcester, when the royal fugitive hid himself in an oak tree, is commemorated on 29 May, Oak-apple Day. Lively processions in celebration of this event take place at a number of villages in England. At Chelsea Royal Military Hospital, which King Charles founded for Army pensioners, war veterans decorate their caps with oak leaves and march past the statue of the king in the quadrangle. At Wishford, in Wiltshire, a procession is held which is a relic of a primeval fertility rite which has since become associated with the privilege enjoyed by the villagers of picking up wood in Grovely Forest near-by. This privilege is incorporated in a charter dated 1603.

WHITSUNTIDE

Cheese-throwing at St. Briavels, Gloucestershire

TINY cubes of bread and cheese thrown on Whit Sunday from the ramparts of the castle in the presence of the villagers commemorate the granting to

341

the villagers of the right to cut timber in a Forest of Dean enclosure of one thousand acres called The Hudnalls. Tradition says the privilege was granted by the lord of the manor about 1206 on condition that a local girl should imitate the ride of Lady Godiva. It is said a girl accepted the challenge, riding round The Hudnalls and through the village covered only by her hair tresses.

Cheese-rolling on Cooper's Hill, Gloucestershire

ON Whit Monday a large cheese is sent rolling down the steep slope and local lads chase after it. Whoever grabs the cheese before it stops rolling gets a small money prize. This centuries-old custom is believed to perpetuate local rights to grazing land.

Dunmow Flitch Trial

THE Dunmow Flitch Trial at Little Dunmow, Essex, on Whit Monday was instituted in the thirteenth century by Baron Faltzwalter, who ordered that any married couple which had neither quarrelled nor "repented, sleeping or waking, of their marriage in a year and a day" should claim a flitch of bacon from the prior and canons of Little Dunmow. Many married couples still take part in the mock trial.

Morris-dancing

MORRIS-DANCING is actually of Moorish origin and is said to have been introduced to England by Queen Eleanor of Castile. One of the chief centres is Bampton, in Oxfordshire, where the troupe has an unbroken tradition of over five hundred years. The dancers wear white costumes and floral hats, with little bells jingling at their knees.

The Court of Arraye and Greenhill Bower, Lichfield

THE custom of holding this court originated about 1285, when every English town held an annual defence meeting and landowners brought in their troops for inspection. At Lichfield the court is still held in the Guildhall and men clad in armour are paraded and inspected. Originally the ceremony took place on Greenhill, to the north of the city, the original site for the inspection of the men-at-arms.

JUNE

Common Riding

AT Hawick, in Roxburghshire, the ceremony of common riding is held annually in June. It dates back to the time when the community grazed their stock on land possessed in common and when it was necessary to ride the marches of the common so as to preserve it against encroachment. At six o'clock in the evening the burgh officials parade through the town accompanied by a drum-and-pipe band. The men of the district then elect their chief, known as the cornet. A blue-and-gold flag, a replica of the one captured by Hawick gallants from a band of English marauders at Hornshole, about two miles from the town, is presented to the cornet, who carries it on the riding through the marches next day. This includes the ceremony of cutting a sod of turf to mark the extremity of the common.

Fire-worship

THE village green at Whalton, Northumberland, is on Midsummer Eve the scene of an interesting survival of pagan fire-worship in Britain, when a huge fire is lit in honour of Baal, a sun-god of the early Phoenicians. The same site on the village green has been used for at least a century, and youths and girls dance round the fire until the flames die down. Midsummer fires are also lit in parts of Cornwall and Ireland, it being widely believed at one time that such fires increased the fertility of the soil and drove away evil spirits that might blight the crops.

JULY

Tynwald Parliament, Isle of Man

ON 5 July each year there meets at St. John's, Isle of Man, the world's oldest open-air Parliament, where the new island laws are read out to the assembly, first in English and afterwards in Manx. Attended by the lieutenant-governor, the bishop, the twenty-four members of the House of Keys (the island legislative body), and civic and church officials, the meeting is held on Tynwald Hill, where it was originally founded by the ancient Norsemen who once ruled the island.

Vintners' Procession in the City of London

OFFICIALS and members of the medieval Guild of Vintners walk in procession to their service at the church of St. James Garlickhithe, preceded by two porters with besom brooms. Clad in white smocks and top hats, the porters recall the days when London's streets were so foul with garbage that such sweeping was necessary.

Swan-upping on the River Thames

ALL the swans between London Bridge and Henley are divided between the King and the London Livery Companies. For the last four hundred years swan-markers, appointed by each party, have rowed up the river to take up the young cygnets for marking. The Royal Swan Warden attends in his official barge.

Rush-bearing

ONCE a year, at Ambleside, Westmorland, articles made of newly cut rushes are carried to church in procession headed by the local village school children. This custom is a survival from the days when the floors of churches and homes alike consisted of dry earth which the people covered with rushes or straw.

343

At Grasmere the ceremony formerly took place at the end of July, but for more than fifty years it has been held on the Saturday nearest the Feast of St. Oswald, 5 August, to whom the church is dedicated.

AUGUST

St. Wilfred's Procession at Ripon, Yorkshire

THE impersonation of St. Wilfred, the patron saint of Ripon, in an annual procession on August Bank Holiday Saturday, commemorates his return from exile to the local monastery about the year 670. The saint is depicted in his episcopal robes, carrying his mitre and crozier, and riding on a white horse led by a monk and preceded by a band.

HARVEST-TIME

Harvest Supper at Manor Farm, Elsted, Sussex

TO mark the end of harvesting, a harvest supper is held at Manor Farm, Elsted, Sussex, to which the farmer and his wife invite all their workers and families. The manor barn is gaily decorated for the occasion and it is customary for the traditional toast to "the Master and Mistress" to be proposed by the oldest hand on the estate.

Harvest Home at East Brent

ALL the villagers and usually a large number of visitors indulge in feasting and jollification, following a service at the parish church, artistically decorated for the occasion. Flags, flowers, and evergreens decorate the village, and a band leads a long procession of villagers to a huge marquee, where they have a meal and drink a toast to a bountiful harvest next year. Afterwards they indulge in sports, dancing, and games. Similar celebrations, on more modest lines, are held in other Somerset parishes.

At Ackworth, Yorkshire, at harvest-time and Christmas each year, a sheaf of corn is dedicated to the "birds of the air" and hung from the pastoral crook of St. Cuthbert's statue over the porch of St. Cuthbert's Church. This is done in memory of the saint, a great lover of the birds, whose body rested in Ackworth Church when the monks of Lindisfarne fled before an invasion of the Danes, taking St. Cuthbert's coffin with them. For seven years they wandered from place to place and tradition says that wherever they rested a church was built and dedicated to the saint.

Abbots Bromley Horn Dance

EACH year at the beginning of September, twelve "Deermen," with huge reindeer horns held aloft, dance through the streets of the village of Abbots Bromley, Staffordshire. The official date for holding the dance is determined by the date on which Abbots Bromley "Wakes" Sunday falls—always the first Sunday after 4 September—the dance taking place on the following Monday. The origin of the dance is now uncertain, but some maintain that

RUSH-BEARING AT AMBLESIDE, WESTMORLAND

it is held in commemoration of the granting of hunting rights in the Forest of Needwood during the reign of Henry III. The reindeer horns, which are kept in the parish church from year to year, are of great antiquity and are supposed to have been left in the district by Norse huntsmen.

The Sheriff's Ride at Lichfield, Staffordshire

BY Charter of 1553 the Sheriff is required on this day to perambulate the bounds of the city to ensure they are intact. He is followed around by a retinue of about one hundred horsemen, who declare that the Ride "covers sixteen of the jolliest miles in the land."

Barnstaple Fair, North Devon

BARNSTAPLE Fair, the most important in Devon, opens on the Wednesday before 20 September. It is over seven hundred years old. On the first day of

345

the fair a ceremonial luncheon is given at the Guildhall at which spiced ale, toast, and cheese are served. The spiced ale is prepared by the senior beadle of the town and its secret recipe has been jealously guarded by a long line of corporation officials. While the fair lasts, a large stuffed glove, signifying the Hand of Welcome, is displayed from the Guildhall. In medieval times the "glove" was hung out on fair days to show that, at this time, outside merchants could enter the town and trade freely with the citizens without interference from the local guilds.

Clipping the Church at Painswick, Gloucestershire

ON the Sunday after 19 September, or on that date if it happens to be a Sunday, the ceremony of clipping is held at Painswick Church, Gloucestershire. The term clipping signifies the parishioners' act of surrounding the church as an expression of their loyalty and affection. A service is held during the afternoon and the children and other members of the congregation, headed by clergy, churchwardens, and choir, march in procession, forming a circle round the outside of the church, and join hands and sing a hymn. A sermon is preached by a minister specially invited for the occasion, who stands outside the church at the top of the steps leading to the belfry door.

OCTOBER

Nottingham Goose Fair

ONE of Britain's greatest medieval fairs is the Goose Fair at Nottingham, held on the first Thursday, Friday, and Saturday in October. It was founded under a charter granted by Edward I and is so called on account of the one-time sale of local geese. The commercial side of the Goose Fair has disappeared, but the three-day fun fair is still opened in the traditional manner by the Lord Mayor.

Mop Fair at Stratford-upon-Avon, Warwickshire

THE word "mop" means a fair or gathering at which farm hands and servants used to be hired for periods of six or twelve months. At Stratford-upon-Avon, on the 12 October, as in many other towns, workers gather in the streets, each displaying some emblem of his particular trade or craft to ensure recognition. In normal times Stratford's fair-day is marked by the roasting in the main street of several oxen and pigs.

Teddy Roe's Band at Sherborne, Dorset

SHERBORNE Fair, on the second Monday of October, dates from 1490, when it was first held to mark the completion of the rebuilding of the abbey church. It is still preceded by midnight revels known as "Teddy Roe's Band," when boys and girls go about the town blowing toy trumpets, banging kettles, shouting, and generally creating the loudest din possible. "Teddy Roe" is said to have been the foreman of the masons who rebuilt the church, and the noise commemorates their rejoicing when the task was finished.

Guy Fawkes' Day

THE bonfires and firework displays which mark the fifth day of November are concerned with history rather than with folk-lore, for they commemorate an attempt in 1605 to blow up the King, Lords and Commons. Robert Catesby originated the plot. Guy (more properly Guido) Fawkes was a soldier of fortune enlisted on account of his military experience and fearless character. The conspirators were ruined men, exasperated by the severe penalties which had been imposed on Roman Catholics by James I. Their plot was betrayed, probably by Tresham, brother-in-law of Lord Mounteagle. On the evening of 4 November the Lord Chamberlain and Lord Mounteagle visited the House of Lords, entered the cellar in which the powder was stored and spoke to Guy Fawkes. After such a warning only a fanatic would have persisted. Guy Fawkes did. He was arrested, tortured, as was then customary, and executed.

All Hallows' Eve

THE night before All Saints' Day, All Hallows' Eve, is traditionally the time when spirits of the earth and air rove about and are most likely to come under the influence of charms. Hallowe'en was observed by the early Druids, who lit bonfires on the hills after dark to appease the god of death, a custom which survived in the highlands of Scotland and Wales until recent times. In the days of the Romans the same date was kept as a feast in honour of Pomona, goddess of fruits, from which come the popular customs of roasting nuts and "ducking" for apples.

NOVEMBER

Payment of Wroth Silver at Knightlow Cross, Warwickshire

AT dawn on Martinmas Eve, 10 November, the Duke of Buccleuch's steward meets the representatives of one hundred parishes at a hollowed stone on Knightlow Hill, Stretton-on-Dunsmore, to collect dues. Each throws a silver piece on the stone, saying as he does so, "Wroth Silver." The Steward then reads a proclamation announcing that the forfeit for default is "twenty shillings for every penny, or a white bull with red nose and red ears." The custom dates from Saxon times when the money paid is supposed to have secured the safe passage of cattle herds within the Knightlow "hundred" against thieves and brigands.

St. Andrew's Day

ST. ANDREW is said to have been adopted as Scotland's patron saint in the eighth century, following a great battle between the Picts and Northumbrians by the Tweed. According to the legend, Angus, King of the Picts, was foretold in a dream that he would be helped by St. Andrew, whose X-shaped cross appeared in the sky during the fighting. After the victory, the white cross set against a blue background was made the Scottish national

347

emblem. St. Andrew is the only patron saint of any land to be mentioned in the Bible. He was the first convert and missionary of Christ and suffered martyrdom by crucifixion in A.D. 69. The day of his martyrdom, 30 November, is one of reunion and rejoicing for Scots throughout the world.

DECEMBER

St. Nicholas' Day

ST. NICHOLAS, the patron saint of boys and sailors, was Bishop of Myra in Asia Minor during the fourth century and was persecuted under the Emperor Diocletian of Rome. In many churches his day, 6 December, is still commemorated by the election of Boy Bishops, who are robed with due ceremony and preside over the services. In olden days it was the custom for people to give presents on the eve of St. Nicholas in memory of the saint.

CHRISTMASTIDE

APART from the general observances of the Christmas season, many interesting local customs are kept up in many parts of the British Isles, except, of course, in Scotland, where Hogmanay celebrations are held on New Year's Eve.

Burning the Ashen Faggot in Somerset Villages

A BUNDLE of ash sticks, bound by green withy bands, was placed on the hearth on Christmas Eve and householders and neighbours gathered round with mugs of ale or cider. The old saying runs, "When the bands that bindeth the ashen faggot do burst, it is time, good people, to take a drink." The custom is said to commemorate a Saxon victory over the Danes in Wessex about 878; before the battle the West Saxons made fires of ash branches to keep themselves warm at night. Ash was the only wood that would burn when green. The only place in Somerset where the custom is now regularly observed is in an old inn at Dunster.

Mummers' Play in North Hampshire

THE thousand-year-old play based on St. George and the Dragon is still acted in many villages, but the troupes of Longparish and Overton, near Andover, claim the longest unbroken tradition. Here, on Boxing Day, the players disguise themselves with weird costumes, made of paper strips, and wear grotesque masks. They perform the play on the village greens and in the local inns and country mansions.

Hogmanay in Scotland

ALL over Scotland New Year's Eve is the liveliest night of the year, and the Hogmanay rites are far older than Christianity. The word "Hogmanay" comes from the ancient practice of making gifts of cake on this day. In some towns and villages the children still go from house to house singing in impromptu rhyme for gifts and money; this is known as "guising," from the fancy costumes the children wear for the occasion.

348

Naturalist's Notebook

WHEN you begin to study nature in Britain, one of the first things that strikes you is the number of things which have been going on that you have never previously noticed. As you learn about nature, your interest grows and with it the enjoyment of what you discover. The variable climate of Britain adds interest to these observations, for it influences the order of events so that things that occur in a particular sequence one year may follow a different course in another.

For instance, no fruit-grower likes too early or too mild a spring because he knows that while the fruit blossom is open it is always in danger from spring frosts. Early blossom, therefore, often means a poor fruit crop, while a season in which the cold continues late retards the swelling of the buds so that the blossom opens late. In this way it suffers less often from a sudden frost, and cold springs are therefore often followed by abundant harvests.

Just as one year may be a good or bad fruit year, so different years may favour this or that plant or animal. Nearly all the plants and animals of Britain's countryside show seasonal variations of this kind, for which there is no single cause. It is the tracking down and piecing together of the complex factors that affect wild life which adds to the interest of study of nature.

In what follows you will find seasonal notes on some of the commoner animals and plants of the countryside of Britain. If you keep your own diary of events and compare them from year to year, you will not only be able to build up a picture of the web of life, but you may also discover new facts.

WINTER

During the unkindest days of winter there is little, apart from hungry birds, to be seen, but during mild days there are stirrings of other kinds of life. In the hedges, the hazel, one of the earliest woodland trees to flower, opens its yellow, hanging catkins. These are bunches of male flowers, and from them the pollen comes out in drifting clouds when the wind blows. The female flowers, which develop into the nuts, are bud-like structures with deep-red stigmas at their tips to catch the pollen, and are borne on the same tree as the male.

In the shade of the hedge, the inconspicuous flowers of dog's-mercury may open at this time of the year. This little herb also has separate male and female flowers which are wind-pollinated. Pollination at this time of the year has to be carried out in this way, for bees and other insects are still sheltering from the weather. It is surprising, therefore, to find flowers in bloom that do

THE BEAUTY OF WINTER

This Yorkshire by-way shows the lovely patterns of snow-drifts. When wind blows snow off the fields, it collects between the roadside hedges, forming deep drifts which may block the road even though only a few inches are lying in the more exposed open country.

not produce the copious clouds of pollen that characterize those that are wind-pollinated. Chickweed, groundsel, and shepherd's-purse bloom in the cool sunshine of winter and they seem to be able to produce healthy seed without cross-pollination. The lawn daisy and dandelion may also bloom in winter and pollinate themselves. This may explain their success against the efforts of the gardener to exterminate them.

In cottage gardens the winter sunshine opens the blossoms of winter heliotrope, with its delicate scent, and the so-called Christmas rose. Aconites and snowdrops in the flower border are sometimes in bloom beneath the snow, and open their petals as the thaw exposes them; but perhaps the most reliable of these winter-flowering importations is the yellow jasmine that puts out its buds on naked stems and opens them in a few hours when you cut the stems and put them in water indoors.

WINTER FUNGI

At this time, too, when flowers are so rare, the flowerless plants show well. In woodlands on fallen logs and in the rotting leaf-mould of the forest floor you can find the fruiting bodies of many fungi. Several different fungi are noticed only at this time of the year, among them the curious black-and-white candle-snuffer fungus and the strange so-called earth stars.

As the days get longer more of the early spring flowers come out. Between their grass-like leaves the crocuses push up their flower buds and open their white, yellow, or purple petals. Even in the bleakest weather, the little whitlow-grass sometimes flowers at this time of the year. A member of the cabbage family, this little plant shows just how hardy it can be, by sometimes opening its four white petals in the depth of winter, and choosing to grow in crannies in walls and other dry and infertile places.

At this time, too, you can expect to see coltsfoot in flower. In the fields, and by the roadside, among the tussocks of frost-bitten grass, clumps of yellow dandelion-like blossoms open at the top of grey-green hairy stems. Coltsfoot is a troublesome weed of arable land but it used to be gathered for its supposed value as a cure for coughs, and some people smoke its dried leaves instead of tobacco. Not many people seem to notice elm trees in flower at this season of the year. This is probably because they do not flower until they are about thirty years old, and the flowers are therefore well above people's heads and, on the naked twigs, show black against the grey sky. But if you can reach them, elm flowers make an attractive indoor decoration. They open on the twigs, and push out their purple stamens so that the wind may take the pollen.

By the waterside, the male and female alder catkins open and so do the yew flowers in the hedges. The male yew flowers give off so much pollen that if you beat the hedge with a stick you can see the pollen rise in clouds. Another tree that flowers early in the year is the Lombardy poplar. This is not an English tree, and the original importers appear to have brought in few female trees. So that when you look up at the tops of Lombardy poplars in late February or March you see only the red pennon-like catkins of the male flowers. Few Lombardy poplars shed seeds, therefore, and each tree is grown from previously existing trees by taking cuttings.

Bird life in the winter in Britain is mainly restricted to the resident birds and the winter migrants. Among the resident birds which are easily recognized, blackbirds and chaffinches are much commoner than most people think; both being about three times more numerous than the common sparrow, and about half as common again as starlings or robins. All these birds will visit your bird table, especially when the snow is down, and in addition song-thrushes, missel-thrushes, rooks, greenfinches and at least two kinds of tit can be seen.

RESIDENT AND MIGRANT BIRDS

At the end of the year such birds as robins and thrushes become more jealous of the territory that they range, and they may sometimes be heard singing to warn off intruders who might wish to share the meagre forage of their hunting grounds. This is a good time to start learning to identify the common birds by their song. In addition to robins and song-thrushes, you can hear missel-thrushes, linnets, wrens, and skylarks, and even starlings try to imitate other birds, or make the fizzing gurgles that pass for their song.

Of the birds that range in flocks during the winter, starlings probably do most harm and peewits most good. Starlings, by sheer weight of numbers, have become a pest to the farmer, for they include in their diet some of his produce. Peewits, however, feed on pests in the soil, and so pay the farmer a handsome rent!

Among the winter migrants, two thrushes—the redwing and fieldfare—are easily recognized. Apart from their appearance, they both differ from thrushes resident in Britain because neither of them sings there and both are nearly always in flocks. Bramblings, also winter visitors, are always in flocks in Britain, where they seldom sing.

As the year advances many British resident birds become more active and conspicuous. Quite early the song of the lark as it rises above the open fields that it frequents can be heard. You will notice the metallic "pink-pink" of chaffinches in February as such birds as tits, blackbirds, and thrushes begin the process of marking out their territory—a process that ends when the hen birds select the actual nesting sites. While most of the starlings are still in their winter flocks, some break away and pair early. Then comes the ominous mating call of the wood-pigeon. As these birds coo in the trees, farmers finger their shotguns, for they know that wood-pigeons' families have expensive tastes—and cost a good deal in corn seed and seedling corn.

While it is still too early for the rooks to start building you will see them moving from their winter roosting sites and making a commotion about the tops of the elm trees as they inspect the old nests. People may tell you that rooks can in some mysterious way foresee the weather, and build high up in the elms if a good summer is on the way. No one has ever verified this, and it is most unlikely.

Many British mammals are active all the year round, and the tracks of rabbits, hares, foxes, weasels, stoats and others may sometimes be seen in the

A SOUTHERN ROOKERY

The rook is found in large flocks all over the British Isles. In this typical rookery the nests are visible among branches still bare of leaves in early spring. A number of the birds are circling; they appear intensely black, seen at a distance, but at closer quarters have a bluish tinge.

snow. Hares and rabbits leave other, and less welcome, signs, and you will soon learn to recognize the damage they do to winter greens and the bark of fruit trees when they are hard pressed for food. When walking through woods you will sometimes see squirrels come out in the winter sunshine. They do not go through the bodily changes known as hibernation, though some people maintain that they do. Squirrels may take long naps during the worst of the weather, but their temperature, pulse rate, and breathing are those of a sleeping animal, not a hibernating one. Voles and hedgehogs also take long naps in the winter and come out on fine days, but dormice and bats really hibernate. Their whole rate of living slows down, and they may die if they are disturbed.

Most British insects spend the winter huddled away from the cold. Many pass the winter as eggs; some as grubs or larvae; some as pupae; and a few in the adult state. Both eggs and pupae, having tough skins, can take considerable punishment from the weather—even being frozen solid—without coming to any harm. It is surprising, therefore, to find that many British butterflies spend the winter as caterpillars curled up in the soil or under debris, while others habitually over-winter as adults with their wings folded, quietly waiting for better times. On fine days these butterflies may come out for a short flight, and so you may see peacocks and small tortoiseshells sucking nectar from early blossoms of arabis or aubrietia in the rock garden.

WINTER MOTHS

Of the moths, the males of the early moth and the pale brindled beauty may be seen on the wing during January. The females in both cases are wingless and do not look like moths. This is true also of the various winter moths whose caterpillars eat the leaves of fruit trees in the spring and early summer. Fruit-growers tie bands of greasy paper around the trunks of their trees in the autumn, so that the female winter moths, crawling upward to lay in the branches, are caught in the grease and perish.

A number of moths have caterpillars which form into chrysalises in the soil, and in digging in the winter you often come across these red barrel-shaped pupae. If collected and kept in a flowerpot of moist soil they will hatch in the spring.

Few other insects are active during the dark days of the year, but most people have seen the winter gnats which come out in the brief sunshine of a mild afternoon. These gnats are different from those that pester us on warm summer nights.

In some years when late winter is warmer than usual, a queen wasp who has been hibernating may be seen, having been tempted out during a burst of sunshine. Such a wasp will not survive the winter if she is too active, as she uses up her fat when she should conserve it for use later. Many people have noticed that a mild winter is often followed by a summer when there are few wasps about. When the sun goes down slightly later each evening, we look for signs that spring is really on the way; and we can feel a little more certainty when we see frogs coming out of hibernation and making their way to their

HOAR-FROST ON THE TREES

Hoar-frost is composed of ice crystals, which cover trees and grass when the
temperature is below freezing point and is the winter equivalent of dew. The
most magnificent displays occur when there has been a succession of exceptionally cold nights with banks of drifting fog.

355

RED DEER IN THE SCOTTISH HIGHLANDS
This herd of red deer is photographed against the winter landscape of the forest of Inverness-shire in Glen Loyne. Like the Forest of the High Peak and many others, this forest is almost treeless and one of the few areas in which red deer are still numerous. Herds of male and female deer always hunt separately, travelling over considerable areas of the wild and barren countryside, only coming together during the mating season in the autumn.

spawning grounds. Sometimes during these spring migrations the roadways are littered with the bodies of these animals who, driven by internal forces to the water where they breed, have been killed by passing traffic.

Soon the nights are loud with the noise of their love-making, and if you visit a pond where the frogs are croaking you will see them crowded in the water, each egg-bloated female with her obedient mate attached dutifully to her back. The spawn is shed and fertilized and the parents then desert it and one another, leaving the spawn in ponds, ditches, streams, and even rain-filled cart ruts.

Perhaps it is this spawn, more than anything else, that tells us that the spring, the season of new young lives, is at hand.

SPRING

When the blackbirds shatter the crocuses, and the daffodil buds show green among the upright blades of their foliage in the flower border, you know that much is happening in the countryside. As the days lengthen and the strength of the sun increases, scillas, polyanthuses, and violets bloom in the gardens, and tiny glands on the wallflower petals secrete the oily scent which sweetens the air.

The dark wet soil of ploughed field and garden soon becomes carpeted with the green leaves of seedlings as they burst from their husks and expand. The gentle rains of spring and the warmth of the sun shower upon crop and weed seedlings alike, causing the stems and leaves to grow with the vigour of youth, faster than they will ever again. The woodland floor is covered, too, with the early blossoms of wood-sorrel, wood-anemone, lesser celandine, and primrose. These blossoms have rested all winter within buds ripened during the previous summer, and are interesting because, being unable to open

PRIMROSE WOOD IN SOUTHERN ENGLAND

In average seasons the primrose flowers in March, though in exceptionally mild weather it is found in southern England as early as February. Occasionally isolated clumps of primroses flower from before Christmas right through the winter. It is a flower of the woodlands, especially prolific in the southern counties, as shown by this scene near the Bath Road at Woolhampton in Berkshire. Primroses in abundance are found, too, on the banks bordering the deep ditches which are common in Essex.

BY A SURREY STREAM

In this picture daffodils are seen at Newchapel, near Lingfield, growing semi-wild in low clay fields bordering one of the streams of the Surrey Weald. In most years daffodils are at their best in the south-west of England in March and in the north by the end of April.

BY THE COAST OF EAST LOTHIAN

Southern Scotland is no less rich in wild flowers than the English lowlands but spring comes later in this more northerly climate. Here cowslips, flowering almost a full month later than in Devon and Cornwall, are in full bloom in a field sloping down to the edge of the sea in East Lothian.

SPRING IN AN ESSEX LANE
Much of Essex is a naturalist's paradise, the clay-lands being ideal for bearing spring flowers in profusion, as certainly as the chalk-lands of the downs are the habitat of the finest British flowers of the late summer and early autumn. In this early May scene between Chelmsford and Dunmow the horse-chestnut trees are in full blossom, the grass verge bordering the road is carpeted with cowslips and the hedgerow trees are showing darker green leaves.

without bright sunlight, they flower early, although it is cool, while the trees above them are still bare of leaves.

As the sap rises within them, the trees, too, become more active. Elder buds open early and the leaves expanding turn from bronzy-red to green. Following the hazel and alder, other catkin-bearing trees come into bloom, and both willow and birch are visited by honey-bees for pollen. The black buds of ash break open and their flowers expand on grey leafless stems, but the beech's bell-like catkins hang in clusters among the young leaves, almost translucent in their loveliness.

Now is the time to see the larches, which are the only common cone-bearing trees growing in Britain that shed their leaves in winter. In the spring, the young green leaf-needles grow in tufts along the russet stems. Cut some of these stems from a mature tree and stand them indoors in water, and soon the red juicy cones expand to make a pleasant splash of colour.

Soon the sides of lanes show white as the delicate blackthorn blossoms open on the dark leafless thorny hedge. Then follow the spring leaves as the buds open and wayfaring tree, bramble, hawthorn, bryony, clematis, and elm put forth their foliage. A strange hint of autumn comes now, for the young crumpled leaves of Lombardy poplar and maple are red, while the oak trees look yellow from a distance. These colours, however, soon change to green as the leaves open fully, and the yellow oak flowers drop.

The white flowers of the hedgerows follow each other as crab apple, dogwood, and holly, cherry, horse-chestnut, wayfaring tree, and hawthorn come into bloom. When the last hawthorn blossom falls, the elder flowers open to whiten the hedges in summer.

Among the later spring flowers of the hedges, those of maple, buckthorn, and spindle are interesting, for although they are pollinated by insects, and the maple especially yields nectar heavily, none is large and conspicuous, so that few people even know what these flowers look like. They appear green to the human eye, but possibly they look different to the bees and other insects, for,

A ROCKY LEDGE OF THE CAIRNGORMS

Wild flowers grow wherever there is a little soil in which they can put forth their roots, even as here, on a rocky ledge near the summit of one of the Scottish mountains. The starry saxifrage, which is bringing springtime colour to this barren rock, is typical of the thousands of rock plants which grow in Alpine and sub-Alpine regions. The flowers of the saxifrage vary in colour from white to yellow and red.

ON A MOORLAND TARN

The black-headed gull nests in reeds around many of the ponds and larger sheets of water in England. The characteristic spotting of the eggs can be seen in this photograph of a gull alighting at its nest.

as is well known, the colour of a flower is important in guiding insects to it. With the reappearance of the honey-bees and other flower-loving insects come the nectar-laden flowers of the hedgerows, banks, and fields.

On sunny banks, speedwells, stitchworts, forget-me-nots, wild strawberry, and trefoil blossom among the young grass leaves, and on the edges of woods ground-ivy, cowslips, herb robert, and crane's-bill come out, while the blue-bells in the deeper shade are still in bud.

There comes a change in open fields as many of them show yellow for a long time now. It is not, however, always the same yellow, nor do the same flowers cause it. For after the buttercups come the dandelions, later followed by bird's-foot-trefoil, hawkbit, cat's-ear, and charlock.

THE BIRDS BEGIN BUILDING NESTS

As the foliage of the trees and hedgerows thickens, it shelters many birds who now build their nests. Many a cock flies round his territory scaring off other cock birds as they, too, mark out their claims. Challenging flights and struttings seem to help in this, and the birds' anger and aggressiveness reach a climax as they burst into song. Thrushes, blackbirds, greenfinches, goldfinches all sing loudly and prepare to mate and nest, so that it is not difficult to find their nests in the hedges. High on the hedge, the little yellow-hammer calls insistently that he has "a little bit of bread and no cheese," and our friends the rooks are hard at work in the trees. Their nest-building is a noisy business as they wheel in flapping crowds about their rookeries in the elms. But the rook is a rapid worker and hardly has building started than it is finished. Robins choose their nests now, sometimes in the most unlikely places, such as old tin cans and iron kettles, and it is strange that there are not more casualties.

Almost before most people have thought of birds' eggs, two summer visitors to Britain have already produced their first brood of youngsters. These two migrant birds are among the first to arrive in Britain and are almost indistinguishable in appearance. The chiff-chaff, whose song is like its name, and the willow-wren are both yellowish-green birds and, like all summer visitors, start nesting as soon as they arrive. With them, and sometimes even before them, comes the wheatear, well known by its white rump and its cheerful "chack-chack." After these early migrants, the main influx of summer visitors arrives. Early in April you may expect the first swallows, and soon after housemartins arrive and are playing mudlarks on the eaves of buildings, as they try out nest-building before getting seriously to work. In April, too, fewer people see the cuckoo than hear the insistent call of the male bird. Still fewer people recognize the coarse bubbling chuckle of the hen cuckoo as she responds to her lover's song. As the days pass the flood of immigrants swells and the air becomes noisy with the song of sedge-warbler, wood-warbler, tree-pipit, blackcap, and nightingale. Britain lies in the line of flight of several migrant birds which, spending the winter in the south, fly to countries farther north than Britain to breed in the spring. Such birds of passage as little stints, bar-tailed godwits and other waders may sometimes, therefore, be seen on

FOXES LEAVING THEIR EARTH
The country-lover may wander over the countryside for years without seeing
a single fox, while in parts of Britain they are frequent enough to cause little
comment. This is especially true in Leicestershire and other traditional hunting
shires, but there are also foxes in plenty on Dartmoor, where their earths are
around the rough tors, and in all the mountainous districts of Britain. Generally
foxes hunt at night, but they come out by day at cubbing time, when additional
food is needed for the vixen and the cubs.

their northbound course. Few people notice that the winter visitors have gone,
for the redwings, fieldfares, and bramblings migrate in order to nest at the
most northerly end of their range, just as other birds do.

After the swallows come the swifts, which, though bearing a superficial
resemblance to them, are not closely related. These tireless birds fly restlessly
from perch to perch, catching insects as they go. Now is the air full of song,
but as the birds pair off the volume of song decreases until, when the nests are
built and the eggs and young are brooded, the parent birds become silent.
Blackbirds, thrushes, robins, chaffinches, and many others are now tirelessly
feeding their young on insect grubs, and the sparrow-hawk is busy flying back
and forth, from the mouse-runs under the hedge to a forked branch high in an
elm.

Mice, voles, and other mammals are all more active as the days become
warmer, but among the earliest of these rodents to breed is the hare who,
sometimes as early as February, carries out his foolish-looking love-capers to
impress his lady. Foxes have mated in the dark days of winter, so the vixen,

364

too, is early with cubs, as are the other carnivores, the stoats and weasels. Moles are active now, and if you keep very still you can watch their molehills forming in the fields, for, although they have poor eyesight, they are very sensitive to the sound of a footfall and lie low if they suspect an enemy near-by. Shrews, which, like moles, feed on small animals, fight fiercely among themselves as they settle their marriage problems. Before long, squirrels' nests, or dreys, are built and occupied, and water-voles are rearing young beside the streams. More often now during the longer spring evenings you notice bats flying in the twilight. They seem to fly straighter than they do during the warmer months, and some people think that this is because there are still few of the night-flying insects about which they catch. Most of the different kinds of bat have only one youngster per year, which they often carry with them on these evening flights.

Dormice wake from their winter sleep, and sometimes on a calm evening you will catch your first sight of a hedgehog picking its way daintily among the weeds of the hedge bottom. Until it notices you it browses busily among the

MUTE SWANS AND CYGNETS

The largest bird of Britain's rivers and lakes, the mute swan is now by habit tame, more often regarded as a graceful ornament than as the strong, magnificent bird he is by nature. Swans are capable of flying long distances and move from one reach of a river to another or, more rarely, across open country to the next stretch of water they can find. They build their large nests conspicuously among the reeds and grasses on the river- or lake-side.

herbage, searching for the slugs, snails, and insects on which it feeds. Should you show yourself, it hurries away, never, however, losing dignity, but with an air suggesting that it has urgent business elsewhere.

After the frogs have laid their eggs, it is still too early in the year for the emergence of many of the insects upon which they feed. The frogs, therefore, go into hibernation once again, until the summer weather has brought the insects out. This second rest helps them to overcome the strain of spawning, which is sometimes so heavy that each year many frogs do not survive it.

Toads spawn later than frogs, and their eggs are in long gelatinous strings, while it is often not until early summer that the different kinds of newt emerge from hibernation and enter the water in order to mate.

Insect life follows the same upward curve, as the days become warmer and longer. Out of their winter chrysalises come the common butterflies—the small whites followed by the large whites. Peacocks, brimstones, and small tortoiseshells come out of hibernation, having passed the winter as perfect butterflies, while the small coppers and common blues that have passed the winter as caterpillars quickly complete their life history and take to the air. By late spring the orange-tip butterfly is also on the wing, and with it cinnabar moths and burnet moths, both of which fly by day. The huge caterpillars of the lappet moth are actively feeding on apple and hawthorn leaves, while the woolly-bear caterpillars of the garden tiger-moth, which feed on stinging nettles, are also found in late spring. Many moths, too, are out at night, and show up in car headlight beams, and may also be seen fluttering against uncurtained illuminated window-panes. Ladybird grubs, which are mauve with orange spots, feed greedily on the aphids which they find in gardens, and rapidly turn into pupae which are found, coloured orange with mauve spots, curled up on walls and fences where they turn into ladybirds.

Inside the hive honey-bees, whose larders are now packed with pollen and the honey made from fruit and hawthorn-blossom nectar, feed up young queens and drones in preparation for swarming. And as May passes into June and the bees surge out of their hives, the roar of their wings as they swarm tells once again that this is the height of the year and that the earth, drenched in long hours of light, is about to bring forth its fruit.

SUMMER

Even before the summer sun rises above the hill, many of the flowers that close their petals against the injury the night dew may cause have opened them. Though the morning is cool the plants respond to the call of light, just as the early flowers of the woods opened even in a cool spring. In the same way the date of opening of the summer flowers sometimes depends more on the length of the day than on the heat of the sun. Thus in the garden the long sunlit days of June see lupins, delphiniums, and stocks, lilac and laburnum, in bloom, while the countryside shows a great variety of flowers in fields, hedgerows, and elsewhere.

Although the summer air is full of insects, the grasses, of which there are over one hundred different kinds in Britain, rely on the wind for pollination.

KENT CHERRY ORCHARD

This mid-April view at Salts Farm, Loose, near Maidstone, is duplicated in thousands of typical English vistas. The cherry is the earliest of the orchard blossoms, coming before the plum, the pear and the apple. In some Kentish views the mass of blossom of the cherry orchards covers many square miles.

IN WINDSOR GREAT PARK

Azaleas and rhododendrons, shown here in full bloom in the gardens of Windsor Great Park, are found only in soils free from lime. Accordingly they flourish in the sandstone country of Sussex, Kent, and Surrey.

One of the earliest to flower, the little annual meadow-grass, is followed by foxtails and timothy grasses, and soon the air is laden with the grass pollen grains that sometimes cause hay-fever.

With the grasses come the clovers and, if hay-time is not too early, the bees snatch a honey harvest before the mower cuts the flowers down. Vetches and bedstraws carpet patches of the open fields, too, and on cornland poppy, charlock, and campion are followed by corn-flowers and ragwort. Waste places also have their flowers, and the later summer sees them decked with the delicate spires of rose-bay willow-herb and yellow toadflax. Willow-herb grows commonly where fires have made clearings in woods. Although its fluffy seeds may be carried in from outside, many of the plants come from seeds already buried in the soil, which, being protected from the worst of the heat, have had their husks damaged enough to make them grow. Like willow-herb, toadflax produces many tiny seeds, but of the millions shed each year only very few grow. No one knows, therefore, why the plant bears its attractive scented and nectar-laden flowers. Though its seeds are stillborn, it spreads alarmingly in gardens, for even the tiniest chip of root may grow into a flourishing new plantation.

ON THE SOUR LAND OF THE MOORS

Poor, sour land in moorland country also carries plants which flower in summer. Here you find heather, and the different kinds of heath whose flowers resemble those of heather. Other summer-flowering acid-loving plants are flea-bane and the little tormentil; and near-by among the tussocks of a grassy bank the delicate harebells hang from slender stems.

Where the water runs iron-red across the moor and lies stagnant and shallow, bog moss fills the pools with a sodden carpet underfoot. Here you can find gentians and bog asphodel; and great colonies of the flesh-eating sundew, whose glistening leaves turn brilliant red as summer advances.

On rivers and ponds the water-lilies are in bloom, and on the bank brook-lime and codlins-and-cream come out. Here, especially where the waterside is cool and shady, you can also smell the sweet heady scent of dame's-violet and meadowsweet.

Scented, too, are the walks beside hedgerows, for the honeysuckle there now opens its flowers and bumble-bee and hover-fly compete for the pollen and nectar within them. High on the hedges the roses are out in early summer, and as they fade the bramble blossoms open, and with them are pink snowberry flowers and those of woody nightshade. On the hedgerows the fruiting season has begun, for already there are green berries of bryony and spindle and at the hedge bottom the wild arum berries swell and show red and green on the same stalk. Agrimony and avens flowers soon fall and, like goosegrass and wild carrot, are followed by dry, clinging hooked fruits.

Unripe fruits hang from trees, too, for the waxy green birch catkins, beechmast, and hazelnuts can now be seen. Other trees that flower in summer are robinia—which some call acacia—sweet-chestnut and lime. A glimpse of the gleaming white robinia flowering in June brings memories of bees among

369

REED-WARBLER WITH YOUNG
Many kinds of bird migrate to Britain for the late spring and summer months
and fresh notes are added to the birds' chorus in the trees. When the young
birds hatch out the shrill sounds of the babies can often be distinguished,
though the mother bird is rarely seen feeding its young. These are reed-
warblers, summer migrants like many other species of warbler, including
the best-known willow-warbler.

the fruit blossom in spring, and as the lime flowers that have been hanging
long in bud open they give another nectar harvest to the bees.

In the trees and hedgerows, the birds are busy rearing their young, and as
spring passes into summer the volume of their song decreases, for more of
them give their energy to feeding their families.

Soon the callow nestlings are covered with tiny spikes, out of which
quickly burst their first feathers. Before long, the young of many birds are
about, wearing the juvenile plumage which distinguishes them from their
parents. Young blackbirds, robins, thrushes, finches, and tits are busy in the
gardens, while young starlings and rooks try their wings among the trees.

Rearing a family is a great strain on frame and feathers, and as soon as the last of the young are able to look after themselves the parent birds shed their old and ragged plumage as a new one grows to replace it. During this moult they look bedraggled and untidy and do not show themselves more than they need. Because of this and also because they do not sing, they are thought to be sad. It is, however, more likely that both their silence and their secretiveness help them to survive at a time when they are weakest.

THE MYSTERY ABOUT YOUNG CUCKOOS

All through this quiet period at least one bird sings almost without rest. As though revelling in its freedom from parental labour, the cuckoo sings throughout June, towards the end of which its voice becomes cracked and faltering. Warblers and blackcaps sing, too, and in the southern parts of Britain the darkness is made lovely by the nightingale. There are late broods of swallows, yellow-hammers, goldfinches, and greenfinches as the cuckoo leaves the shores of Britain and makes its way south. Its young, left behind, follow later, and no one knows how they find their way to the lands where they spend the winter. People have suggested that their foster-parents guide them, and this may be so where these birds also migrate. But the mystery remains, for meadow pipits and hedge-sparrows, many of whom foster cuckoos, are residents and never leave the shores of Britain.

The swifts leave soon after the cuckoos. Their stay in Britain is short indeed, for they are among the latest summer visitors to arrive; and before many people have finished their holidays fieldfares may fly in from the north to spend the winter in Britain. Some people believe that when fieldfares fly south early cold weather will occur. As the birds may go south because of food shortage, which in turn may be caused by cold, the bad weather following the birds can sometimes fulfil the prophecy.

The summer life of mammals follows a course similar to that of birds. They continue rearing their families born in spring, and prepare themselves for the winter. Some mammals have more than one litter, and rabbits, rats, and mice commonly rear three. On the other hand, bats rear only one youngster, and this may be carried in flight until quite late in summer.

Not until late summer do snakes, lizards, or the legless lizards called slow-worms, breed. Though these reptiles are hatched from eggs, those of adders hatch so long before they are laid that the young are born alive, while the eggs of slow-worms and lizards burst their soft shells soon after they are laid, thus releasing the young.

The frog tadpoles in the ponds and rivers, hatched from spawn laid in spring, feed largely on water-weed for the early part of their lives. The delicate frilly gills of their extreme youth soon shrivel and give place to others which line slits opening from the mouth. These slits cannot be seen, for they are protected by a fleshy covering that grows backward over them from the front of the head. Tadpoles are voracious feeders, and as they become older new tastes develop and they do not refuse animal food—even the body of a fallen comrade.

Life in fresh water is less varied than it is on land, and you can learn

371

much during the summer about the animals in ponds and rivers. There are many different kinds of fish; molluscs such as snails and mussels, several kinds of worm, crustaceans, that is, water animals which have jointed shelly armour such as water-slaters and crayfish, and many insects and their larvae.

In summer the male of the three-spined stickleback turns blood-red along his belly and builds his nest of weed. Into this he coaxes the female fish who, after having laid some eggs, is turned out so that others may do the same. No faithful husband, but a gallant, angry, and loving father is the male stickleback as he tends the offspring of his many wives and fights bravely in defence of his little ones. Mussels also protect their young, which hatch within their limy shells. For more than a year these larvae stay there, growing slowly, and when released into the water cling as parasites to the bodies of such fish as sticklebacks. Only when full-fed and ready to turn into mussels do they release their hold and sink to the muddy floor of the stream. Here live the different kinds of pond snail feeding on water-weed, and with them various river worms and flat worms. In the mud, too, among the rotting fallen alder and willow leaves crawl the slaters who, though unable to live out of water, are quite closely related to the garden woodlice. Also crawling here are crayfish which, though not commonly eaten in Britain, are much appreciated in other countries. Though much smaller, these crustaceans resemble the lobsters of the sea and are ruthless carnivores, or flesh-eaters. Besides their beaked claws they have several pairs of legs along their flanks, those nearer the hind end being small and called swimmerets. For some months after it is laid, the egg-mass sticks to the swimmerets of the female, during which time she is said to be in berry. Even after hatching, the young crayfish, if frightened, frequently run back to the parent's swimmerets.

INSECTS THAT COME OUT OF THE WATER

The larvae of caddis-flies, mayflies, dragon-flies, gnats, and midges all live in ponds and rivers and may be seen during summer crawling up out of the water and changing into the adult forms which fly about in the warm air. Some insects, however, have adapted themselves more fully to life in water, and silver-beetles, water-beetles, water-scorpions, water-boatmen, and pond-skaters are among those that seldom leave it, even as adults.

Most of the twenty thousand or so different kinds of insect living in Britain spend the summer feeding, mating, and laying their eggs. The number of individuals of each kind of insect is generally so huge that it is usually easy to find those you seek. Among the best known are beetles, flies, bees, moths, and butterflies.

The clammy white grub of the cockchafer beetle is well known to gardeners, and when full-fed it changes into the adult beetle and comes out of the ground. These cockchafers damage the leaves of trees, and sometimes clouds of them can be seen swarming, bee-like, around oak and birch trees on summer evenings. Almost as active as bees, droneflies are always out in the summer sunshine visiting the flowers for a meal of pollen. They are quite harmless and unable to sting, though many people, mistaking them for the

ON A PERTHSHIRE HILLSIDE

The marguerite is one of the brightest of the wild flowers found in almost every part of Britain. It is a flower closely allied to the garden chrysanthemum, but unlike its garden counterpart usually bears white flowers. This photograph of a view on a Perthshire hillside shows the rarer yellow marguerite blooming in profusion. Most frequently wild marguerites occur along the edges of cornfields in later summer.

bees among which they are found, are afraid of them. Closely related to bees, ants always attract attention, either because they make themselves a nuisance, or because of the crowds of winged ants seen crawling on lawns or occasionally flying about. Most of these winged ants are males, and during these flights each female (or queen) accepts one of them as a mate. She returns to earth, and after entering the ground bites off her own wings. Using the substance of her wing muscles for egg laying, she then lays eggs and so founds a new ant colony, or if she returns to the colony of her birth she lives in harmony with her mother, assisting her in the maternal function.

Hawk, clearwing, tiger, underwing and vapourer moths are some of the many kinds active during the summer months. Some of them, like the graceful humming-bird hawkmoth, are not natives of Britain, but fly there each year from across the sea. This is also true of many of the butterflies, such as some

MANY-HUED BUTTERFLIES

These are two of the loveliest butterflies of the English countryside. That shown on the *left* is the painted lady, which is not a native of Britain but travels each summer from the Continent. Though it breeds in Britain, none lives through the year. On the *right* is the peacock, distinguished by the bright "eye" clearly seen on each brownish wing. Some of this species hibernate and may be seen in the early summer flying with dishevelled wings.

of the whites, and red admirals, the clouded yellow, and painted lady, and the rather rare Camberwell beauty.

AUTUMN

When the grain swells within the ears of corn, and the ripening vetch pods twist open flinging out their seeds, signs of autumn become more frequent. Autumn flowers come out, berries show on trees and hedges, and the leaves change colour and fall. In gardens dahlias, chrysanthemums, and the flowers of the pink daisy-like cosmos open. These plants are natives of countries which, being nearer the Equator than Britain, have shorter summer days. For that reason, they do not flower in Britain until the short days of autumn come.

Among flowers which also open in the autumn are heleniums and perennial asters (which some call Michaelmas daisies). All these autumn-flowering plants belong to the daisy family, which seems to be as well represented among autumn garden flowers as among those of the countryside.

In addition to many of the wild flowers that come out in the summer and go on flowering into autumn, colchicum, orpine, and thornapple are among those that bloom only late in the year. Colchicum, or meadow-saffron, is also sometimes wrongly called autumn crocus. Though not unlike the crocus in appearance, it differs from it in having six stamens instead of three and also in its time of flowering. It contains a drug, colchicine, which is used by scientists so to alter the nature of plants that new breeds are produced.

For most plants, however, autumn is not the time of flowering, but for preparation for the dark, cold days ahead. The food made in the sunlight drains from the leaves of plants into their fruits and seeds. Annuals such as chickweed, poppy, charlock, and groundsel expend all their stored wealth in this way, and die exhausted after shedding the seed, which survives into another year. Perennial plants, however, also store much food in the different parts of their bodies. Beneath the ground, daffodil and snowdrop bulbs swell as their leaves wither, and the roots of many herbs are never fleshier than at this time of the year.

Where the hedges have been white in spring and summer, they are now reddened by the autumn fruits that hang there. Crab apple, spindle, barberry, hawthorn, and hip turn red as they ripen in the slanting sunlight and gentle frosts, and the black berries of the wayfaring tree can be seen among the bunches of its red unripe fruit. Other blue or black berries are those of dogwood, bramble, and elder, and the poisonous fruits of the little black nightshade.

People sometimes say that a hedgerow loaded heavily with berries forecasts a hard winter. They believe that in some mysterious way provision is made in advance for the welfare of the birds. Careful observation over even a few years, however, disproves this; the most likely cause for an abundant crop

THE COMING OF AUTUMN

Here is an early autumn scene in the wooded gardens of the Royal Horticultural Society at Wisley in Surrey. The tall reeds growing round the lake are ripe for gathering. It is in late summer and early autumn that the great reedbeds around the Norfolk Broads are gathered.

of berries being the weather—not of the winter following it, nor the summer preceding it, but that of the summer of the previous year.

Then, if there are long hot dry spells, the plants make more sugary food than usual and use it to make flower buds instead of leaf buds. These buds rest through the winter, and if, when they open the following year, the flowers are pollinated, many berries will form from them.

In the same way, the number of plants of any kind growing in a district may depend on the number of certain birds and other animals there. As is well known, the berries of many plants are distributed by the animals that eat them. The seeds, being unharmed by the animals' digestive juices, pass out with the droppings far from the parent plant. The seeds of other plants are also dispersed by animals, but they are hooked and, instead of being taken within the body, cling to the animals' fur as they pass by. Examples of this kind, such as agrimony and avens, have already been mentioned, and you will often find in addition the hooked fruits of burdock, which grows in shady places on waste ground.

SEEDS THAT FLOAT ON THE WIND

Autumn is the time, too, for all the seeds that float on the wind. The hedges of the lane sides are misty with fluffy fruits of traveller's joy or wild clematis, and as you walk along paths through the bracken you will see among it the tall spires of willow-herb now austere and grey. Their flowers have fallen and when the pods open they let out the minute fluffy seeds that carry the plant for many miles—even into the heart of cities.

Many plants that shed their seeds in autumn have more haphazard methods of dispersal than these. Poppy, foxglove, and many others have tiny seeds that are flung from the dry split fruit-husk as the plant sways about. As many of the seeds are wasted by this method, these plants produce large numbers of them. Poppies, for instance, are said to produce about sixty thousand seeds per plant, while foxgloves shed an even larger number. The seeds of some of these plants, though sown in autumn, are normally unable to germinate until they have passed through the frosts of winter. For this reason you seldom find seedlings of white goosefoot or wild oat in the autumn, though the soil may be full of their seeds.

Light and darkness, as well as heat and cold, guide plants through the bodily changes in autumn. Light damages the green chlorophyll of the leaves and at this time few plants repair the damage. For this reason the leaves change colour, and into them the trees pour their waste oils, gums, and tannins, accumulated during their summer labours. Resins ooze from the buds and, hardening in the cool air, glaze the overlapping scales which protect the shoot tips from the winter. Even though October may be warm, the waning sunlight yellows the leaves of birch, lime, hazel, and ash, while elm and oak turn brown, and the beech leaves glisten copper-red. Cherry and sumach are scarlet, while maple and hawthorn are yellow, orange, and red by turn.

As the soil cools around their roots, the trees take up water more slowly, and in order to conserve it they shed their leaves, through which it would

STARLINGS IN THE FAR WEST

The last day of October witnessed this vast congregation of starlings above a
Pembrokeshire moor near Fishguard. Starlings are noisy gregarious creatures,
nearly always seen in large flocks, or "murmurations." Many of them live in
Britain all the year round, but some migrate in autumn while fresh flocks fly
in from the Continent.

otherwise be lost. A single sharp night frost fractures the slimy layer which is now all that holds the leaf stalks to the trees, and in the thawing warmth of the morning sun the leaves flutter down.

In autumn, many birds gather together in their new winter plumage, and before long the skies are noisy with flocks of rooks and starlings, which are often seen feeding together during autumn and winter in different parts of the same field. Lapwings and pigeons flock up, too, and the farmer would prefer to be without the latter, though he is glad to see the former.

Before leaving Britain, the migrant birds gather into flocks, and blackcaps, nightingales, swallows, and martins follow the swifts that have already gone. The urge to leave Britain at this time of the year is sometimes even stronger than the birds' parental instincts, and martins especially may leave late broods of nestlings to die. Chiff-chaffs and warblers leave, singing as they go, and the young cuckoos find their way instinctively to their winter homes.

The passage migrants seen in spring flying northwards now return to their winter home. Some of these birds, though breeding in the Arctic Circle,

AN EARLY AUTUMN SCENE
Early autumn is the season of mists and cobwebs, and those hazy moist mornings which turn into brilliantly fine and sunny afternoons. There is a special beauty in the shafts of sunlight shining through the mists, a beauty which is just as visible in city parks as in open country. This apparently rural scene is a view in Wanstead Park, Essex, on a late September morning.

A GREY SQUIRREL
Nowadays the grey squirrel is found in many parts of Britain, yet he is not native to the country. Formerly the red squirrel was the only one of the family which made its habitat in Britain until the grey was imported from America. The grey is hardier and multiplied more rapidly than the red, so that now the red squirrel is comparatively rare. Squirrels do not hibernate, but take such long sleeps during winter that they are sometimes thought to hibernate.

fly even farther south than the Equator and may be seen as they pass through Britain in the autumn.

Flying southward, too, are the winter visitors to Britain, such as the fieldfares, redwings, and bramblings. The black redstart, once a rare winter visitor to Britain, has changed its habits somewhat during and since the Second World War, and several pairs of these birds now stay there throughout the year and nest.

Even the birds that most people think of as resident in Britain migrate to a surprising degree, so that the skylarks, thrushes, blackbirds, and starlings seen in autumn and winter are seldom the same as those seen during spring and summer. The summer races of these birds have gone south for the winter and their places are taken by others that fly in from the mainland of Europe. In the same way, rooks, crows, and jackdaws crowd into Britain for the winter from across the sea, though few of those that have spent the warm weather there depart. During the autumn, there is still food in plenty for the birds, and as they feed on weed seeds, greenstuff, and insects, the song of robin, hedge-sparrow, starling, lark, and wren may be heard.

Mammals, of course, do not migrate as birds do, but like them they put on warm winter clothing. In addition to thickening their coats in autumn, they accumulate a layer of fat below the skin which protects them from both cold and hunger.

Squirrels and field-mice also lay by stores of nuts and grain, and squirrels especially seem possessed by a mania as they hurriedly make one store of nuts after another. Most British mammals do not hibernate, though some of them sleep for long spells during the winter, and as the weather becomes colder the carnivorous mammals, especially, become hungrier and bolder. For this reason, you may see stoats, weasels, and foxes about in the daytime.

Snakes, lizards, frogs, and toads are all unable to control their body temperature and become more lethargic as the weather gets colder. Because of this and also as a defence against food shortage, autumn sees a reduction of their activity and they all hibernate during winter.

Among freshwater fish, the salmon is not affected adversely by approaching winter as the land animals are, and autumn sees lusty cock and hen fish swimming strongly into the rivers from the sea. Upstream they go, past rapids and waterfalls to the shallow upper reaches where they lay their eggs.

Insect life gradually declines during autumn. Ants descend into the deeper galleries of their nests in the soil, and honey-bees, after having slaughtered all the drones, gather closer around their queen within the hive. Wasps drag their young from the nests, leaving them outside, while they themselves crawl away sleepily to die. Of the wasps, only the queens survive the winter, and autumn sees them entering houses, where they hibernate during the winter. The beautiful green lacewing fly is also often seen indoors at this time of the year, and in the same way peacock and small tortoiseshell butterflies seek the protection of buildings. These butterflies, together with red admirals and commas, are, however, active late in autumn, especially when the sun shines on the flowers of Michaelmas daisy and orpine from which they suck nectar.

The caterpillars of such butterflies as the common blue, small heath, small copper, and ringlet pass the winter curled up away from the cold, but those of the whites change into chrysalises.

A CATERPILLAR WHICH BURIES ITSELF

One of the most beautiful caterpillars seen in autumn is that of the pale tussock-moth, which, if kept without food, spins a silken cocoon, inside which it turns into a chrysalis. The delicate green privet hawkmoth caterpillar also does this, but makes no cocoon, and if kept in a flowerpot of soil will bury itself.

Throughout the spring, summer, and autumn, the daylight gives strength to animals and plants alike. The greenness of all plants, from the tiniest cells of a pond-scum alga, to the broad leafy canopy of oak and beech, soaks up the energy-giving rays. Using this source of power and the simple gases and minerals of the earth, plants build up their structure and in turn become the food of animals. Thus does the aphis suck the sweetness from the briar and the fly devour the aphis. Death comes to the fly in the spider's grip, and the spider's body feeds the toad. The flesh of the toad sustains the bird which, weakened with age, hungers, and dying so returns its substance to the earth. As summer passes into autumn and the hours of sunshine dwindle, the source of power weakens and the animals and plants prepare for winter. Many store food, surviving for another season, but many more die, leaving only some tiny fragment of themselves, which, resting safe in the soil through the winter, expands in the warmth and light of a new spring.

Index

Numbers in italics indicate illustrations

384